Emil & Berta

The Origins of the
Waldorf School Movement

Emil's favorite verse:

Live in the love of the deed.
Live in the understanding of the other's deed.
This is the law of the free human being.

– from a page in Emil's diary, 1930

Emil & Berta

The Origins of the
Waldorf School Movement

by
Sophia Christine Murphy

Waldorf
PUBLICATIONS
RESEARCH INSTITUTE FOR *Waldorf* EDUCATION

Printed with support from the Waldorf Curriculum Fund

Published by:
Waldorf Publications at the
Research Institute for Waldorf Education
351 Fairview Avenue, Suite 625
Hudson, NY 12534

Title: *Emil & Berta: The Origins of the Waldorf School Movement*
Author: Sophia Christine Murphy
Editor: Eilís O'Neill Maynard
Proofreader: Melissa Merkling
Layout: Ann Erwin
Photo enhancement: David Mitchell
Cover photo: Emil and Berta with students and children on the steps
of the Waldorf School in Stuttgart, Germany: Emil in the foreground
on the right; Berta on the left above two teachers and behind a small
child with blond braids.

Preface

Emil Molt was a successful entrepreneur and philanthropist in early 20th century Germany. Inspired by Dr. Rudolf Steiner, he and his wife, Berta, founded the first Waldorf School in Stuttgart, Germany. Today Waldorf schools can be found on every continent of the world. In their time Emil and Berta were among those who made Germany strong before the First World War and who tried to bring a new spirit to the country after it. They were social, widely traveled, engaged in pressing political issues and, above all, deeply committed to the spiritual teachings of their mentor, Rudolf Steiner.

Emil and Berta Molt were my grandparents.

This biography is based on Emil's memoirs, his private diaries and correspondence as well as my parents' anecdotes and conversations with people who knew them. It reflects my years of preoccupation with both of them, which has allowed me to bring their story to life.

– Sophia Christine Murphy

Acknowledgments

This book is a combination of Emil Molt's private diary notes and correspondences, historical research, my parents' anecdotes, and conversations with people who knew Emil and his wife, Berta. The bibliography at the end contains much of the reference material I worked with. Steiner's written work did the rest.

Thanks to the many people who helped, especially my husband, Finbarr; my son, Kieran; daughter, Deirdre; cousin, Christoph Kimmich; Sandra Landers; Patrice Maynard; her daughter, Eilís; and many others.

– Sophia Christine Murphy

Contents

Foreword 9

Part One:
The First Twenty Years 1876–1896 13

Part Two:
Triumphs 1896–1916 49

Part Three:
Transformation 1916–1936 138

Epilogue 348

Appendix:
An Appeal to the German Nation
and to the Civilized World 354

Bibliography 358

Addendum 363

Waving goodbye at the pier

Foreword

How I came to write the story

In 1937 drums rolled in Germany, soldiers marched in parade, and a demonic little man had begun his mission to take over the world. I was three months old when my mother, Edith Lichtenberg Molt, left her native country to find freedom thousands of miles from home. She boarded a boat in Bremen with me in her arms, crying as she waved goodbye to her parents on the pier. She was afraid that she would never see them again and she was right. On the ship, I was rocked in a hammock for ten days next to my mother's bunk. She was seasick and heartsick as the boat made its way to New York, where my father, Berta and Emil's son, Walter Molt, waited. He had fled Germany three months earlier and had taken over management of the fledgling Weleda company in Manhattan.

My parents first settled in the New Jersey suburbs where my sister Ursula was born. After a few years they moved to the Threefold Farm community in Spring Valley, New York. One of my earliest memories was of Christmas Eve. My sister Ursula and I had to wait at the head of the darkened stairs until we heard a chiming bell. Then, our hearts beating with excitement, we were brought into the warm and fragrant living room. There was a tree decorated with real candles—unusual in America. My parents sang "Silent Night" in German: *Stille Nacht, heilige Nacht* and other songs because German was the language we spoke at home.

Later, I remember the word *war* and my mother lying on her bed sobbing over a black-rimmed letter from Germany. We were practiced in responding to potential air raids—a nearby blaring siren meant dropping everything, closing padded curtains, and turning off lights. Military planes often flew overhead. That was when I learned that "German" was a bad word, not to be mentioned in my little country school.

In 1953, when I was sixteen, my parents decided that Ursula and I should spend two years in the school our grandparents, Emil and Berta Molt, had founded in Stuttgart. We arrived in the spring, as in those days the new school year in Germany started after the Easter holiday. Initially I was a bit of a celebrity—teachers saw my grandparents in me, and my classmates saw an American in jeans. But I soon merged with it all, loving my fellow students, my teachers and the extraordinary school.

After the war, with classmates and an American soldier

The teachers, some of whom had been pioneers of the school's founding, taught a wide range of subjects wisely and with imagination. We learned surveying by going into the mountains and doing it; we visited cathedrals and other ancient monuments and played in the school orchestra. My classmates talked together, learned together, danced, and hiked together. I saw the aftermath of the war in bombed-out buildings and a mountain in the making, built with truckloads of war rubble still being carted out of the city. They called it Shard Mountain, *Scherbenberg*, or, more affectionately, *Monte Scherbelino*. The war had only been over for eight years, but for me it was remote. To this day I do not understand why I never asked my parents or my classmates about the war. Living in the moment, it simply didn't occur to me.

I did have another link to that past: my godfather, Walter Rau, whom I met for the first time in Stuttgart. He had a kind, attentive face and a luminous smile, and he owned a soap factory named after him. Often, he would pick me up in his chauffeur-driven car and take me to an elegant coffee house for cake and conversation. I loved his wide interests and he told me much, but we never spoke of the war nor that it was he who had rescued the diaries and documents from the bombed and burning Molt house. I learned sign language for him because he was stone deaf.

Walter Rau

After graduation I studied and traveled until I met my husband, Finbarr. Then we took over the management of the Weleda company in Manhattan. Later we moved to the Threefold Farm community and located the business nearby. Our children attended the new Green Meadow Waldorf School.

Much later, in the 1980s, I woke up one morning feeling the urgent presence of my grandparents calling to me. I realized that their story had been obscured by the passage of time. I rang my mother, who had moved to the Italian part of Switzerland, and asked if she had any documents of their lives. She told me most things had been lost in the war and that the rest she'd given away. There were some of Emil's old diaries, but she thought them too painfully private and said she planned to burn them.

"The past should be laid to rest," was how she explained it. This made me panic. I decided I would have to rescue the diaries, so I boarded a plane with a half-empty suitcase and went to visit her. She showed me the diaries, tucked away in an old chest in a back storage room. One night, at the end of my visit, the diaries found their discreet way into my suitcase and, after a few days, into America.

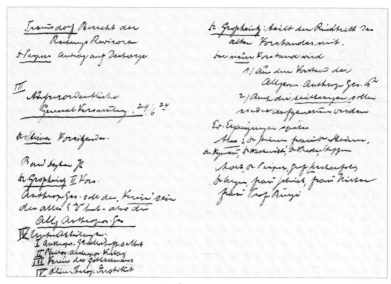

A diary page

My plan was to translate the diaries from German into English, but when I examined them, I was overwhelmed by the tiny handwriting and couldn't bring myself to start the process. Instead I translated two printed booklets describing Emil's early life which he had dictated to Berta on his deathbed. In 1991, I published this partial biography of Emil and Berta's life leading up to the founding of the Waldorf School. After moving to Ireland (the land of poetry and inspiration), I tackled that tiny script in the diaries and spent two years transcribing it into English. After that, I started researching and writing, going to sleep at night with questions about Emil and Berta on my mind and waking up some mornings with answers. I lived their life stories intensely while putting my own life on hold, working to fill in the gaps and always believing this project was important for the present and for the future.

Part One

The First Twenty Years
1876-1896

Schwäbisch Gmünd

Schwäbisch Gmünd (pronounced *shvaybish gmint* and simply called "Gmünd") is a town situated east of Stuttgart in Württemberg, a small region in the southwestern part of Germany. It has rich soil, pleasant rivers and scenic rolling hills that serve as the setting for ancient legends and contain many romantic hidden corners. "Württemberg" means "the host by the hill" and, until 1870, it was an independent kingdom. Its people were called Swabians or Schwäben. Traditionally they considered themselves an ethnic rather than a political group, and prided themselves on their frugality, warmth, humor and unique dialect. Swabians were

Schwäbisch Gmünd

farmers and merchants. They loved their homes, yet traveled the world. They were—and still are—freedom lovers, philosophers, poets and storytellers.

The Swabians are descended from two main ethnic groups. The Celts came first, arriving from the east along the Danube in pre-Christian times, and were followed by the Alemanni, who migrated from the north. These migrants gradually displaced what was left of the Roman Empire and spread as far as Switzerland in the south and the Alsace in the west. They received spiritual instruction from Irish missionary monks who often built their monasteries on the ruins of Roman forts.

The bakery

Around 1878, a wood-paneled bakery stood at a crossroad in the center of Gmünd. It had gleaming counters and alcoved windows. One window always held a display of fine breads and biscuits and the other often displayed a frail two-year-old boy with a little wooden horse. He could often be seen munching on a sugar bun. When her lunchtime break was over, his mother would open the door with its tinkling bell to welcome customers into her warm and fragrant shop. She was a thin, energetic woman in her late thirties with a white cap over frizzy hair and an apron covering her dress from buttoned-up collar to ankle-length hem. Her customers were dressed more stylishly—corseted, with hats and gloves. These ladies loved their afternoon tea, and their daily adventure was going to see what new delights the baker had prepared for them. "Good afternoon, Frau Molt," they would say. "And how is your little boy today?"

The boy knew that this idyllic setting was not all it seemed. No matter the season, he heard his mother anxiously cajoling his sleeping father to get up to start his workday in the early darkness—breads for the mornings and cakes for the afternoons. Every day was the same—even Sundays were busy, as churchgoers wanted their warm, sweet rolls with their leisurely *Milchkaffee*. The boy was used to frequent outbursts in the bakery when his father's finger got scorched or an ingredient was missing in the latest creation. But by the time the customers arrived, the day's offerings were in place, and the portly and choleric baker was resting in the flat above the shop, recovering from his impatient battles with dough. His name was Conrad Molt, his wife was Marie, and the little boy was Emil Hugo.

Conrad Molt's background

Conrad Molt was born in 1840, the offspring of teachers in Obergröningen, a remote but close-knit little town northeast of Gmünd. His father died when he was eight and his uncles helped his mother raise him. Conrad, although bright enough, could not compete with his classmates in sports and on the playground because of a weak heart. Consequently, he suffered the jeers of his more robust classmates.

Conrad made a sympathetic friend in the kindly local baker, who let him help out after school for pocket money. The youth loved the warm and comforting bakery. He had talent and was proud of his part in the finished breads. After graduating from school, his classmates rushed to sign up for their stint in the military, and, although Conrad was among them, he was found physically unfit. His parents said he would make a fine teacher, but the thought of facing more jeering children terrified him and he insisted he wanted nothing more than to be a baker. This caused quite an upheaval in his house.

Conrad's uncle said trade was not in the Molt tradition and was below their station in life. He reminded Conrad, while pointing to the framed coat of arms hanging on the wall, that his illustrious ancestor, Joseph, held an honorary lifetime title as Württemberg Schoolmaster to the Nobility. Conrad,

Molt coat of arms

who liked history and had done his share of research into the family, replied that Joseph's son, while teaching, had also been a weaver. Furthermore, the weaver's son, Georg (Conrad's great-grandfather), had been a shoemaker—all facts that proved artisanship was just as much in Conrad's blood as teaching. This argument earned him chastisement. A few months later Conrad packed a satchel with clothes and some food from the larder, put his savings in his pocket, and climbed out of his window into the night, knowing he could never return. In that parochial time when a son was expected to continue in his father's profession and marry within a radius of ten miles, Conrad's rebellious behavior brought shame upon his family.

Marie Friederike

Meanwhile, Marie Friederike Goeller—the daughter of respected Protestant pastor, Johann Peter Ludwig Goeller, and an unmarried, headstrong young woman—had recently moved to Schwäbisch Gmünd to manage the boarding house of a distant aunt. Late one rainy night, Marie heard a loud knock at the door. She wrapped her dressing gown over her nightgown, straightened her nightcap, and looked out the window. Conrad Molt stood in the rain looking half drowned. When she opened the door, he asked if she had a room, and Marie took pity on him. She led him into the kitchen, warmed a bowl of soup for him, and then showed him to a room.

For the next week, Conrad was in bed racked with chills and a fever. While Marie nursed him, he regaled her with embellished stories of travel and adventure in Germany and France, claiming that he had learned the art of pastry-making "from the greatest chefs of Paris." He prided himself on his smattering of French and told her his motto was *toujours travailler* (always work). He offered to repay her kindness by baking for her customers. When she asked about his own home and found out he could not return, she was flooded with sympathy that soon blossomed into affection for him, spurred on by the sweet morning aromas from the kitchen. Conrad recovered from his illness, although for a time he remained pale and unfit. He responded to Marie's affection, but said he couldn't possibly wed without having a means of income. This inspired Marie's entrepreneurial spirit, and she decided to leave her aunt's employ, offering her small savings to help set Conrad up in his own bakery.

In the early 1870s the couple found a suitable location with a bakery downstairs and apartment upstairs, and had just set up shop when a short war with France broke out. They felt lucky to have each other, and Marie was glad that Conrad would not be obliged to fight. But both felt themselves to be foreigners in Schwäbisch Gmünd, without the support of their extended families. Marie, a Protestant, compensated by attending church regularly and exchanging pleasantries with her customers. She also kept in written contact with her own family. Conrad, however, was still estranged from his clan and did not make friends easily. He withdrew into his bakery. They both dearly wished for a child, but Marie, overworked and no longer very young, suffered several miscarriages.

Family life

On Good Friday, April 14th, 1876, Marie at last gave birth to a frail and asthmatic son. In his early hours, the infant was so sickly that Marie begged Conrad to run for the pastor, who came to the house and baptized the baby Emil Hugo according to the parents' wishes. Conrad, who had hoped for a strong little warrior unlike himself, fell into a dark mood, afraid of what the next hours might bring. But the child survived. A doctor prescribed regular doses of Malaga wine, which Marie administered religiously. Her full powers of motherhood awakened, she kept her little son close by in the shop, first in a basket and then on the window ledge so he could look out at the world. She kept an eye on him, all the while lavishing bits of sweet bread and cake on him. The Malaga cure was medieval and the sugar diet more modern, but Emil seemed most nourished by his mother's love.

The relationship between Conrad and Marie was not particularly inspiring or romantic—the practical requirements of the business kept

Emil's birth house

them both busy. Often the bakery stayed open late, and free time for
family outings was rare. Although Marie spoiled her son, his upbringing
was prosaic and authoritarian. His parents didn't read him fairy tales,
instead focusing on prayers throughout the day. When Emil made
a mistake and spilled his milk or broke a cup, his father's anger was
terrifying. Punishments included confinement in a dark storage closet
for what seemed like hours, or banishment to the bedroom with the
door locked and window blinds drawn, turning daylight into witching
shadows. A more robust lad would have withstood such treatment, but
young Emil was frail and unusually sensitive, and these recurring events
gave him nightmares for years to come.

On better days Conrad's outbursts were mitigated by kindness. He
sometimes took Emil to feed his tame pigeons, and taught him to play
the drum. Once Conrad brought home a child's fiddle, which Emil
doted on until he carelessly left it lying on a sofa and a portly visitor sat
on it by mistake. Whenever Conrad heard the sounds of a military band,
he would snatch his son up, put him

Conrad's snuff box

on his shoulders, and run down the street to watch the cavalry riding by in full dress uniform.

In the streets of Gmünd

As Emil grew, he eventually left his window seat, venturing out with his little dog, Assorle, to join the neighboring children. He was a pale, wheezing, blond boy, but he had access to a never-ending supply of warm sweet "seconds" from Conrad's kitchen, for which he was much in favor with the other children. On Sundays, Emil delivered breakfast rolls to some of the larger households in town, after which his mother packed up some pastries as an extra treat for his friends. The neighborhood boys played in squares and alleys that fronted stately houses or ran down winding cobbled streets to a stream by an old Roman wall. This border wall had never kept anyone out and was therefore called *gaudium mundi*, the "joke of the world." Emil loved exploring his medieval town, which was known for its gold and silversmith shops.

Almost all of Emil's playmates were Catholic, and it seemed natural for him to follow them to Mass in their rich and mysterious church with its ornate statues and aroma of incense—so very different from his mother's plain and sparsely furnished Protestant church. But Emil harbored a secret dread of being made into an altar boy like his friends, so he never stayed in church very long.

First loss

In 1882, the summer of Emil's seventh year, his 43-year old father, hot from his work with the oven and anxious about an unexpected rush order, ran out into a rainstorm for butter. He came back feeling chilled. Perhaps his heart wasn't up to the strain, or his frustration got the better of him, but he came down with pneumonia and died within a few days. Marie was devastated, and Emil felt somehow responsible for this tragedy, racking his brain over which of his many little sins had caused this great calamity. His father's death was a significant turning point in Emil's life, setting him on the path to the next stage of his journey.

Life in Alfdorf

After Conrad's death, Marie didn't feel up to running the business on her own. She sold the shop and, with Emil, found temporary refuge with her brother, Gustav Goeller, and his family. Goeller was the minister in a tiny Swabian village called Alfdorf, not far from Gmünd. He became Emil's guardian, and Conrad's friend, Julius Daiber, was appointed to oversee the modest inheritance.

The village of Alfdorf was so small that it consisted of only one long street surround by a few scattered farms. Most inhabitants were farmers, although there was a butcher, a baker, a turner (whose specialty was spinning wheels), a potter, and a bookbinder. The village was mostly Protestant, with a few Methodists and Pietists, who had their own ministers and chapels and were generally looked upon with great mistrust by their neighbors. A nearby little Gothic castle was home to the Baron von Holtz and his family. They provided endless occasions for gossip by the locals.

Uncle Gustav and his family lived in the rectory in the center of the village. His house was an imposing building set back slightly from the road and somewhat apart from the other houses. It was marked by a

The rectory, with church in rear

20

linden tree with a circular bench around its trunk and an unused barn that stood behind the house—a playtime paradise for children. Near the barn was a large kitchen garden, lovingly tended by Pastor Goeller. Adjacent to this stood a beautiful old baroque church, the "Sanctuary" as it was called by the household.

The pastor was a strict but kindly man. Although well read, he was an unquestioning believer, holding firmly to Protestant tenets. He had no time for Catholics and disliked Methodists and Pietists, whose children he would have preferred not to confirm. He, along with the schoolmaster and the mayor, was a political conservative and admirer of Chancellor Bismarck, the man who had brought them peace and a unified Germany. Being conservative at that time meant preserving tradition in form of state, society and church. The schoolmaster, the mayor and Uncle Gustav all abhorred the liberal Democrats with their revolutionary principles and commitment to gymnastics.

Gustav's wife, the gentle and highly intelligent Friederike, was related to the famous physicist, Julius Robert Mayer. In more modern times she would have been given a college education, but then she was simply the pastor's spouse, mother to his children, and hostess to the many people that either boarded in or visited the house. Two of her sons were already grown and had left home. Adelheid, her only daughter, was a graceful 17-year-old girl and her mother's helper and companion. The youngest son, Hermann, was Emil's age and shared a room with him.

An ordered life

From the intensity and chaos of the bakery, Emil's life at the Goellers' now took on a strict order. Meals were served at the same time every day, and every hour had its assigned task. Within days of his arrival, the boy who had spent his time running around streets of Gmünd now found himself tethered to a school bench with the other boys, across from the girls who seemed to him to occupy a different universe. The only good fortune was that Emil and Hermann were treated with great leniency, thanks to their status as the Pastor's boys.

Hermann, thoughtful and quiet, loved his schoolwork and enjoyed studying in his room. Emil, on the other hand, was a nervous, impulsive child who hated his lessons. Seeing Hermann at his studies sometimes infuriated him to the point that he would attack him, provoking a physical fight. Despite being the aggressor, Emil usually got the worst of it.

Between fights, Emil and Hermann played in the meadows around Alfdorf, diverting the many small streams into mouse holes. Discovering where the water came back out of the earth was fascinating to them. On rainy days they played in the unused barn behind the house, producing plays and shows with stick puppets. Once, Hermann tried making an organ out of some old organ pipes they found in the loft. Emil, already the businessman, sold advance tickets to the concert, but Hermann's pipes refused to play. It was reported that their audience was kind enough not to laugh at them.

Once a week, Emil and Hermann had to climb the stairs to Uncle Gustav's study on the top floor, where he prepared his Sunday sermons

Town hall and school

amidst clouds of pipe smoke and an abundance of potted plants. Pastor Goeller, in a tasseled house cap, instructed the boys in Latin while seated at his mahogany desk. Emil hated these lessons, looking longingly out the window at the blue sky, the ink stains in his copy book betraying his impatience. Once Uncle Gustav went so far as to punish Emil by putting him over his knee, for which Emil never forgave him.

On Sunday mornings the whole family went to church, which had a lovely Rococo interior with two rows of benches. The beautiful organ faced the entrance, and the church council had chairs in the front row in order of rank. The pastor's family had their own box on the balcony. To the right was the "royal" box of the Baron von Holtz and his family. The latter were always mentioned in the closing prayers. In winter the church was so cold that the congregation had to bring along foot-warmers and candles.

Three things in particular were fostered in the Goeller household: social games, books and the celebration of festivals. Because of their large circle of friends and the relative loneliness of country life, much time was spent playing games of all kinds, and performing little plays.

Learning by listening

The Goellers had a great knowledge of books and explained them. Historical events were learned as games or verses—a practice so lively that Emil maintained a love of history for the rest of his life. Sometimes in the evenings Aunt Friederike read aloud from novels, many of which romanticized brave deeds, courtly knights and noble damsels. She excelled at hosting festivals, especially at Christmas when all the younger cousins came through the silent village swathed in snow to celebrate together, warmed by a roaring fire. Emil resumed playing the fiddle, and it was not long before he was able to accompany the children's singing.

Some Sunday afternoons, the pastor took his family out into the countryside to prune the trees in his orchard or to gather fruit. Other times he had his horse and trap hitched up and drove around to hold services in places without churches. Or, weather permitting, he would walk, taking the children through fragrant woods and golden wheat fields. On the way back, they often stopped at one of the picturesque farmhouses belonging to the Baron von Holtz, where refreshments were served. From there they could admire the view of the hills with their own village in the distance and the Stauffer castle ruins above it.

Uncle Gustav knew the name and story of every hill, many of them crowned by ruins of old castles. Emil loved these walks and thought this landscape with its soft colors must be the most beautiful in the world. One day, however, relatives came to visit and they all went climbing to the ruins of the old Stauffer castle. It was dark as they came back down, and Emil found it hard not to appear weak; the forest with its rustlings and ghostly shadows filled him with dread, reminiscent of the dark bedroom in Gmünd with its witching shadows.

Some evenings, the Goellers would go to the Rose Tavern to meet villagers over a glass of beer and an occasional game of ninepins—but not before Mr. Epple had come with his *Mäpple* (mail pouch). He was the night watchman, sexton and mailman all in one, and he always carried a horn and an antiquated spear. Each evening he brought the mail to the Goellers' house and the children were allowed to watch the ceremonious opening of his pouch. After that, the evening Bible verse was read and Hermann and Emil would shake hands with everyone and go off to bed.

Living in the country

After a year of living with the Goellers, Marie found three rooms and the use of a kitchen in a merchant's house, and she and Emil moved in. Although their new home was not far from the rectory, it was outside the village amidst open fields. Emil still attended the village school, but he felt freed from the constraints imposed upon him at the Goellers, and he started spending time with his new neighbors, the farm boys. Their threshing machines, stables and haylofts fascinated him. He went along for plowing and haying, and on butchering days was given bowls of hearty broth. Many of his new friends had their own woodworking benches and were good at carving wooden swords, bows and arrows.

Their favorite occupation was ringing the four church bells hanging in the tower—it took one boy to ring the smallest bell and four to ring the large one. It was great fun being pulled by the weight of the bell right up into the old belfry with its owls and bats.

On dark winter evenings, the farmers sat together spinning ghost stories. One said he had seen lights on a fresh grave, another a spirit haunting a certain spot. Their tales were so real that, for a time, Emil needed his entire courage to walk home alone in the dark.

In this new setting, Emil became stronger and happier and his asthma disappeared. He also became wild and undisciplined, often skipping school and coming home with bruises and torn clothing. He started disobeying his mother, running out when she wanted him in and laughing at her when she tried to chastise him. She was still in mourning and did not have the strength to manage him, often also feeling lonely and unwell. When Emil was nine, her doctor diagnosed a heart valve defect and Emil understood that he must control his behavior and be kinder and gentler for her sake.

In 1884, when Emil was eleven years old, he reached the end of his country schooling. The question now arose how to provide for his further education. Marie decided to move to Stuttgart because schools were better in Württemberg's capital. Marie had a sister living in Stuttgart who managed a boarding house. She had an enterprising spirit matching Marie's, and she encouraged Marie to open a specialty shop selling products from Alfdorf. In April 1887 they found an ideal location, a vacant shop and apartment within easy walking distance of Emil's new school, the Realgymnasium. Marie, back among townspeople, was happy to indulge her flair for business. She sold milk and beer from the baronial estate, sausages and meat from the local butcher, cheese, and her own homemade noodles. She was as successful in Stuttgart as she had been in Gmünd although she needed her entire strength for it. Emil helped his mother with some chores like turning the handle of the heavy noodle machine, but generally he was left to his own devices.

Stuttgart

For Emil, the Realgymnasium was even worse than his former school in Alfdorf. Its dull routine was led by tired, frustrated, elderly teachers whose only exercise was applying the strap—sometimes the whole class had to stand in line to receive their raps. Lessons followed each other at 45-minute intervals without a break. A class would race up from gym, out of breath, with cold hands in the winter from throwing snowballs, and go right into Latin. As soon as the students finally settled down, the lesson would change again to something quite unrelated. Field trips and museum visits were not included in the curriculum, and most youngsters spent holidays cramming for tests.

The best thing about school was that it ended at midday. Then Emil ran outside with his friends, supplementing his education with life in the streets. They perfected the art of ringing doorbells and blasting keyholes with peashooters without getting caught. Another game was putting firecrackers on the rails of the horse-drawn streetcars and then watching from a hiding place as the horses reared. Once Emil caught his foot between two rails while attempting to change the directional points, only just managing to free himself before the streetcar was upon him. He and his friends lurked in shadowy alleyways, smoking cigarettes made of chestnut leaves or, if they were lucky, collecting tobacco dregs which Old Man Hunnius discarded behind his tobacco shop. Hunnius made zesty cigarettes with black paper and gold mouthpieces for the Russians living in Stuttgart.

The popular King and Queen

In the 1880s the city of Stuttgart, with its winding Neckar River, was still relatively small. There wasn't much poverty nor much stark ambition in Stuttgart. It was a contented town of about 85,000 inhabitants, surrounded by vineyard-covered hills.

King Karl I of Württemberg and Queen Olga had their seat in Stuttgart. She had been a grand duchess in Russia, and she brought with her a colony of wealthy Russians who added pomp and worldliness to the city. Their palace stood in the park-like center of town, where the King often took unaccompanied evening strolls, being greeted casually with, "How are you today, Mr. King?" by other strollers.

The King was a jovial and sociable monarch, who found frequent cause for public celebrations with parades and fireworks. One time he came riding through town, flanked by Chancellor Bismarck and General von Moltke. The boys, seeing them in all their pomp, were stage-struck. They bought old bayonets and fitted them into makeshift wooden hilts, adorning themselves with ribbons and buckles and marching in their own parades because, for them, war meant pageantry and romance. Emil was their natural leader, not because he was the strongest or the oldest, but because he observed the soldiers most closely. Once, while waiting for the changing of the guard, he had a flash of insight. He realized: *I have relatives, I have a mother, but I am a self, separate and unique.* The thought was so vivid that years later he could still picture himself as a twelve-year-old boy, standing alone among the many people with this insight.

The orphan

In September 1889, after a summer holiday spent visiting his mother's relatives in her hometown of Waldenburg, Emil returned to Stuttgart to find Marie bedridden and in extreme pain. He walked into her sick room and, when he saw her suffering, he was completely overcome. Marie put her arms around him and broke into tears at the thought of leaving him. Over the following days her condition worsened, and Emil was not allowed into her room, seeing her only on the eve of her death. The boy sat by her bed in a state of utter despair while the relatives from Stuttgart and Alfdorf made funeral arrangements. Pastor Goeller and the others tried to comfort Emil, but he hardly heard them. A few days later Marie was buried next to her husband in Gmünd. Emil stood by the grave, conscious that now, at thirteen and a half, he was truly alone.

The family discussed who should take on the troublesome boy. His uncle and aunt in Stuttgart, the Jägers, offered to keep him for a couple of years in exchange for room and board, paid for out of his inheritance. It would allow him to finish school. Their invalid son, Oskar, as old as Emil, was confined to a wheelchair and needed a companion. They hoped Emil could make himself useful while they were at work. Mr. Jäger was curator in a nature museum, Mrs. Jäger took over Marie's shop while continuing to run her boarding house. They meant well, but they were stern and unapproachable. The morning after his mother's funeral, Emil came downstairs to greet his uncle, holding out his hand.

"Good morning," he said, as taught by his mother. "Shaking hands is unnecessary in this household and you should avoid it in the future," Uncle Jäger answered. This reaction made Emil extremely uncertain. He missed his freedom too—afternoon duties were laid out for him. He wheeled his cousin Oskar out every day and sometimes let him fly down the hill in his chair. Once a neighbor came rushing in to tell his aunt that Oskar and Emil were on the roof. These adventures did Oskar no harm. In fact, his health improved to the point that he no longer needed his chair. But the Jägers did not attribute Oskar's health to Emil.

School as drudgery

School was a further misery. For the most part the teachers favored a few good students and barely tolerated the rest, routinely punishing their pupils with beatings, humiliation and extra work. Coming home from school, Emil often had swollen hands from the teacher's switch, and each morning on his way to school he imagined the terrors the day would bring. School, combined with the state of mourning he was in, thwarted any inclination to learn. He also languished physically; the Jägers' evening meal of bread, sausages and beer did not agree with him.

Early in the new year of 1890, Emil decided he could bear school no longer. He remembered the advice of a friend: "If you keep staring at your nose for a long time, you can make yourself throw up." Emil tried this during an especially hateful lesson, and it worked. The teacher sent him home immediately, and the Jägers called for a doctor, who diagnosed him with mild hepatitis. Emil was delighted to stay in bed for a few weeks, but by then he was so far behind in school that he had no hope of catching up.

The Jägers called an emergency meeting with the Goellers to tell them that they no longer wanted Emil in their house but did not know what to do with him. The Goellers could not take him back because there was no secondary school in Alfdorf. Somebody recommended a small institute in the town of Calw in the Black Forest that specialized in the education of difficult boys, and the family agreed that Emil must be sent there with funds from the sale of the shop in Gmünd. In the first week of April, Pastor Goeller came to Stuttgart to collect Emil. He helped him pack his few belongings, and Emil said farewell to Oskar, of whom he had grown quite fond. At the door, Mr. Jäger finally shook Emil's hand and wished him well. Mrs. Jäger patted him on the shoulders, hiding her relief behind her handkerchief.

Confirmation

His confirmation in Alfdorf, alongside his cousin Hermann, was the final rite of passage during this sorry time in Emil's life. Standing in front of the altar, his voice shaking and the eyes of the entire congregation on his back, he forgot half the Bible verse he was supposed to recite. His embarrassment was so intense that the festive meal following the ceremony and the rest of the week until his departure were torture. Emil decided the adults were right to consider him a hopeless case.

The Lyceum in Calw

Emil's fourteenth birthday on April 14th, 1890, dawned bright and sunny. He rose early, his belongings already packed, eager to set off on the next stage of his life. This first train trip was the best birthday present. It was made even better because his favorite cousin, Adelheid, Hermann's older sister, was coming with him. She had become a lovely, gentle young woman with large dark eyes and a bright smile which caused a great tender feeling in Emil. They boarded the train in Gmünd and the cousins sat opposite each other with their refreshments. They laughed and chatted, commenting on the changing landscape. Through the train windows they saw sleepy little villages alternate with large tracts of grain and cabbage fields peppered with the odd horse in harness. Eventually the scenery gave way to dark, pine-covered slopes as they entered the silent Black Forest. Then suddenly the medieval town of Calw appeared below them as the train wound its way down to the station.

The stationmaster gave them directions to the Lyceum and, having found it, they were directly sent in to see the headmaster, Professor Weizsaecker. This dignified personage, who had corresponded with Pastor Goeller, fixed Emil with an appraising yet kindly look and suggested he secure lodgings before returning the next day for an entrance exam. He recommended the house of Professor Kies and his wife, located near the school. Mrs. Kies was housemother to seven boys and had room for one more. For that first night, however, the cousins stayed at a thatch-roofed inn, dining together and exploring the town in the evening light. The next morning, Adelheid assured Emil that he would do well and waited while he, nervous and unsure, took the exam. He passed the test, if barely. Much relieved, Adelheid helped him unpack in the room he now shared with two other boys before hugging him and leaving for home.

Easy adjustment

Emil settled into his new environment quickly. The other boys, used to students coming and going, accepted him easily. The school was clearly different from the one in Stuttgart, with airy rooms and a pervasive atmosphere of learning. In Emil's very first class, old Professor Staudenmeyer asked a student a question he could not answer, whereupon the other students whispered the answer across to him fairly loudly. Emil was astonished at this bold behavior until he realized the professor was fairly deaf. Yet the students respected their teacher and learned well from him as they did from the other teachers—all gifted educators who expected discipline without the need for corporal punishment. Emil thrived in this atmosphere, discovering that all it takes to learn is enthusiasm for the subject.

In the afternoons, the boys went out walking, cocky in their white Lyceum caps. Their favorite destination was the train station, where they treated themselves to secret glasses of beer or pieces of chocolate from the bakery and watched the passing girls. Emil admired the girls from afar, imagining them as the romantic lofty beings of Mrs. Goeller's historic novels, but he never met up with them. Sometimes the boys wandered through gardens and meadows to the hills, past the "enchanted well" and the old gallows, which afforded many pleasant shivers. In the evenings they studied together, overseen by the head student. They never copied notes and always encouraged each other in their work.

Seventh class

In the fall of 1890, Emil began seventh class, the highest in the school. Here, the teachers treated the boys more like equals. In the spring final exams arrived and Emil worked hard to prepare. When testing day arrived, he felt he did quite well despite being nervous. When the grades were finally announced, his results, including in math—his weakest subject—were so good he was speechless. After his mother's death and the confirmation disaster, he had given up on religion, but he now felt his mother's presence strongly and sent a prayer to heaven for her. In just over a year he had transformed himself.

At the end of his time at the Lyceum, Emil's class performed Goethe's *Götz von Berlichingen*. Emil was given the part of Götz's sister, Maria, an indication of how slender and delicate he still was. Indeed, he acted so convincingly in his powdered curls and frilly dress that a lieutenant of the local platoon mistakenly paid him court after the performance. Two of Emil's classmates, still in costume, borrowed a couple of horses and galloped whooping through town waving their stage bayonets.

Then it was time to say goodbye to teachers, landlady and schoolmates, most of whom traveled back to their own homes. They promised each other to stay in touch, but Emil lost contact with all of them except for two, who remained his friends for life. The first was the famous writer Hermann Hesse, who was sent to the Lyceum after running away from a priest seminary in Maulbronn. The second was August Rentschler, who later joined Emil in his business.

Emil stayed on in Calw waiting to hear from his relatives about what his next step should be. His uncles and aunts, while surprised at his good grades, did not want him back. His best course, they agreed, lay in business—a career people chose (they said privately) if they were unable to do anything else. Why even travel to Stuttgart at all? They'd heard that the Georgii company in Calw was looking for an apprentice and encouraged Emil to apply. Emil's uncle promised to write a letter of recommendation to Mr. Georgii.

Emil knew the venerable Georgii emporium well with its three large display windows and a bronze sign that read: E. Georgii, Bookseller. It stood in Calw's central square and was the favorite shopping establishment in town. Lyceum students loved its variety and often came in to browse among the many tempting foreign products. Typically, students only ended up buying something small, like a penny notepad to make their purchase of cigarettes more discreet.

It cost 15-year-old Emil a great deal of courage to present himself to the owner, but he brushed his jacket, smoothed down his hair and went. In the store, Georgii's wife, Pauline, smiled at him kindly. "Hello Emil," she said. "My husband is expecting you." She took him to the back where Emil Georgii was sitting at his accounts. He listened to Emil's awkward speech, questioned him thoroughly and then told him to go home and wait for a reply. Two suspenseful weeks passed, during which time Georgii made extensive inquiries about Emil. Finally, Emil was invited back and Georgii told him he had the position.

Emil the apprentice

The plant

The Georgii business was an early prototype of the modern general store. Three stone steps led to the entrance, and Mrs. Georgii was on hand to greet her customers inside. The retail store and offices were on the main floor with sections of the store closest to the entrance devoted to stationery and art supplies, including postcards and illustrated cards with verses in them. The store's books were Mr. Georgii's special pride—he had once apprenticed in a book-bindery, and he looked after this section himself. Behind these goods were imported foods, both dried and preserved, including coffee, sugar, salt, tobacco and wine. At the back of the main floor was the bank, overseen by Georgii with the help of his oldest apprentice. To the left was Georgii's son Paul's office and an insurance and emigration bureau. The family and the apprentices lived on the three upper floors of the house.

A mighty building in the rear, accessible via a large double gate, was linked to the store by a courtyard. It contained warehouse spaces on the ground and first floors and a school for girls on the second. The attic was used for tobacco storage, and the bales were hauled up with a winch. This warehouse stored building supplies and farm equipment.

Tradesmen and farmers loaded these onto horse-drawn carts brought in through the gate. Grain, wood and other goods were weighed on a scale hung from a high beam with stones as counterweights.

Mr. and Mrs. Georgii and sons

Proprietor Georgii was a muscular giant of a man with a full head of white hair. He was well into his sixties but looked ten years younger. His vitality permitted him to take on various civic duties alongside his demanding business. He served on the city council as surrogate mayor and for years headed the fire brigade. He was a passionate hunter, going out in the early morning with his gun slung across his shoulders and his knapsack on his back, returning triumphantly with a hare or venison in the evening. Despite all this activity, Georgii was one of the first to arrive at work in the morning and the last to leave in the evening. The larger portion of his Sundays was also given over to work. He combined punctuality with thoroughness and a sense of duty and was able to impart these qualities quite naturally to his apprentices.

Georgii and his wife had two sons. Paul, the youngest, was his father's trusted helper. He oversaw all purchases and accounts and ran the firm's own bank. The older son, Emil, was extremely handsome and charismatic. Having recently returned from Greece, he started making cigarettes on the premises in partnership with G. Harr, a friend based in Greece who procured the tobacco for him. Cigarettes were just coming into fashion and his was the first cigarette manufacturing company in Germany. His parents were proud of him, and Emil Molt, who only knew a small part of southern Germany, was much in awe of Emil Georgii's worldliness and elegance.

Rules of apprenticeship

In the 1890s, an apprentice belonged, body and soul, to his master and his establishment. Rather than receiving pay, the agreement called for an upfront apprenticeship fee of 600 Marks, paid by Emil's trustee to

Georgii. It covered three years' apprenticeship, plus room and board in the house. Additionally, the usual pledges regarding confidentiality and loyalty to the master had to be signed.

On Emil's first day, the other two apprentices, Oskar and Emil, introduced themselves and immediately knocked him to the floor in a kind of crude initiation to their world. They quickly decided to call him by his dreaded middle name, Hugo, since the house already had too many Emils. Oskar Wendel, the younger of the two, was a short, stubby fellow. He took Emil under his wing like a rough nanny, pointing out the rules with punches rather than words. They all shared a room just big enough for three beds and three chests with washstands and ewers with water that froze in winter. Candles provided light after sundown.

Emil Lauffer, the oldest apprentice, was in his final year of apprenticeship. He was tall and strong and had a penchant for sneaking out at night in violation of the rules. During Emil's first week, Lauffer ordered him to join one such an expedition. Lauffer did not have a key but knew that the front door remained unlocked while Georgii and his sons were out. He also knew when they would return. When the house was quiet, the three apprentices tiptoed downstairs and paid the local pub a visit. Returning, Lauffer whispered, "Boots off, take care on the stairs." The two older apprentices had already passed the first floor when Emil stepped on a faulty stair and it creaked. The sound terrified him into dropping his shoe. The door of the first apartment opened and Emil ran behind a wardrobe. But his shadow gave him away, and Georgii's younger son Paul found him. Emil stood before him in abject misery and begged not to be reported, sure that his career as apprentice was at an end. Maybe Paul remembered the trials of his own youth, as he gallantly kept the secret and there was no retribution. After that, nothing in the world could have enticed Emil to participate in such a caper again.

The workday

For the apprentices, the workday began at seven in the morning and ended at eight at night. In the morning, one apprentice would tiptoe to the master's open bedroom door to get the warehouse keys. Then all three went downstairs, opened the shop shutters, and proceeded to sort merchandise and clean the space, well aware that the master's wife would find any overlooked dusty corner later on. If, by mischance, the master woke up before them and the apprentices heard him winding his old wall clock and bounding downstairs, they would throw on their clothes without washing or putting on their removable collars and run down after him.

Breakfast was prepared by Katarina, the cook, and consisted of coffee and rolls. Emil soon learned to supplement breakfast by pocketing a slice of bread and later dipping it into the sugar sack in the wholesale warehouse behind the shop. Each day he helped stock shelves and fetch beer, wine and champagne from the large cool cellar full of barrels and hundreds of bottles. The apprentices hid a cup behind one of the barrels in the cellar so that they could "test" the quality of the wine.

The store's sacks of gunpowder, almost too heavy for one person to lift, were stored in a warehouse on a hill outside of town. The two husky older apprentices, smirking, told Emil that the newest boy must fetch the gunpowder when a customer ordered it. They were sure Emil's narrow shoulders would find carrying the gunpowder an impossible task. That's when Emil discovered the virtue of brain over brawn. He found a small wagon, pulled it up the hill, loaded the gunpowder sack, and rolled back down the hill, quick as the wind, sitting on the sack. He was rewarded with a small tip for his prompt delivery. With that extra money, he went straight to the store's book section and bought the first book of his library. It was a small collection of songs called *Wanderlieder* (hiking songs) by Josef von Scheffel.

Serving customers

At first Emil found serving customers in the shop difficult. He was shy with young women and terrified by older women—especially when they stared at him intently, as if to say, "Hurry up young man!" Mrs. Georgii noticed his awkwardness and taught him tricks for memorizing names. She also coached him in the art of conversation and polite inquiry. From Georgii, Emil learned thrift. The master turned every incoming envelope inside out to reuse it, saved every string, and pulled out and straightened every nail. Yet despite his phenomenal attention to detail, Georgii never lost sight of the whole organization. As a member of the local council, he found time to put in an appearance at every big event in town. If, on his way back home late at night, Georgii found Emil still working, he didn't say, "It's late, run along to bed," but rather, "Oh, you're still here too!"

On Saturdays and Sundays there was more work—books and magazines to be unpacked, invoices to be logged, and a thousand other odd jobs. In spite of the lack of free time, Georgii insisted that his apprentices learn French and English and go to gymnastic classes because he believed these skills to be essential to the well-being of the new nation. Of course, he also knew that gymnastics could help prevent teenage boys from getting into mischief.

Emil profited from these lessons, developing a love for gymnastics. He became agile and strong and quite skilled, eventually winning a few prizes in district competitions. Beyond brief visits to the local pub for a glass of beer, Emil had little social life. The only real excitement came from the occasional fire—Georgii, as fire chief, expected his apprentices to help, and they outdid each other in racing to the scene and proving their bravery and daring. Sometimes, at the end of these long days, Emil was so tired he crawled into bed without undressing. But his loyalty and admiration for his fatherly master were so strong they kept him going.

At the end of Emil's first year working for Georgii, the oldest apprentice was replaced by a new one, whom Emil initiated more gently than his predecessors would have. He now moved into the office of his master's younger son Paul, to learn the basics of bookkeeping, inventory, and buying and selling. He taught himself stenography and a careful style of handwriting for letters and ledger entries. Paul was an excellent example of a person who loved his work for its own sake rather than for profit, and his methods became a model for Emil, who soon learned that behind every transaction there is a person. This knowledge made arithmetic, formerly his worst subject in school, come to life for him.

In his third year of apprenticeship, Emil became his master's right hand, helping him run the business. He took care of most of the company's correspondence while standing at an upright desk, translating his stenographic notes into presentable handwritten letters. Carbon paper had not yet been invented, so every letter was hand copied for the company's records, and an accidental ink stain on the original meant the whole thing had to be redone.

In a remarkably short time, Emil acquired an excellent understanding of the entire enterprise. Looking back over his apprenticeship, he recalled that his pervasive feeling during his first year was, "I must do it," which changed to, "I should do it," in the second year. By his third year, Emil could tell himself with conviction, "I can do it," and that gave him confidence and strengthened his will.

During Emil's last month as an apprentice, Georgii approached him with an unexpected invitation to stay on for an additional year as a paid employee of the company. Emil, who had no plans for what to do next, accepted gladly. His boss gave him a room of his own, a key to the front door, and a salary. Otherwise, Emil's tasks remained the same, with the exception that Sundays were now free for hiking and exploring.

Finding his soul-mate

At eighteen, Emil knew many people in Calw by sight, but he was still shy and, lacking a family environment, mostly quite lonely. But in the autumn of 1894, the local rifle association held its annual fair. It was one of the big social events in Calw with prizes for marksmanship, relay races and a band. Emil went to the fair with his gymnastics classmates, and they soon joined up with a group of girls. Two of the best-looking girls were sisters dressed in identical dark blue skirts, plaid blouses, and fur-trimmed boleros. They stood chatting and laughing with friends. The older girl was striking and fiery, the younger pale and quiet with large dark eyes and thick hair tied back in a loose knot. At first, Emil was drawn to the older sister, but then his attention turned to the younger, delicate sister with the gentle look. Her name

Berta Heldmaier

was Berta Heldmaier, and to Emil she looked like one of those rare and unattainable princesses featured in his aunt Goeller's novels. Later Emil wrote about Berta in his diary:

> *From the first moment it was no ordinary flirtation. It was too elemental and in spite of some detours, too assured. Later we both remembered a feeling of absolute recognition. How else would it have been possible that two such young people, without prospects, knew with such certainty they were destined for each other? One day I want to write the story of our love. At the moment it seems too profane to commit this most intimate affair of the heart to paper....*

Berta's story

She was one of three daughters of Pauline and Georg Heldmaier. Her older sister, Emma, was born in 1873, and Berta herself was born in June of 1876. The youngest daughter, Pauline (called Paule), was born a year later.

When Berta was a healthy and happy three-year-old, she suffered a severe reaction to a preventive tuberculosis vaccination and was bedridden for seven winters in a row with a kind of lung catarrh. The illness kept her from school and made her quiet and withdrawn, worrying her mother to distraction. Berta's dreams during this illness were intense—one morning in a dream state she went to the top of

Berta's teacher

the stairs in her nightgown and launched herself from the top step with outspread arms, believing she was flying over the world. Luckily her father happened to be walking by on his way to breakfast and managed to catch her as she came sailing down.

Too often she watched longingly from her window as her friends skated on the river or sledded in the snow. Luckily she had an excellent teacher who helped her catch up with her schoolwork after each winter absence. When she was sixteen, Berta was able to graduate with her class, but for the rest of her life she remained frail.

The Heldmaiers

Berta's father, Georg

Berta's father, Georg, was a master locksmith and an inventor who owned various patents for stoves, baking molds and other metal objects. Like Georgii, he was a devoted Democrat and an ardent gymnast. He was also well known in town for his beautiful daughters.

Berta's mother, Pauline Staudenmeyer, was born in 1840, the daughter of a master plasterer in Calw. Hunger years followed her birth when even bread was barely affordable. For a

Berta's mother, Pauline

time the child Pauline did piecework for a match factory. In 1865 she went to Frankfurt as a lady's maid and was there when war broke out between Austria and Prussia. The Prussians march into Frankfurt to the horror of the townspeople. Pauline's employers, like other citizens, fled, leaving her and the cook to mind the house. Pauline lost her taste for living "abroad" and returned to the safety of

Calw where she eventually married the young master locksmith named Georg Heldmaier.

Making hats

Pauline had a sense of style and a liking for financial independence. Her reputation as a maker of fashionable hats brought her an ever-growing clientele. After a while she had so many orders she needed help from her daughters. Berta, who longed to go to college, was obliged to stay at home with her older sister, Emma, to help their mother. The work was demanding, especially before Easter and in the autumn when the new season began. The sisters often sat from early morning until late at night stitching and shaping while their mother struggled with her accounts. Only 10-year-old Paule was exempt from this work because of her age.

The garden

On fine summer days, the girls sometimes relaxed in their mother's garden above the town where their father had built a gazebo as a gift for his wife. In the colder winter months Emma, with her mother's enthusiastic support, often invited friends to their house for social evenings and parlor games. Berta liked these social affairs, but being shy, she preferred exploring the world through books. Emma had plenty of admirers, and Berta, who

Berta and Emma as children

considered herself plain, had her share too—including young Hermann Hesse and her cousin Gustav Rau. To the sorrow of both of these young men, Berta was always attentive and friendly but never flirtatious with them.

Berta's review of her life

Much later, reviewing her life, Berta wrote in her diary:

My sister Emma was known for her beauty and she had many admirers. My little sister Paule was strikingly pretty too. I myself was frail and pale, often tired and lacking energy and it depressed me dreadfully that I had two such lovely sisters, the talk of the town, while I was regarded with pity. Once I told a friend: "Why did God make me so ugly that my mother can't love me?" Later when I read the story of the ugly duckling I thought it was my own life.

When Berta met Emil at the fair, she was immediately taken with him, but she had no idea how she might go about meeting him again. She knew that Emil worked at Georgii's, but due to the social constraints of the time, she couldn't simply go there and ask for him. She dreaded meeting him by chance in the street. Emil also agonized over the dilemma. He realized he had never seen Berta in town, and what excuse could he possibly give for knocking on her door? Berta became even paler and more withdrawn in the wake of this meeting. Her mother finally noticed and asked what ailed her.

"I'm all right, Mother," Berta replied. Pauline, worried about Berta's health and, annoyed at the lack of communication, talked it over with her husband, who suggested asking Emma to investigate.

The intrigue

Emma took Berta on a long walk, cajoling her into confessing that she had fallen in love at the fair. Berta begged Emma not to tell her parents—they would never approve of her interest in a complete stranger. Emma, surprised and then delighted by this new game, immediately set her mind to finding ways for Berta and Emil to meet. When the girls returned from their walk, Pauline was astonished to see Berta looking happy. Emma told her mother that the walk and the fresh air had done Berta a great deal of good.

One day, Emma happened to be browsing through the Georgii establishment. To her satisfaction, she found Emil busy behind the banking counter. She told him she would like to come back the next day with her savings book to make a deposit, and asked when would be the best time. He gave her a look and then said between one and two, the time he knew the Georgiis were at lunch. The next day, Emma showed up at the store with her sister. Both Berta and Emil were extremely formal and constrained. She, red-faced and stuttering, barely raised her eyes to him.

Young Berta in traditional dress

A few days later, Emma was back at the store saying she wanted to open a savings account for their little sister, Paule. She had a small box of biscuits for Emil, baked by Berta. Next, Emma decided to have Emil meet the family. She asked his friend, her cousin Gustav Rau, to invite Emil to his father's tavern for the annual New Year's Eve party.

The party

Emil prepared himself for the visit by asking Gustav Rau about the Heldmaiers, finding out there might be music and what songs the girls liked to sing. On the night he brought along his fiddle and was the life of the party. Years later, Berta wrote about that night in her diary:

> I met my husband when I was 18, having first seen him at a festival but never having really talked with him. On December 31st, 1894, my sisters and I went to my Uncle Rau's pub to wish the family a happy New Year. There we met Emil, who complained that all his friends had gone on holiday whereas he had to stay and mind the Georgii shop. Emma invited him to our house for that evening.

When he arrived I shook hands with him and felt an electric shock, right down to my feet. I was shattered without knowing why and sat down behind the Christmas tree to hide my tears.

Adopted by the family

The party went very well and Berta's family liked Emil—he chatted enthusiastically on the topic of gymnastics with Berta's father and complimented Berta's mother on her hats, offering to help with her bookkeeping. Soon he was a welcome guest in the house, coming over after work and staying late, lending a hand with various odd jobs. The new world of women thrilled and fascinated him. The house was an irresistible magnet, and the girls, lacking a brother, lavished affection on him. Early in the morning he would walk up a hill from where he had a view of the house, then walk down past it, whistling the first five notes of a hunting tune as a signal. His reward? Waves and smiles from all three sisters in the upstairs window. He taught Berta stenography discreetly, as a kind of secret language between the two of them.

Old Georgii, curious where his employee might be spending his evenings and knowing it was not in the pubs, went on the lookout. One night he passed the Heldmaier house with its brightly lit windows and fiddle sounds and was astute enough to figure it out. He probably put in a good word for Emil with his fellow Democrat, Heldmaier, but Berta's parents were already glad to offer the orphan from Stuttgart some family life. Emil appeared on equally friendly terms with each of them, and Berta was able to keep her secret with Emma's help. Only Gustav Rau divined what was really going on and withdrew from courting Berta in defeat, not without bitterness.

Emma's engagement and an outing

In May 1895, Emma became engaged to Karl Hofstetter, a handsome young traveling salesman with an elegant black mustache. Hofstetter took Emma to Reutlingen to formally present her to his mother, and

Berta was invited along as chaperone. Since she should not travel without an escort, the Heldmaiers were grateful when Emil offered to take on this task. The young people spent a wonderful two days on this trip, touring the dusky corridors of Lichtenstein Castle and taking a romantic evening walk by a moonlit lake, serenaded by frogs.

Such freedom was not possible in Calw. Once, Emil and Berta planned to meet discreetly in the little garden at six in the morning, ostensibly to harvest some fruit. She never showed up, and later Emil found out that her father had noticed her getting ready to leave and, when he heard she was going to meet Emil alone, asked her not to because of what people might think.

The kiss

Emil found such old-fashioned behavior intolerable, but eventually his moment to meet with Berta alone arrived. September 2nd, 1895, was the anniversary of the battle of Sedan (against Napoleon) when all Germany celebrated the founding of the Empire. That day, Berta went to the garden accompanied, as usual, by her little sister Paule. Emil "happened" to meet them there and pulled some coins out of his pocket, offering them to Paule and suggesting she go into town to buy fireworks. Paule could not resist this temptation and ran off, thrilled. At last, Emil and Berta had an hour to themselves. He asked her to marry him and she said yes. They sealed the promise with a kiss. Berta continued to hold their secret close.

A letter

Meanwhile, Emil had soon to serve his obligatory year in the army. In order to fulfill the tradition of journeyman after an apprenticeship, he packed his haversack and said goodbye to the Georgii family. All were on hand to wish him well except his old master. *Does he not care that I am leaving?* Emil wondered. But then Paul Georgii handed him a letter from his father dated September 12th, 1895.

45

It said:

Dear Hugo-Emil: I don't like saying goodbye, so I am writing. You have done well and I wish you much luck. Be good as ever and continue your gymnastics; then you will remain healthy in body and soul. If you need advice or help come see me. I especially appreciate that you stayed with us for this additional year. Farewell, I remain your well-intentioned master. E. Georgii.

Naturally, this document was written on the back of a packing slip and delivered in a recycled envelope together with the following reference:

I hereby declare that Emil Molt, son of the master baker Molt of Gmünd (deceased), has completed his apprentice training in my establishment and worked for an additional year as an employee to my full satisfaction. I recommend him highly as a capable, hard-working, reliable and honest young man. Emil Georgii

This brought tears to Emil's eyes.

The Journeyman

In mid-September, Emil left Calw and hiked through the Black Forest. He then bought a "hobo" train ticket for twenty Marks that allowed him unlimited travel throughout Württemberg.

Military service

On October 1st, Emil entered the garrison in Neu Ulm, home to a Bavarian regiment, and spent the following year there. He chose this regiment having heard that military life in Bavaria was not as harsh as in Württemberg or Prussia. The region also came with extra holidays, since Bavaria was predominantly Catholic. Emil's youthful vanity delighted in his sharp uniform with

Emil in uniform

its blue jacket and tight white trousers (the Greek colors, worn because this regiment once accompanied the Bavarian Prince Otto to Greece to be crowned King). Emil, having arrived very fit from Calw, enjoyed the training sessions and the marches—army discipline was easy after his rigorous apprenticeship. He was good at target practice too, as long as his superior did not roar at him and make him lose his aim. Because of his excellent penmanship, the company's headquarters soon co-opted him as secretary, which absolved him from some of the rougher duties.

The whole town catered to the garrison, providing restaurants, boarding houses and entertainment in abundance. Emil observed that the army discipline of daylight hours was mightily undone by nighttime revelry—consumption of large amounts of alcohol and sexual exploits. His shyness and the thought of Berta kept him from the mischief of his fellows, and frequent visits to Calw were enough to remind him of his ideals.

Another healthy distraction came in the form of Emil's cousin, Paula Sepp, who lived nearby with her husband. This childless couple introduced Emil to science—an absorbing topic for progressive minds in those times of new research and widening religious doubt. The Sepps had discarded tradition, which at first frightened and then intrigued Emil. He admired their capacity for clear and unimpeded thinking. Eugen, the husband, studied nature as his hobby and took Emil on walking tours, describing every plant and insect they saw. Both Sepps were musical and loved the theater, and they often invited Emil to performances. He never saw them anxious or melancholy, and regarded them as wonderful masters in the art of life.

In January 1896, halfway through his military time, Emil enrolled in an officer training program. Had he continued the course through the summer, he would have become a reserve officer, but he decided instead to spend the time with Berta. Later, Emil wondered whether he had made the right decision, but ultimately decided that his duties as an officer would have stood in the way of his marriage and career.

Applying to Greece

In July of that year, Emil met Friedrich Bauer, an employee of Hamburger & Co in Patras, Greece. This firm was the one Emil Georgii Jr. had worked for. Emil was intrigued, asking Bauer whether there might be a position for him at the company. Bauer suggested sending the firm a request in writing, which Emil did with Paul Georgii's help. He soon received a reply saying that Emil would be welcome after the summer. Emil was delighted by this good news, knowing how much he would learn by going abroad. His happiness was dampened, however, at the thought of parting from Berta.

On August 8th, 1896, Emma married Karl Hofstetter, and Emil, on leave in his blue and white dress uniform, was best man. An announcement in the paper invited the entire town to the evening reception, and it was an opportunity for Emil to try out his skills on the dance floor with Berta. But as the evening wore on and the wine flowed, Emil and Berta were shocked by the sexual innuendos and crude jokes loudly aimed at the new couple by their guests. Despite the treatment they were subjected to, Emma and Karl were obliged to remain at the party, hosting the entire evening as well as a wedding breakfast next morning. Berta and Emil promised each other quietly never to subject themselves to such an ordeal at their own wedding.

Part Two

Triumphs
1896-1916

Off to Greece

On October 8th, 1896, a small procession headed for the train station in Calw. All five Heldmaiers, the ladies in their newest hats, and their father consulting his pocket watch, accompanied 19-year-old Emil on his way to foreign lands. The ladies had lovingly prepared several days' worth of food for Emil and packed it up for him. After numerous last-minute instructions at the station—be sure to wear your hat in the sun and don't forget to write—Emil was on board and the train moved off in a southerly direction. He sat glued to the window until the last of the waving handkerchiefs disappeared, then watched the changing landscape until he was joined by an acquaintance on his way to Zürich, Switzerland. Arriving there in the evening, both young men took rooms at an inn, then attended a concert with music so romantic that Emil's heart overflowed for the love left behind in Calw.

The next morning, he continued his journey over the spectacular Swiss mountains to Milan, where the son of one of Georgii's employees met him and gave him a tour of the city and its newest buildings. The tour didn't include any of the cultural sights such as DaVinci's *Last Supper*, so Emil passed through this ancient and classic country completely unaware of its historic and artistic treasures. Instead, he was on a constant quest for picture postcards to send back to his sweetheart.

At Ancona, Emil had his first sight of the Adriatic Sea, and at Brindisi he boarded an overnight steamer. He did not spend much time in his bunk, preferring to stand on deck, watching the moonlit waves and thinking about Berta. The next morning, the boat landed in Corfu, where Emil spent a few hours waiting for his next connection. He strolled the narrow lanes, wrapped in the comforting warmth of the place, and watched artisans stitch leather or shape earthenware in front of their doors. A small ferry took him the last leg of his journey to the great commercial town of Patras. The harbor, packed with ships loading and unloading merchandise, ebbed and flowed with milling crowds of busy people. He had imagined quaint little buildings surrounded by palm trees and tropical vegetation, but instead the town was large, prosaic and businesslike.

Everything is new

Hamburger & Co, Patras, was housed in an imposing, modern harbor building opposite the elegant Hotel Angleterre. It was the most important export and import company in Greece, with its own ships and several hundred employees. Everyone knew the owners—the brothers Franz and Albert Hamburger—who were among the large German diaspora, assimilating easily and contributing to their chosen society. They exported raisins and wine and imported merchandise from Germany, England, France and Italy.

Emil was introduced in the main office and put straight to work at a standing desk. His first task was translating a letter into French from German, which he did badly. Confident that he was coming to Greece with skills, he now saw that, essentially, he had to start at the bottom of the professional ladder again and would have to overcome once again his old insecurities. Ordering food in a restaurant was an adventure too—the dishes were as strange as their names, prepared in oil and lacking the vegetables his Swabian stomach craved. Emil was sick for a week. The wine research he'd done in Georgii's cellar was not much help to him either—he was baffled by the offerings in Patras. The first time he drank ouzo, he was with a gang of coworkers who nearly collapsed laughing at his expression when the fiery liquid flowed down his throat. He laughed and took another swallow, knowing he would have to learn fast. Because he was young and determined, he did learn, studying Greek by night and observing his surroundings closely by day.

The extended Hamburger family was impressed by Emil's energy and invited him to their cocktail parties and dinners. They were all very musical and pressed him to take violin lessons, which he did for a while but then gave up because learning sight reading was too arduous. He soon became bored by society life, though, preferring to go out on the town with less high-powered friends who were his own age. He loved the haunting music, the dancing and the promenades along the harbor in the cool of the evening. Sometimes, late at night, having become extremely merry, he and his friends would leapfrog through the streets without anyone taking any notice. *I can overcome all obstacles*, Emil thought while doing this, delighting in the easy freedom of life in Patras compared to the constraints of Germany.

Exploring the countryside

On his days off, Emil explored the countryside alone or with companions. From the Hamburgers' library he borrowed books on ancient Greece and found reading them made history come to life. Wherever he went, he found warm hospitality. Once, passing through a village, he was given an escort of two soldiers because the mayor suspected brigands were in the area and wanted to protect Emil.

On another magical day, he and his friends hired sturdy mountain ponies and rode high up to a monastery perched in the rocks. Singing and confident, they climbed past treacherous precipices with no thought that their ponies might lose their footing. A friendly monk greeted them and brought them past the gardens and the wine press into the cool kitchen for refreshment. Afterward, the monk took them to a chapel that nestled like a bird's nest in a breach of the rock. The friends were astonished by the treasures inside, brought there to safety long ago when the Turks invaded the old Byzantium. The sun was still high when they left, and it beat down on Emil's uncovered head. He had forgotten Berta's warning to always wear a hat and would one day regretfully trace his early baldness back to the burning Greek sun.

At work Emil learned the import and export business, and about diplomacy and negotiation. He evaluated products and equivalences in foreign currency and was constantly impressed by the scope of the enterprise, so much greater than the local business in Calw. He loved the warmth of the land and the warmth of the people and began to feel so much at home that he imagined bringing Berta over to live with him in Patras. He even started sending her lessons in basic Greek. His employers liked his work and increased his salary. They promised him a rising career, and he signed a contract for four years.

Military threats

Then, in 1897, tension between Turkey and Greece began to mount. In a letter, Emil described the crisis to Berta:

> *Here is what I've been told: The ancient island of Crete is controlled by the Ottoman Empire [Turkey] but is largely populated by Greeks. The Islamic Turks and the Christian Greeks do not get on well and spring is always a time of unrest in the Balkans. This year the Greeks revolted, perhaps sanctioned by Athens, perhaps prodded by an interfering larger power. They marched and Athens sent ships and troops to help them. At this critical moment England, Austria, Germany, France, Italy and Russia stepped in, blockading the island. In Chania, the Turkish army, trained by the German Baron von der Goltz Pascha, shot at the insurgents and unfortunately a vessel built by Germany, the 'Augusta Viktoria,' got involved too.*

Emil and his friends suddenly found themselves less welcome than before, and they followed political developments with some trepidation. Mainland citizens demanded that their sovereign support the Greeks on the island, shooting and demonstrating in front of the foreign embassies. The monarch, originally Danish and with close family ties to the crowned heads of Europe, was faced with an uncomfortable choice between a revolution that might end up deposing him or an ultimatum delivered to the blockading powers—his kin. He knew very well that the Turks had the advantage of a fully equipped army and that the Greeks, with their outdated armaments, were not prepared for modern warfare.

Meanwhile, the great powers bartered endlessly among themselves. The Greek citizenry did not much care for international machinations, and because popular international sympathy was largely with them, the harbors soon saw young volunteers pouring in from all over Europe to riot alongside them.

On Easter Sunday, 1897, war was declared. Emil and his friends were out hiking and happened to be sitting on top of Mount Omblo looking down on Patras when they saw the battleship *Spezia* pull out of the harbor. They had been given a tour of that very ship just two days before.

The kingdom of Greece was small, and Turkey, occupying Albania and parts of Thessalia, Macedonia and Thrace, easily routed the Greek army. Soon, the citizens saw large numbers of wounded Greek soldiers arriving back home in dreadful shape. At that point, their courage turned to panic and they blamed their king. Luckily for him, the war ended after only thirty days, but the conflict was a prime example of financial and political interests manipulating sources of discord that would eventually lead from one war to the next.

Emil's reports to Calw were addressed to Berta but meant for the whole family, while a second sheet, intimate and written in shorthand, was for her alone. Each day he waited anxiously for a letter from her and was rarely disappointed. It troubled him greatly that she was still working late into the night, missing out on sleep, and he longed to take her away from Calw. They both discussed their future in their letters, wondering whether it would include Patras because Emil was so happy there.

Emil Georgii's offer

Then one day a letter arrived from Georgii's older son, Emil. He wrote that he had relocated to Stuttgart and had bought a little cigarette factory with his father's help. "It's a partnership and it is perfect," he wrote. "I oversee manufacturing and sales. My partner, Harr, lives in Greece. He buys and ships the tobacco. Please join me," he urged. "The prospects are excellent because cigarettes are relatively new here and becoming fashionable very fast, with only a handful of companies producing them. I urgently need a good sales manager." Emil spent a few days pondering. Should he leave his promising new life in Greece for a fledgling venture? He finally opted to take on the challenge, expecting the Hamburgers to oppose his

Tobacco plant

decision. Of course they did, saying he had an obligation to them. "I will find a replacement for you and train him to your satisfaction," he told them. They offered him a generous salary increase—enough to start a household as a married man in Patras. He thanked them profusely but said, "I am beholden to my old master, Georgii, and his son needs my help." At this there was no further argument.

Emil wrote to Georgii senior who soon found a good replacement for Emil's position. Emil trained the new employee thoroughly over the next months, creating a seamless transition that left the Hamburgers satisfied. Before leaving Patras, he sent a formal letter to Berta's parents asking for her hand in marriage. Feeling himself on the way to financial security, he wanted his intentions to be clear. To his delight, both parents answered, welcoming him into their family.

In order to see at least a little more of Greece before he left, Emil requested a few days' holiday around the beginning of the new year. He took a train to Athens via Corinth and Megara. He felt a certain devotion as he passed Eleusis. Riding along the gulf, he saw the snow-capped peaks of Parnassus and Helikon. In Athens he was astonished to feel an intense familiarity with the town and its landscape: *It is as though I've been here before*, he mused as he found his way easily past squares and buildings. On New Year's Day, under a clear blue sky, he walked to the Acropolis. He felt joy at approaching the Erechtheion and was moved as he stepped into the Areopagus where St. Paul had preached to the Athenians.

Parting from Patras was painful for Emil—Greece had thoroughly won his heart. He was now proficient enough in the language to be able to communicate with producers and distributors and had acquired basic conversation in Italian, French and English. His dealings with people of different nations made him feel like a citizen of the world and prepared him for his own future tobacco business. He had gained familiarity with international trade and social economics, and the war had taught him the tragic consequences of powerful political agendas and passions. He promised himself that he would return often and not lose touch with his friends and employers. His German friends gave him a farewell dinner at their club, then brought him, singing, to the steamer that would take him home. On February 28th, 1898, he boarded the Lloyd steamer *Elektra* for his return.

Looking back at this period in his life from many years later, he saw just how wisely he had been guided. Had he stayed on in Patras and brought Berta to live with him, they would have been ruined, as were the Hamburgers. They and all the other Germans in the country were expelled during the First World War.[1]

On Saturday, March 5th, 1898, Emil arrived in Stuttgart. On the cusp of turning 22, he was now a mature and worldly young man with a sound grasp of business practices. He had assumed significant responsibility at a young age, and now the careful, prudent side of his Swabian nature gave way to the adventurous and ambitious

Emil returns to Stuttgart

1 In1923 Emil met Albert Hamburger again at a eurythmy performance in Vienna. He learned this talented and highly cultivated family had found its way to anthroposophy.

side. Eagerly he set off to meet his new boss. It was a fine day on the edge of spring. His light Greek suit wasn't quite warm enough, but he felt exhilarated by the cool air and the charm of this city—which seemed smaller and more provincial than he remembered.

At the cigarette factory, Emil Georgii Jr. greeted Emil and they chatted for a while in the manner of old friends. Then Emil left his suitcase and returned to the station with just a knapsack on his back and boarded the next train to Calw. Berta, waiting at the station with her sister, was delighted to see her fiancé looking tall, tanned and worldly while he was surprised to see Berta looking even lovelier than he remembered. Paule was no longer a child but a budding teenager.

The Heldmaiers besieged him with questions while he unpacked small presents and mementos, each one with a story. He told them more presents were on the way (he had spent most of the money he had saved in Patras on presents). Late in the evening, he left that warm and cozy house, stopping briefly at the local pub to see his former drinking mates. As before, he spent the night at the Georgiis', where he was welcomed and questioned once again. Georgii, the old master, seemed delighted for Emil to be working with his son who, he said, could benefit from his influence. This amused Emil—it was a typical father's remark, he thought, as though the son still needed looking after.

The next morning Emil went to church with the Heldmaiers and then walked along his favorite woodland path above the town in the sunshine, the three sisters laughing and talking around him. Every minute was sweet, and he felt himself the happiest man in the world. In the evening he returned to Stuttgart and settled into a room in the house of relatives—temporary lodging while he looked for an apartment.

Early Monday morning Emil presented himself at the factory for his first day of work and was shown around by his new boss. Having learned retail in Calw and wholesale in Patras, Emil now found himself faced with the totally new challenge of learning about production in an industrial setting. Emil Georgii's company included forty people, some salaried employees and some hourly workers. The latter were overseen by Sophie Wiedman and were responsible for cutting, sorting and filling paper cigarette cylinders with tobacco. Emil was shown his office, which adjoined the production space located next to the bookkeeper. Then Georgii took him to the first

Cigarettes

floor to show him the warehousing, packing and shipping departments, as well as a room for specialty workers proficient in fitting thin gold-leaf mouthpieces. Karamousas, the tobacco master, had an apartment on the top floor, and his job was purchasing and mixing tobacco and maintaining standards.

Emil Georgii, handsome and elegant, was brimming over with ideas. He described everything to Emil with enthusiasm, dwelling on his dream of the perfect machine that was to revolutionize production. In fact, Georgii's pride and joy was a large, rather ponderous packaging machine run by several young women. At the best of times, this machine was slow, and in damp weather it didn't work at all. But Georgii assured Emil he was designing improvements that would soon replace all hand labor. Georgii did not seem concerned about capital, and when Emil asked him how he meant to finance his machines, Georgii said that his wife's family was wealthy and eager to help. In fact, he had hired Emil so he could be free to pursue his inventions. After this introduction, Emil Georgii clapped Emil Molt jovially on the back, wished him well, and went off traveling.

Although Emil's main responsibility was selling, he realized he could not do so without fully understanding the product and the business. On his second day of work, he walked into the production area and found the ladies lounging at tea now that the boss was away. He told them he would have to check their quotas, which earned him scornful looks, and then he was pointedly ignored. Seeing his new authority challenged, he countered by addressing them with exaggerated politeness, which made them laugh and relent. From then on, they regarded him as their boss.

Emil's next hurdle was Karamousas, the tobacco master, whose feathers Emil ruffled by showing up in the stockroom, looking into bins and asking questions. The hot-blooded Greek suspected him of spying and reported this back to Georgii, who was not at all pleased to hear that Emil had ventured into what he considered his and Karamousas' private domain. These reactions did not stop Emil from doing his research—his persistence was finely honed since his apprenticeship.

Georgii had asked Emil to balance the books for the year 1897, but the bookkeeper, Karrer, became very defensive when asked to produce the books. He refused to hand them over, saying the previous year still needed work. Emil decided to try a different approach and invited Karrer out for a glass of wine to get to know him better. Then Karrer, a charming man at least fifteen years Emil's senior, became friendly and chatted freely. He said he hated bookkeeping and much preferred spending time with clients. Emil soon realized their roles should be reversed: Karrer should do sales while Emil ran the internal affairs of the company. They talked it over and agreed to try it.

Over the next few weeks, Emil immersed himself in the details of the business and was able to produce an all-encompassing report on the business's previous year. When Georgii returned to Stuttgart, Emil called on him at his house, telling him that, in spite of the tobacco master's resistance, Emil needed complete freedom of movement. Much later that night, convivial and jolly, Georgii toasted Emil for doing a fine job, saying he trusted Emil completely. But the next morning at 7:00 Georgii showed up at work to check up on Emil. One step ahead of Georgii, Emil had made sure to get to work by 6:00am, and Georgii was surprised and impressed to find Emil already busy at his desk when he arrived. After this, Georgii offered him a modest raise as well as free use of the upstairs apartment that Karamousas would shortly be vacating for a more spacious one in town.

Engagement

Emil now felt financially secure enough to announce his engagement to Berta. He wrote her a letter and then impulsively rushed to the nearest tailor to order a tuxedo. On July 13th, 1898, he arrived in Calw with a big bouquet of flowers for Berta. He placed an engagement notice in the local paper and took Berta to the jeweler for a ring. They also paid a visit to a recently established photographer to have their pictures taken. Emil's packages had arrived from Greece and he insisted they be photographed in the full traditional Greek costumes he'd sent. At first Berta wanted a more conventional photograph, but then, overcoming her shyness, she laughed and wore the costume for another shot. For months afterward, these pictures were the central adornment in the photographer's window and a subject of endless local commentary.

Engagement photographs

The engagement was celebrated in great style the following day (Berta's birthday) with a festive dinner, music and dance. Then, their relationship properly established according to all rules of society, the couple was finally allowed to appear in public arm in arm without causing a scandal.

Georgii's plan

When Emil first returned to Stuttgart, Emil Georgii had encouraged him to invest what was left of his small inheritance in his firm. Emil did so, trusting Georgii. But when he had finally deciphered and balanced the company books, he discovered significant losses and realized that the investments from Georgii's relatives, as well as his own, were in serious jeopardy. Georgii looked pained when confronted by this surprising news and said he needed to think things over. Fairly soon he came back with a plan to increase capital—he would create a private label manufacturing company.

On paper, this idea looked perfect: a central organization producing separate brands for participating shareholding firms who wouldn't have to worry about equipment or labor. Georgii's machines were part of the business plan, and he envisioned them selling well in Germany and abroad.

Georgii spent the entire summer preparing and looking for investors, and on October 1st, 1898, the new company, called United Cigarette Works, was launched with a capital investment of 450,000 Marks. The main investors were Georgii, his wife and brother-in-law, Ostermeyer, and fourteen very respected cigar manufacturers. The latter were eager to expand into the new business of cigarettes. Georgii drew up a ten-year contract for himself as general manager with a handsome annual salary. Emil, who would be running both companies, Georgii und Harr as well as United Cigarette Works, was not included in the contract.

Nobody noticed the inherent flaw in Georgii's plan, which was that if shareholders purchased discounted cigarettes from their own company, they were minimizing the return on their investment. Later, Emil wondered why he hadn't seen this at the outset. It was his first taste of what happens when conflicting expectations drain the life out of an organization.

Next, Georgii bought a commercial building—an old framework house that needed extensive renovation on the east side of town. He equipped it generously, and months went by before everything was up and running. The new brands needed planning and design and required a large inventory of boxes, labels and cigarette papers—all of which Emil had to coordinate.

Emil was constantly kept busy by the needs of the moment. He usually did not get his own work done until everyone else had gone home for the night. For lunch he sometimes went to a local restaurant, phoning in his order ahead to save time. A group of young architects enjoyed meeting there and he got to know them well, especially a man named Emil Weippert ("I shall start an Emil club soon," said Emil). In the evening, if he got hungry, he would run next door to the little grocery at the corner for a sandwich, then continue working until well past midnight. Once the motherly shopkeeper said to him, "I saw your light on late again—and when I woke up this morning you were still at work. You must be earning a pile of money." Emil answered: "If I got paid for all my work, that much money wouldn't even exist!" He was voicing a fledgling thought which he only fully understood many years later, namely that work and payment are separate entities, work being one's contribution to society and payment being the sustenance needed in order to execute that contribution.

A little house with a view

In 1899, Georgii and his wife decided to move closer to the United Cigarette Works, and they bought a piece of land on the east side of the city. While their villa was being built, they lived nearby in a new development with charming houses. One day in April, Emil came to Georgii's office with worries about the company's massive expenses.

"Every beginning has outlays," Georgii answered cheerfully. "You shouldn't worry so much—the sales will soon justify the expenses. Why don't you come spend the evening with us and take your mind off the business?" Emil accepted the invitation and, upon arriving at Georgii's, promptly fell in love with the neighborhood. He asked his architect friend Weippert to look for available apartments in the same complex Georgii was living in. A few days later, Weippert brought him the keys to a little two-bedroom, ground-floor flat with a glass veranda in front and porch and garden in back. It was an enchanting home with climbing roses and an open view to both sides, over vineyards to the west and distant hills to the east. The road was unpaved and gas and electricity had not yet been installed. In spite of that, and because it was so unspoiled and inexpensive, Emil leased it.

On Whitsun in 1899, Berta was allowed a rare holiday and given permission to travel alone for the first time in her life. Emil and the Sepps met her in Goeppingen, and, although the day started out rainy, the group was in the best of spirits. They rented a carriage and drove up to the Hohenstaufen castle. The sun came out and they walked to the Rechberg Mountain and from there to Schwäbisch Gmünd. It was Emil's first time back since leaving as a schoolboy and the picturesque town had grown in size. The four of them visited the house where Emil had been born and the graves of his parents. They toured the town, admiring the old Roman wall and staring through the windows of the jewelers' shops. After lunch in the Hotel Rath, they strolled along the little river while Emil reminisced until it was time to part. The Sepps went home and Emil took Berta back to Calw. On their way back, they made a detour to Stuttgart where, to Berta's great surprise and delight, he showed her the little house he had rented.

Emil stayed the night at the Heldmaiers—a new privilege that came with their formal engagement—sleeping in Berta's room under the eaves while she slept with her sister. Hers was a simple enough little room, but it was paradise for someone as much in love as Emil.

Wedding and honeymoon

As his wedding day approached, Emil asked Georgii how much time he could take off, and Georgii replied that the decision belonged to Emil. As a result, Emil took just one week. The Heldmaiers organized a bachelor party the evening before the wedding and it was a lively, carefree affair. The next morning the couple went to the registry office for their marriage license. Berta wore a silk dress in blue and white (the Greek colors) which Emil had given her, and a little blue hat with an ostrich feather made by her mother. After lunch, at one o'clock, the couple met at the church and now Berta was dressed in white. On seeing her, Emil was speechless, sure that Calw had never before seen a bride so lovely and so pure. The town minister officiated with solemn and kindly words, and the church choir, of which Berta had been a member, sang for her wedding and for her farewell.

Wedding menu

After the ceremony the newlyweds and their guests formed a long procession on foot that passed by the Heldmaier house and over the bridge to the Badische Hof restaurant for the wedding feast. Emil splurged and bought champagne for everyone, and coffee was served in the sunlit garden. After the meal, Emil wanted to leave right away with Berta to forgo the hours of lewd jokes and dancing they'd witnessed at Emma's wedding. But Herr Heldmaier insisted they stay out of courtesy to their guests, just as Emma and her husband had done. Emil, determined to have his way, prepared himself for a fight but had the presence of mind to ask Georgii Sr. and his uncle Staudenmayer for help first. These two gentlemen took Heldmaier aside and the latter eventually gave way, twinkling and beaming and saying he would probably have done exactly the same thing.

After bidding their closest friends farewell, the couple slipped away in a carriage, past a surprised Emma. They went home, changed into travel clothes, and drove to the station to meet with Berta's best friend, Berta Stroh, and her new husband, Adolf Schmid—they had just been married the same day. The two couples were so fond of each other that they had decided to spend their honeymoon together. For all of them, it was an extraordinary sensation to be on their own as newlyweds.

The Schmids decided to stay in Horb for their wedding night and got off the train after a few stops. Emil wanted royal treatment for his bride, so they continued to Stuttgart, where they checked into the Marquardt, the best hotel in town. The train ride was unforgettably poignant for Emil. The weeks before the wedding had tired Berta so much that she fell asleep with her head on his shoulder. *How glad I am*, he thought, *that I've taken her away from her exhausting life.* They arrived at the hotel and were shown into a truly splendid room, where they felt like a prince and princess in a fairy tale.

The next day they met the Schmids again and traveled to Zürich. All four were exceedingly merry. They found rooms in a small hotel at the center of town and stayed for a few days, climbing the smallest Swiss mountain they could find and savoring local restaurants. Emil said that since honeymoons are unique events, they had the right to splurge, so, just once, they ate at the exclusive Baur au Lac, haunt of the rich and famous. They even managed a straight face when they saw the prices on the menu.

Emil was determined never to appear the penniless husband. He considered it his duty to introduce the delights of the world to his adorable young bride, previously so restricted to her home. She, for her part, longed to see and experience what she had only read about.

They took their ease for three more exquisite days. Then they returned to Stuttgart, where they found their little house littered with crates and boxes of furniture and utensils, donated by parents and relatives. They were grateful, but it was a rude reentry into practical life. Emil went back to work while poor Berta was left to unpack and sort—a task that took a long time because Emil was only free on Sundays and preferred spending that precious time with his wife instead of the furnishings. Still, she did manage in the end and made the house cozy with the help of her sewing and embroidery skills. Sometimes they ate out and walked in the hills, but mainly they lounged at home, absorbed in each other.

Each day Berta went to the local market or to town looking for unusual delicacies with which to create special meals for her husband.

Having subsisted on sandwiches and restaurant fare before his marriage, Emil loved her home-cooked food. The more he praised her cooking, the more inventive she became. Sometimes they strolled out in the moonlight after supper, entertaining each other with news of the day. Evening was their favorite time, when their life felt most warm and secure, and larger world events interested them not at all.

Then, in the summer of 1900, Berta's father, Georg Heldmaier, died suddenly. The family, including Berta, had to help put his affairs in order and comfort the bereaved Pauline. Shortly after his death, Berta became pregnant and was proud and happy to become a mother. But her health took a turn and she suffered a miscarriage, a loss that affected her greatly. Never robust in the best of times, she remained ill for months, and the doctors were not able to help. Finally a young naturopath, adept at a holistic approach to healing, took over her care and helped her back to her feet. But for a long time she mourned her lost child.

Anxiety rising

As one year moved into the next, dissension and doubt grew in United Cigarette Works. Some shareholders became suspicious that the venture was built on sand. They had not received any dividends and, although they were experts in the cigar trade, their cigarette sales were slow because they were inexperienced at marketing them. The sales manager, Karrer, recognized the problem and tried to alleviate it by starting a cigarette trade association as a center for information and assistance. He asked Emil to be its treasurer, which Emil was glad to do as it enabled him to network with like-minded people.

With anxiety stirring in his professional environment, Emil sat down with his wife to look over their own personal finances and found they were living beyond their means. In almost four years working for Georgii, Emil had not received a salary increase, and now he was providing for two. Assured that Georgii valued his competence as manager, he handed him a list of his income and expenses and requested a raise. Georgii, thinking Emil's salary quite adequate, said, "I surely can't tell the Board you're starving." His answer appalled Emil and made him realize that his future with the company was as shaky as the shareholders' dividends.

The company's financial report for 1901 predicted a coming catastrophe, and the chairman, Ostermeyer, raged against his brother-in-law Georgii, saying he must step down as director. "Henceforth he can do what he likes with his life and his machines," Ostermeyer stormed. Emil was worried about his own small share in the business, but when he expressed his concern to Ostermeyer, he was told, "It's your own fault for investing in this company." This infuriated Emil and he applied moral pressure.

"You're a millionaire," Emil said, "and I am a young beginner." Then Ostermeyer promised to pay him back his shares, adding that Emil would shortly be answerable to a new director. On sudden impulse, Emil said, "That may not be necessary. I know this company inside and out. Try me, you have nothing to lose—and for the beginning I won't even ask for a raise." The proposition appealed to Ostermeyer, and the Board agreed. That was how in 1902 Emil, at 26, took on the role of company director and obtained the freedom of action he so badly wanted.

Georgii could not bear the thought of his erstwhile employee and his father's former apprentice replacing him. To salvage his dignity, he took his own firm, Georgii und Harr, as well as the sales representative Karrer, out of the United Cigarette Works and remained as an independent client with major concessions.

Meanwhile, Emil had his mind on other matters. He fired Karamousas, hired a younger tobacco master, and eliminated the still imperfect and unpredictable machines, replacing them with more efficient hand labor. As a further measure, he asked Berta to help him with the bookkeeping. She was delighted to do so, feeling lonely at home. For her excellent work and to supplement their income, her boss (Emil) paid her a very modest salary. Finally he wrote off and discarded thousands of old labels, engraved cigarette papers, cartons, and stale cigarettes, making a clean sweep of the warehouse.

Emil and Berta working together

Georgii complained so bitterly about these radical measures that the Board hired a consultant for an objective evaluation. The man they chose was the successful and respected Mr. Mandelbaum of the firm Manoli in Berlin. His analysis of the previous state of the company's affairs was devastating, but he was full of praise for Emil and his courageous decisions. "Come and visit me in my firm any time if you need advice," he said cordially, and Emil was glad to do so some months later.

Buoyed by Mandelbaum's endorsement, Emil slowly developed a healthy working basis for the United Cigarette Works. The Board members were pleased and invited him to join them as a member of the Board, granting him an annual salary of 4000 Marks, which was raised to 8000 Marks a year later.

Berta, now a work colleague, became involved in finding ways to improve the business. It was her idea that Emil visit each of their shareholding companies at least twice a year to form a closer working relationship with them and to advise them on sales. Emil began enjoying these outings and was welcomed wherever he went. Often he took the night train—in those days sleeping compartments were cozy and affordable, and he always took light reading along. His favorite novel featured Constantinople (Istanbul), much of the plot taking place in an elegant hotel called the Pera Palace. It was a fantasy location for the leisure classes in an exotic setting, and at the time Emil would never have believed that he would one day be an honored guest in that very establishment.

Stabilizing the business

Emil's great achievement at the end of 1902 was a dividend of 5% paid out to United Cigarette Works shareholders. It did not endear him to Georgii who, although independent, was still a shareholder. In fact, Georgii became so antagonistic that he made Emil uneasy.

"I believe eventually Ostermeyer will want me out because, after all, he is Georgii's brother-in-law," Emil said to Berta. She advised him to do his best and to keep his eyes open for other opportunities.

Accordingly, Emil set out with great energy to find new clientele beyond the shareholders—in the form of wholesale customers. He was so persistent in this quest that one client remarked with a sheepish grin that the only reason he started dealing with United Cigarette Works was to gain respite from Emil's letters.

Emil was just as persistent with his suppliers. He wanted to immerse himself in all aspects of the business, so he often traveled to Dresden with his tobacco master, spending a day smoking, evaluating and writing comparisons until the choices were made. Dresden, at that time, was the tobacco capital of Germany, and Emil and his tobacco master became well known there. As soon as they stepped off the train, the grapevine would announce their arrival, and they would be inundated with samples and offers as soon as they arrived at their hotel. Emil chose the most reputable importers, invariably making friends with them. His favorites were the four Enfiezioglou brothers. They were gentlemanly and trustworthy Greeks who loved their tobacco. They demanded a high price, but their quality was always the best. At the end of a day of sampling and bartering, Emil and the Enfiezioglou brothers would get together for a friendly meal. Once they completed a deal, Emil was confident that his exact selections would arrive in Stuttgart.

Aware that he could never master all there was to know about tobacco, Emil focused on becoming an expert at identifying quality—feeling its crispness, looking at its color, smelling its aroma, and tasting it. A session evaluating 50 to 70 samples per day was not unusual for him. The nicotine kept him highly alert but it took a toll on his health. Once, suffering acute nicotine poisoning, he begged Berta to accompany him as his nurse on a business trip to Rotterdam. Another time, while climbing a hill on vacation, he suffered a fainting spell. These incidents made him realize he had to cut back and delegate more to his tobacco master.

Finding staff

Emil was always on the search for experienced employees. Once, a Berlin client told him about a local colony of Jewish immigrants from Galicia. "They are the best workers," he said. "You can rely on them." Emil paid the colony a visit and looked up its elderly rabbi. Soon he and the rabbi were sitting together at tea and Emil was extolling the virtues of southern Germany. He had to be persistent—the potential workers were not thrilled at the idea of leaving Berlin for what they considered the "provinces." But he made them a good offer and promised to pay their train fare. When the first group arrived in Stuttgart, he met them at the station and took them to their lodgings before taking them on a walk through town. In an effort to make them feel at home, he introduced them to the local rabbi and invited them all to a meal. The newcomers settled in well, enjoying their work and letting their friends back in Berlin—many of whom later followed—know that they were happy. Emil became friendly with the local rabbi, and if ever there was a problem with one of the workers, he and the rabbi solved it together.

Visitors to the company—even competitors—always found a welcome. Emil freely showed them through the firm without worrying about competition. One of these visitors was a brash little American named Gutschow, sent on a fact-finding mission to Germany by J.B. Duke's American Tobacco Company. He came padded with expense dollars and seemed insignificant at the time, but later he would play an important role in Emil's business life.

Science as new religion

For many people in Germany at that time, science was the new religion. Educated society loved discussing Haeckel, Darwin, and the achievements of modern experimentation, but blushed when the words "spirit" or "soul" were mentioned. Emil's association with the Sepps had opened his mind to the wonders and riddles of natural science, but both Emil and Berta had existential questions that they felt could not be explained by science alone. In her diary, Berta wrote:

> During my childhood I had a personal relationship with the Redeemer and promised to be faithful to him, but during confirmation class I struggled with doubt, wishing the minister could prove the existence of God although I didn't dare ask him. At communion, I became very unsure. I couldn't understand the sacrificial death of Christ and the words: "He who is unworthy but eats and drinks (of the sacrament) will be judged." I felt myself to be so unworthy. I battled with myself, listening to sermons which seemed full of contradiction. Once I mentioned this to my sister and she called me godless. She said one must just believe, but I kept asking myself, why has God given me reason if I can't use it? Religion should be able to tolerate someone thinking about it.

While Berta tried to maintain the faith of her childhood, Emil had completely discarded religion. For a time, he had gone to church with Berta and her family on Sundays and afterward discussed the merits of the sermon with her. But once married, they both stopped going altogether.

Attempt at mind control

Once, during the time of Berta's convalescence after her miscarriage, and when the cigarette business was at its shakiest, Emil read a news article about an upcoming lecture that offered to help attendees achieve success through mind control.

"That might be the thing for me," he said half in jest. "I could use a little control." He went to the lecture and heard about a method of focusing thought through concentration, but was taken aback to find out that the speaker was a theosophist (theosophy being a religious sect, as far as he was aware). "If I had known that," he told Berta afterward, "I would not have gone." Still, the lecture was interesting and he was animated recounting it to her. He even decided to put what he'd heard to the test. "I have had a difficult letter on my desk for a week," he said. "Let's see if the theory works." He concentrated his thoughts on the letter and, sure enough, after a few days the best way of dealing with it emerged in his mind. He was not a dabbler and engaged in no more of such experiments, but the exercise convinced him that thoughts have power and can be schooled.

Berta was curious to know more about theosophy, so Emil did some research and came up with a succinct definition: "Theosophy means 'Wisdom of God' and it was started in New York in 1875. It is said to be an esoteric philosophy of life rather than a religion and has branches in most European countries." Berta found this interesting, and when another theosophist speaker, named Jaskowsky, came to Stuttgart, both she and Emil went to hear him speak.

"He mentioned *soul* and *spirit* and no one blushed," said Berta as they were leaving. "I had no idea so many people take an interest in such things."

"Look, there's José del Monte," Emil said as they stepped outside. "He makes boxes for our cigarettes. Let's say hello." Berta smiled at the energetic little man walking toward them. While not handsome, his open face exuded honest kindness.

"Were you just at Jaskowsky's lecture?" del Monte asked in surprise. "If you're interested in that kind of thing, you should hear the philosopher and theosophist, Dr. Steiner. I'll send you tickets when he comes to Stuttgart."

Some time later he sent them the promised tickets. They went and found the large hall full of an interesting array of people. All seats were taken and several people stood at the back. Del Monte sat next to them. As they waited in their seats, the murmur of conversation suddenly died down and an elegant, slender man with black hair and black clothing walked lightly down the aisle and stepped onto the podium. Rudolf Steiner surveyed his audience for a moment and then began to speak with a slight Austrian accent.

Rudolf Steiner

He was animated and cordial, presenting his material in an imaginative yet authoritative way. Only once did doubts assail Emil, when Steiner mentioned the Saint John Gospel. *Now this man, whom I was just beginning to admire, brings in the Gospels, which I gave up on long ago,* he thought.

Nonetheless, Emil listened with growing interest as Steiner talked about the origins of the world and the solar system not as a random explosion, but as a gradual evolution under the wise guidance of spiritual beings. He said that the visible world and the cosmos were equally imbued with spirit and that anyone could grasp these ideas by means of thinking. He praised natural science as a great achievement, but said that, in the end, it would lead nowhere unless coupled with a study of the spiritual laws underlying physical phenomena. He did not proselytize or use worn-out phrases; he was warm and courteous and perfectly matter-of-fact. This lecture had nothing to do with dogma, Emil felt; this man was quite obviously talking out of direct experience.

When the lecture was over, the Molts walked to the door with their friend del Monte and thanked him profusely for having invited them. He was happy too, as no one else in his circle of business acquaintances was in the least inclined toward philosophical conversation. As the three of them walked through town talking, Emil realized that his previous rejection of religious ideas had more to do with outdated church tradition than with the truths underlying them.

"How can we find out more about this man?" asked Emil.

"My uncle, Adolf Arenson, knows all about him," replied del Monte. "I'll be seeing him on Sunday for afternoon coffee. If you'd like to come along, I'm sure you'd be most welcome." The Molts were delighted, both at the opportunity to hear more about Steiner and to become better acquainted with this kind business associate, del Monte.

Tea at Bad Cannstatt

Adolf Arenson lived in Bad Cannstatt, a spa town on the outskirts of Stuttgart. When the Molts reached the house with del Monte, they heard a piano accompanying an exquisite song issuing from the open window. They stopped and listened and when it ended, rang the bell. The singer, a graceful woman, greeted them and invited them into the sitting room. Of early middle age, with a warm and charming face and lively eyes, she introduced herself as Deborah Arenson. She bustled off to the kitchen to ask for fresh tea and coffee, and meanwhile del Monte broke the ice by introducing everyone. Sitting at the piano was Deborah's husband, Adolf, older than she and immensely compelling, with the wisest face they had ever seen. He rose and shook their hands, then introduced them to his two teenage daughters and his young friend, Carl Unger, all three sitting on the couch. His third child, a little boy, sat under the piano on the floor, holding a pet cat. The Molts were instantly drawn out of their shy reserve.

Adolf Arenson, they learned, was a native of Hamburg who had built a successful business in Chile before returning to Hamburg and marrying his cousin, Deborah Piza. He was now in his second career as a musician, composing and writing operas. The couple had moved to Cannstatt together and joined the Theosophical Society. Carl Unger, born near Stuttgart, was Arenson's junior by 23 years and his future son-in-law. His grandfather was the noted mathematician, Ephraim Salomon Unger, and his father was a banker. When he was 14, Unger, an agnostic and a lover of natural science, came to study music with Arenson and they became friends. Arenson, who was interested in reincarnation, mentioned this to Carl, who accepted the idea only after months of reflection, concluding that it in no way negated his understanding of science.

"Carl is a medical miracle," said del Monte. "He carries a bullet right next to his heart." Unger laughed and explained that a comrade had mistakenly shot him while he was in military service.

"Yes," said Arenson. "He thought he was about to die and decided the experience would give him a chance to test his views about life after death. But luckily for us he survived!"

"I started a company making precision instruments with the goal of becoming financially stable enough to pursue my philosophical interests," Unger said. "Both Arenson and I became active in the Theosophical Society and started a study group."

"And," added Arenson, "shortly after that, we met Steiner and, from then on, have preoccupied ourselves with his ideas."

"And, friend del Monte, how do you fit into this story?" asked Berta.

"I was also born in Hamburg," he said, "but spent most of my life in Chile, only coming here in '98, encouraged by Uncle Adolf. He helped me start my box company and I have had great luck with it, not least because of my best customer, the United Cigarette Works. I enjoy living here near my family and enjoy the stimulating new ideas that have found such receptive ground in Stuttgart."

"Let us pause for supper," suggested Deborah, "and afterward we will tell you about Rudolf Steiner."

"Are you sure we're not overstaying our welcome?" asked Berta, not wanting for a minute to leave. She was assured the cook had made a hearty soup, enough for everyone. After the meal, Deborah asked the girls to put their brother to bed, and the adults moved back to the sitting room.

About Rudolf Steiner

"Our friend and mentor, Rudolf Steiner," Arenson explained, "was born in German-speaking Kraljevec in 1861. His father was a railroad employee and the family lived an extremely frugal life. From a very young age, Steiner was able to see into the nonmaterial world and was astonished to find out that not everyone could do so. He was a very apt student in school, and his teachers helped him go on to higher education. Becoming fascinated by geometry and physics, he realized they were outer expressions of the spiritual forces that he experienced. To ground himself further in the physical scientific world, he attended technical college in Vienna. After graduating, he edited Goethe's scientific works in Weimar. Steiner went on to teach students and adults and slowly developed a following. Eventually he moved to Berlin and continued lecturing and writing. Annie Besant, head of the Theosophical Society,[2] asked him to head its German section. He accepted because, as he said, the Society had a basis in spiritual research and its members were open to the ideas he was presenting.

"One of his early books, entitled *How to Know Higher Worlds*, is an esoteric self-development handbook. Another, *Christianity as Mystical Fact*, describes the evolution from the ancient mysteries to Christianity. He has brought a counterbalance to the materialism of our time with an ever-widening description of the cosmos and humanity's role in the world. We do what we can to support his teachings."

It was late by the time del Monte and the Molts left. In those few hours everything had gained new depth and meaning for them, but Emil also felt small, realizing how deficient he was in philosophy and a classical education. He had great respect for his new friends, believing them enlightened far beyond what he could ever hope to achieve. *I can read to try to decrease my learning deficit*, he thought. *But can I ever catch up with them?*

---

2 The Theosophical Society was founded in New York in 1875 by Helena Petrovna Blavatsky, Henry Steel Olcott and William Quan Judge. After Blavatsky died, Annie Besant became head of the Esoteric Section.

Carl Unger and Adolf Arenson were among the first to embrace Rudolf Steiner's scientific and epistemological groundwork, and together they were able to cultivate these ideas through working with interested groups of people. They also had sessions for young people on certain weekday evenings in the Arenson house. Initially, neither Berta nor Emil felt inclined to join their Theosophical Society. Those members seated in the front rows—mostly women with flowing gowns and flamboyant hair styles—at first disturbed and deterred them from stepping any closer to the Society itself.

But then Berta joined Adolf Arenson's and Carl Unger's introductory study course, making notes to share with Emil. Each session left her more enthusiastic. Sometimes Emil fetched her and was introduced to various members of the group, but he always excused himself from attending, saying that he did not have time and that his wife would share the new ideas with him.

Rudolf Steiner started coming to Stuttgart more frequently and began to define his own philosophy using the terms "spiritual science" and "anthroposophy" (human wisdom), rather than the term "theosophy" (divine wisdom). Often he introduced his lectures by saying that in previous times, esoteric knowledge had been secret and restricted to only those who were suitably trained. It was then a means to exert positive influence over political and social institutions, indirectly, through its fruits. He described the printing press as the invention that brought what was previously hidden into the public domain. It opened up philosophical discussion of existential questions, such as where does humanity come from? What is its goal? What lies hidden behind visible forms and what happens after death? Steiner talked about karma and reincarnation and how, after death, the soul prepares for the next birth, framing the results of its previous lifetimes into its future destiny.

In 1905 Emil was able to win over the owners of W. Mueller, a prestigious cigar wholesale company in Hamburg. The owners, Ludwig Mueller and his brother-in-law, Max Marx, became customers and shareholders of the United Cigarette Works, which would manufacture their own private-label cigarettes. Together with Emil they searched for a suitable brand name for their new line. Emil went to Hamburg several times with suggestions, but nothing caught their fancy. Then one day they sent him word that they'd bought the brand "Waldorf Astoria" with its wreath-and-crown logo.

Waldorf Astoria logo

The name "Waldorf Astoria" originated with John Jacob Astor (1763–1848), native of a small town south of Stuttgart called Walldorf. Astor emigrated to the United States at a young age and made a fortune in the fur trade. In the 1850s the Astors' house was the most elegant in New York City, and John Jacob's descendants built the famous Waldorf Astoria Hotel to commemorate him. The family's Waldorf Astoria Cigar Company expanded into cigarettes and later sold cigarettes in Germany. For whatever reason, the principals did not understand the German market; the company failed and was put up for sale.

Emil loved the logo and the cigarettes—the American style was bold and contemporary and the cigarettes had names like "Chicago," "New York," "Boston" and "Washington"—all so different from European cigarettes whose artwork featured Oriental themes. Emil was convinced that the American look would be popular and easy to promote with the help of Mueller and Marx, and he considered this new product a windfall for the United Cigarette Works. He leased a second production facility and trained new staff under the tutelage of his works manager, Sophie Wiedman, now named Kaiser since her marriage. Before long, the first shipments of Waldorf Astoria cigarettes—hand-rolled with cork tips—were on their way to Hamburg.

Hiking in Austria

The Molts celebrated the successful business venture by packing their knapsacks and hiking in the mountains of Austria for three weeks. They had a wonderful time walking the hills, discovering edelweiss and other flowers, exploring hidden valleys with small animals for company, and staying in rustic inns and hostels. They had gone hiking in the beauty of nature before, but this time they found that their new understanding of the cosmic forces underlying nature added a dimension to their experience. Although this walking tour challenged Berta's physical limits, they came home fit and feeling reborn. Before the vacation, Emil had been in medical care due to heart and liver ailments, but the trip brought him back to health. Berta's health was so improved that she became pregnant shortly after returning. She stopped working at the company after some months, and Emil had a telephone installed in the house so she could call him at any time.

At work, orders from Hamburg were pouring in, often delivered personally by Max Marx, who enjoyed coming to Stuttgart. A cordial relationship developed between him and Emil. Although they were different in many ways, they were alike in that both were courageous, enthusiastic men with a zest for life and a bit of brashness. Emil often brought Marx home for dinner. One night Marx mentioned how nice it would be to have one's own manufacturing facility. Emil agreed— he could do much more if he were not serving so many bosses. They promised that if such an opportunity ever arose, they'd let each other know, and it happened sooner than either of them imagined.

Karrer asks for help

On a day in late fall 1905, the salesman Karrer, still working for Georgii, came to Emil on a confidential mission. He had found a new client in the prestigious firm of Abraham, based in Hamburg. Emil knew of the Abraham brothers, Richard and Emil—they imported Havana cigars and Egyptian Dimitrino cigarettes. They were much talked about in the industry as being very wealthy and living in the most exclusive section of town.

The German government was planning to impose a stiff tariff on imported cigars and cigarettes as a means of protecting domestic production. The Abrahams, concerned about the impact this would have on their business, began discussing the possibility of either manufacturing their own cigarettes or entering into a partnership with an existing German company. They asked Karrer for advice and he immediately saw an opportunity for his boss Georgii, thinking that the latter might be delighted to sell or merge Georgii und Harr with the cash-rich Abrahams.

Karrer couldn't figure out whether Georgii would be willing to include the United Cigarette Works in such a deal. "What do you think I should do?" he asked Emil. Emil told Karrer he should simply inform Georgii of the opportunity and let him deal with it in any way he wanted. He hoped Georgii would not drop the United Cigarette Works. Georgii, whose business had not improved, recognized the opportunity but came back with what Emil knew was an unacceptably high purchase price. Karrer was extremely embarrassed and, feeling out of his depth as a business negotiator, he begged Emil to accompany him to Hamburg to present the proposal. Emil was concerned—he thought that if the deal turned sour it could easily harm his company as well as Georgii und Harr. He ultimately agreed to go, but only as a friend and advisor, limiting his role to that of listener.

An audacious business proposition

As they expected, the Abraham brothers rejected Georgii's proposal. At that instant Emil, recalling his conversation with Max Marx, realized that between his own expertise and Marx's Waldorf Astoria brand, they had exactly what the Abrahams were looking for. He called Marx, saying he happened to be in Hamburg and would like to pay him a brief visit. Marx knew and respected the Abrahams, having done business with them in the past, and when Emil unveiled the idea of a collaborative venture, Marx was not opposed to it.

Emil went back to the Abrahams with the idea and they, too, were interested. Now he was faced with the diplomatic matter of bringing the two parties together. It was beneath the dignity of the great Abrahams to seek out the more modest offices of Mueller and Marx, while Max Marx saw no reason to run to the Abraham offices, since he owned the

Waldorf Astoria trademark. Richard Abraham solved the problem by inviting Marx, together with Emil and Karrer, to join them for a social Sunday lunch at his brother's luxurious villa.

The Abraham brothers were gracious, receiving their guests on a veranda overlooking a garden. Emil and Karrer were impressed, and so indeed was Marx. As experienced businessmen, the Abrahams came straight to the point, and Emil was able to demonstrate the viability of the undertaking with the help of a financial outline. Toward the end of the luncheon Karrer, who by this time was interested in the project for himself, began to worry that Emil may have given away too much information and that the Hamburg gentlemen would sideline the two of them. But when Marx and the Abrahams reached an agreement to start a new company with cigarettes manufactured by Emil, Emil said, "I will only participate if I have a stake in the company." The others were astonished.

"What share do you want in the business then?" Marx asked. For a moment, Emil was at a loss for words, but (as he later noted) his good angel came to his assistance with a bold and simple answer.

"Exactly as much as you!" he said. He knew he would have trouble raising the money to invest, but to his own surprise he remained calm in the moment.

Each of the three Hamburg gentlemen agreed to invest 20,000 Marks, as did Emil. Karrer then offered 5000, which brought the startup capital to 85,000 Marks. They appointed Emil as general manager of the new company (Marx vouching for him) at a salary of 6000 Marks per annum and 15% of net profit. Karrer was retained as sales manager with a salary of 7000 Marks per annum and 4% of net profit. Emil insisted that he manufacture in Stuttgart where he had his contacts. They decided that the head office, as well as sales and marketing, were to be in Hamburg. After all this was agreed to, the name "The Waldorf Astoria Cigarette Company, Hamburg/Stuttgart," was decided upon. Then they finished with an elegant champagne luncheon.

Phoning Berta with the news

Afterward, Emil was elated. He telephoned Berta when he could, describing the extraordinary turn of events and the wise guidance that brought him there at the right moment. For the first time he realized what was to become a motto in his life—*Alone I can do nothing; I can only be productive working together with others*. She was impressed, knowing that this new venture was just what he needed, but she wanted to know how he was going to raise the funds. On the train back to Stuttgart, Emil decided to ask his bank manager for a loan, believing he would not be able to get more than 10,000 Marks.

Berta asks her mother

But Berta was determined to help. Knowing that her father had left her mother a modest legacy, she invited her to a day of shopping in Stuttgart. Over tea she told her mother what Emil had done in Hamburg and asked whether she would be willing to give them a loan. Her formerly unbending mother smiled at her radiant, pregnant daughter and said she would be glad to help. *This gift is better than any I could have had in my childhood*, thought Berta. The bank manager, seeing the merit in the plan, promised Emil the rest of the money, and by the time the payment to Hamburg was due, Emil was able to send the full amount to his new colleagues.

Breaking the news to the United Cigarette Works

After this, Emil asked for a meeting with Herr von Eicken, the current chairman of the Board at United Cigarette Works, and broke the news that he would be leaving the company in January. He promised to find and train a good replacement for himself. Von Eicken was astonished and admired Emil's courage for trying to start a new company just when taxes were about to be imposed.

"It is the perfect time, since the importing companies will have to raise their prices," said Emil with conviction.

Finally, and with heavy hearts, Karrer and Emil went to present Emil Georgii with their news. Having his proposal turned down by the Abrahams only to find out that Emil, of all people, had negotiated a different deal was too much for poor Georgii. Additionally, he said, a new manager for the United Cigarette Works could be found, but losing his best traveling salesman was a calamity. Emil felt terrible for his former friend and for the disappointment it would cause the Georgii family in Calw. He promised to help in whatever way he could, but it was cold comfort for Georgii. Karrer resigned from Georgii und Harr immediately and began looking for a building for their startup in Stuttgart. He found a suitable location near José del Monte's box factory.

When it came time for Emil to leave the United Cigarette Works, he was surprised to find that sixty of his best workers had decided to come with him. The new company opened for business on January 1st, 1906, and the first brochures attracted considerable attention and sales.

Instant success

Round Germany as a central support the rest of the European economic system grouped itself, and on the prosperity and enterprise of Germany, the prosperity of the rest of the Continent mainly depended... — John Maynard Keynes,
The Economic Consequences of the Peace

Emil's new business, the Waldorf Astoria company, grew rapidly, and the staff scrambled to keep up with production. Soon, one building was too small for the company and another was purchased—then a third. Overnight, Stuttgart acquired a reputation as the cigarette capital of Germany, and the firm became a magnet for people from faraway places looking for work. Ishirian, one of Emil's Armenian employees, sent for ten of his compatriots; they arrived, smiling, without a word of German. Mytilencos, a Greek worker, showed up after leaving a job in Zürich. His specialty was hand-filling up to 3000 cigarettes per day. A highly efficient Orthodox worker named Rossbach took work home on

Production

Sundays so he could celebrate Shabbat on Saturdays. (In those days the work week was six days, with only Sundays off.)

Demanding top quality

Emil insisted on using only the top-grade tobacco that was offered to the high end of the market. Often he argued with his Hamburg associates because their preference was a quick sale at discount prices. Emil gave in briefly just once when, encouraged by his Munich distributor, he brought out a line of two-penny cigarettes in competition with the popular Bavarian brand "Sport." But he soon realized the impossibility of having an exclusive brand while selling cut-rate on the side and discontinued the practice. He justified the decision to shed this cheap line to his partners by describing how the shareholders of the United Cigarette Works had demanded cheap cigarettes and how badly it had affected their return on investment. With the company riding a wave of increasing demand, Emil was able to show his partners a healthy profit.

When new shipments of tobacco arrived in Stuttgart, spirits at Waldorf Astoria were high. Bales were stored with just the right humidity. A group of women sorted and mixed the leaves by hand, aerating and stacking them ready for the cut. Their fingers had to develop a fine feel for the appropriate degree of moisture. One worker was an expert at sharpening knives with which to cut the tobacco, using a French sandstone. He could tell which knives needed sharpening based on the "ft ft" sound they made as the tobacco was cut. After cutting, the tobacco was lifted and shaken to achieve the right "woolly" consistency, retaining its glorious color and aroma. The dust, dubbed "Turkish earth," was vacuumed away and used for compost. Finally, the tobacco master mixed tobaccos from Macedonia (for body) with strains from Smyrna (for aroma) and Samsun (for balance and strength), blending with finesse to produce Waldorf Astoria's high-quality cigarettes. The noblest tobacco of all was from Xanthi in Macedonia and was so costly and rare, it was available only to certain clients. Emil deemed it the crown of tobacco creation in both taste and aroma—a far cry from what cigarettes later became.

A difficult birth

In preparation for her confinement, Berta stopped doing the bookkeeping for the company, but she retained her interest in the business and Emil found her to be a wonderful, levelheaded advisor. In order to stay close to Berta during this time, he trained a new person to take over the parts of his job that involved travel.

On May 5th, 1906, Berta, who had planned to give birth at home, was rushed to hospital where she endured a breech birth with an enormous loss of blood. The child was frail with a tenuous hold on life, just like his father and his grandfather had been before him. Berta remained in recovery for a long time, unable to nurse her child, and she never conceived again.

It took a while for the baby, baptized Walter Georg Conrad, to become used to a world that offered him such a difficult entry. He did not tolerate cow's milk, and the beef bouillon the doctor prescribed gave him a rash. The baby grew more frail and Berta was distracted with anxiety. One day, in desperation, she called Emil and asked him to come home. The doctor had recommended clearing the baby's nasal passages by blowing out the nose with a balloon syringe. When Berta hesitated, the doctor did the procedure himself, bursting several blood vessels in little Walter's forehead. When Emil got home and asked the doctor why Walter's forehead was

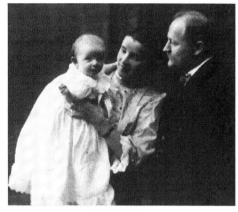
Baby Walter

blue, the doctor claimed (before he was thrown out the door) that Berta had put a blue cap on the baby. Berta tried a few other doctors with no success. Then, on the advice of a neighbor, and without consulting her husband, she called in a homeopath. Dr. Stiegele calmed her nerves and gave the baby remedies that helped immediately. When she told Emil, a strong skeptic of homeopathy, how their son had improved, he became a supporter.

Leaving the little cottage

Now that the Molts had become a family and were experiencing financial success, they said goodbye to their beloved little flat and leased a six-room apartment nearby. It included a maid's room and central heating and was suitable for entertaining. They had little furniture to begin with, but over time they decorated it tastefully.

In August, when Walter was over the worst of his illness but still wakeful and cranky, Berta heard that Steiner was coming to Stuttgart to give a series of evening lectures.[3] Hungry for mental stimulation, she asked her mother to stay with them for two weeks to tend the baby while she and Emil went to the talks. Pauline came, and for those two weeks Walter was a model child, contented during the day and settling

---

3 August 22–September 4, 1906, *At the Gates of Spiritual Science.*

in to bed peacefully at night. Berta wondered how this was possible when she was having so much trouble with him.

"It is always the way with grandparents—my mother was able to do the same when your sister was small," Pauline said. Mother and daughter treasured these two weeks together.

A scrape with the law

That summer a new cigarette tax was announced. Every package of existing stock needed a tax band glued onto it, so all the Waldorf Astoria employees, including Emil, sat down one night after work to complete the project. It turned into a kind of party with tea, biscuits and much singing. Suddenly, there was a heavy knock at the door— the police had noticed the lights on and suspected illegal after-hours labor. The officers were invited to stay for tea but served Emil with a summons for disobeying trade laws instead. The next morning Emil had to go to court. The judge wanted him to sit in the dock, but he refused, preferring to stand with what was left of his dignity. Defiance did not help his case, and he was pronounced guilty and fined heftily. Worse still, his name appeared in the official offenders' book. Years later, as an appointed commercial judge, he asked to have that old blemish removed from the book so he could hold his head up in society again.

After this brief run-in with the law, Emil made the most of the tax challenge by launching a new premium line. It included "Victoria Cup,"

Tax sticker

Waldorf Astoria Cigarette

in a tin, and "Bridge," with 24-carat gold mouthpieces so precious that the cigarettes were later requisitioned as currency when the war broke out.

In spite of higher prices, sales did not suffer, perhaps because imports were now virtually unobtainable and because the name Waldorf Astoria seemed to exert a magical appeal. Trucks painted with the initials W.A.Z. (Waldorf Astoria Zigaretten) carrying cigarette deliveries became a ubiquitous sight.

A strike and a resolve

Emil chose his supervisors for their social and technical skills, and his employees at the Waldorf Astoria factory were generally a happy lot. Emil also employed an old friend, Wally Almendinger, to serve as ombudswoman for any questions or problems that arose. Even so, in the following spring of 1907, the tobacco fillers went on strike. The supervisor was unable to explain why it happened or to negotiate successfully with the workers. Naturally, management was in a predicament with orders pouring in and no one to fill them.

"Berta," said Emil, "I can't let them get away with this. I'm going to Patras to get us some new workers." Berta pointed out the difficulty of the undertaking and the uncertainty of its outcome, so he promised himself he would focus entirely on his task and not fall prey to distractions. Off he went, denying himself a window seat on the train to avoid getting carried away by the scenery. *If I'm successful,* he said to himself, *I will join the Theosophical Society.*

During a stopover in Milan, Emil bought a ticket for Brindisi and checked in at the post office to see if he had any mail. He found a telegram that said, "Return to Stuttgart. Strike over." Although a little disappointed to miss out on a trip to Greece, Emil returned to Stuttgart and found everyone amazed and relieved at the resolution, with things at the company back to normal. Emil dismissed the supervisor involved in the strike and hired the wise and competent Karschinierow, who understood his workers well.

Emil joins the Theosophical Society

After this trial, Emil paid a visit to Adolf Arenson and joined the Theosophical Society. He joined as an associate member because he felt he wouldn't have enough time to participate in meetings, but from that moment on he became totally involved. Berta, who had joined earlier, was delighted.

The next time Steiner was in Stuttgart, Arenson introduced the new members Berta and Emil to him. He was very cordial, welcomed them, and remarked that he had noticed them at his lectures. They requested a personal interview, and he invited them to come to the Hotel Marquardt, where he was staying. They prepared carefully for their visit, knocked on his door with beating hearts, and were warmly received. Emil told him how he experienced the lectures as lifting him out of the mundane and said he wanted to preserve that mood on a continual basis. Berta mentioned the study evenings and how helpful they had been in her daily life. Rudolf Steiner looked pleased and suggested some meditative exercises with a verse for the morning and one for the evening as preparation for the transition between waking and sleep. He also encouraged Emil to join the Society as a full member: It would give him more strength for his work. Berta, her social sense overcoming her shyness, told Steiner he would be welcome to dine with them when in Stuttgart. He was extremely grateful for the offer and shook her hand warmly.

From then on, the path of inner development became the central aspect of the Molts' lives, and as a result Emil's attitude toward his workers, his colleagues, and even the work itself changed. Despite being busy at work, he now found he could make time for spiritual pursuits without compromising his business. He even ended the year with a very good balance sheet.

Giving up alcohol and meat

One morning around this time, over breakfast, the Molts decided to give up alcohol and meat. It no longer felt right for them to go to a lecture after a meal of sausages and wine. Ordinarily, it would have been hard to give all this up without a relapse or two, but the couple encouraged and monitored each other, convinced that this step was important for their spiritual development. The most difficult repercussions of this choice were mockery from colleagues and inadequate restaurant menus. In 1907, vegetarians did exist, but Emil had always considered them strange. Now he tried at all costs to avoid being classed as such. On top of that, he found that ordering mineral water instead of wine was an embarrassing ordeal. But over time, meatless cuisine became more popular—even fashionable. Berta hired a creative cook and together they planned menus so luscious that people found excuses to visit the Molts for lunch or dinner.

The Ticino

At Easter in 1907, Emil took a week off with his friend Weippert, exploring the Canton Ticino in the Italian part of Switzerland. He fell in love with the southerly landscape, its mimosas and magnolias and the lovely Lago Maggiore, with its head in Switzerland and the length of its body in Italy. It was his first glimpse of a place that was to play an important part in his later life. Berta stayed behind because young Walter had the chicken pox.

Renting a garden

That summer, the Molts and Weippert rented a small garden near their home, which served as a playground for Walter. One Sunday they were in the garden enjoying a picnic when the sky announced a summer thunderstorm. The Molts did not want their delicate little boy to get wet, so Emil put him in the stroller and raced home through the streets, swerving around impediments while Berta gathered up the lunch. In those days, men simply did not push strollers, and Emil found it dreadful. "Never again will I have anything to do with that hateful piece of equipment," he said. Walter, however, thought it great fun, laughing all the way back.

Walter in the garden

Walter still needed a great deal of attention. At night he woke up so frequently that Berta kept his cot next to her bed to comfort him without disturbing his father. For months she walked up and down with him. Walter thoroughly enjoyed these nightly diversions. Every time he woke up, he would call energetically: *"Mutterle, Mutterle, Händele halten"* (Mama, Mama, hold my hand).

"You should put an end to this," Dr. Stiegele told her, finally. "Take Walter's cot into another room, as far away from your bedroom as possible." This tactic worked. The boy slept and the parents finally had some peace.

Sunday gatherings in Cannstatt

Sunday afternoons, Berta and Emil went to Cannstatt, where Arenson and his wife, Deborah, had begun hosting a weekly open house—a kind of literary salon with refreshments. These events brought together people of all ages.

"What did you discover this week?" one would ask the other. "What are your new ideas, your dreams?" The group talked about theosophy, literature and music, and these conversations were a rich source of inspiration for Emil especially, who wished to combine his business life with this more artistic, spiritual side.

The General Assembly of the Theosophists

Later in the fall of 1907, the Molts went to Berlin for the General Assembly of the Theosophical Society. During the afternoon break, Dr. Steiner served as a gracious host, welcoming newcomers and helping them circulate among older members. Eliza von Moltke, the wife of General Helmuth von Moltke,[4] head of the German General Staff and one of the Kaiser's closest advisors, was on hand serving refreshments. She warmly invited the Molts to stay for supper at her house. There she told them she thought a new era of peace and spirituality had begun, but that her husband was not convinced. "To him," she said, "the bloody events in Russia are like a torch illuminating a dark future. He believes that peace is still far off." The Molts were astonished to hear that von Moltke had frequent conversations about spirituality with the Kaiser, and that the latter subscribed to the idea of reincarnation.

A split

Emil enjoyed this meeting in Berlin but he felt he had not been entirely wrong in his original perception of the Theosophical Society, which increasingly seemed split into two definite philosophical streams. One was the purist, more mystical and Eastern theosophical movement with its center in Adyar, India. The other was Rudolf Steiner's spiritual science with a Western, Christian approach that Emil and Berta were drawn to.

Joining the esoteric school

In 1908, when Berta and Emil had only been members of the Society for a short while, Steiner invited them to join his esoteric school. They accepted and were sponsored by their friend, Camilla Wandrey. Emil was also elected treasurer for the local branch of the Theosophical Society, which he considered an honor. Meanwhile, Steiner's public

---

4 The nephew of the victor of the battle of Sedan.

lectures were drawing an ever-larger audience. A summer highlight was the lecture cycle, "Universe, Earth and Man," held at the Stuttgart town museum. At one of these lectures, Emil met a sympathetic young artist by the name of Hilde Hamburger. He asked her whether, by chance, she knew the Hamburgers of Patras, and she answered, "Of course I do, they are my uncles!" The Molts were often surprised by such synchronistic meetings. It was a topic for Sundays at the Arensons, and they called the phenomenon "a timeless circulation of friends." The more the Molts participated in gatherings surrounding Steiner, the more their interest in anthroposophical learning grew.

Modernizing

While handwork was still a big part of production at Waldorf Astoria, increasing demand made some mechanization necessary. Cutting and rolling machines had become technically efficient, but they ruined the tobacco, which emerged unrecognizable in taste, aroma and color. Eventually an English machine called Legg mastered the gentle touch required, and Waldorf Astoria bought one in 1908. It was kept in a locked room, and for a while the handworkers regarded this new mechanical device with suspicion.

A trip to the East

As the Waldorf Astoria cigarette enterprise rose to prominence in Germany, both Max Marx and Emil felt the need to observe tobacco cultivation first-hand. Added incentive to travel was the fact that Emil's newly hired tobacco master, Ethiocles Sterghiades, had just invited him to participate in his wedding in his Greek hometown. So in June 1909, Emil and Marx boarded the Orient Express for the 40-hour trip to Constanza. They took their ease on the train, passing the Swabian highlands, then the Alps, then the Danube River and the forests around Vienna.

During the night, Emil was asleep in his bunk dreaming of Rudolf Steiner when suddenly he was rudely awakened by a terrific screeching of brakes and a jolting stop. Just after Budapest, his train had transferred to the wrong track and nearly collided head-on with an oncoming train. It would have been catastrophic but at the very last moment, both engineers were able to stop. Interestingly, Steiner was nearby in Budapest that very night preparing a lecture called "Man Between Death and Rebirth."

The next day, none the worse for their experience, Emil and Marx traveled through the endless fields of Romania and the bare landscape around Bucharest to arrive in Constanza at the mouth of the Danube. There they found a graceful steamer waiting for them. Aboard the ship, Marx and Emil were served fine food and each was offered a spacious stateroom. Emil rose at dawn the next morning and went out onto the deck where he found himself swathed in a ghostlike mist in the middle of the appropriately named Black Sea.

The sun emerged from the fog as they slowly sailed into the mouth of the Bosporus, and Emil was overwhelmed by the sheer beauty of the scenery—seeing Europe to his right and Asia to the left, the shoreline featuring the old watch-towers, Anatoli-Hissar and Rumeli-Hissar. *How fine it is*, he thought, *that my product, which I consider less a commodity and more as something poetic, takes me to the most beautiful cultural and historic parts of the world!*

Constantinople

The ship landed at the Golden Horn, from where Emil and Marx could clearly see the three cities that made up Constantinople at the time—Stambul to the left with the seraglio and the Hagia Sophia towering above it, Galata to the right with its ancient round tower built by the Genoese, and the modern European city of Pera before them. On the Asian side of the water, Emil glimpsed Haider-Pascha with its gleaming new German-built train station.

Emil stood lost in the past for a moment, imagining Alexander the Great passing through on his expedition into Asia. He thought of the ancient Greeks building Byzantium, the Romans conquering the Greeks, and Constantine breaking with Rome to establish the Eastern Church.

He imagined the Crusaders, the Venetians, and the Genoese all traversing this land before the Turks took the city in 1450 and built an empire. He was pulled from his reverie by a shout and a wave from quayside—Ethiocles Sterghiades was waiting with his uncle, Tassoudis. Marx and Emil disembarked, slipping some baksheesh to customs officials who waved them through without checking their bags. At the time there were laws against importing books, cameras and cigars, and between them Emil and Marx had all three.

From the outset, Emil felt a familiarity with the Turks and enjoyed the noisy, teeming quayside, which reminded him of Patras. Sterghiades had a carriage waiting to drive the new arrivals to—of all places—the Pera Palace Hotel that Emil had read about so many times in his favorite train novel. "I shall go up to the hotel on foot so I can get an idea of the city," Emil said, once he realized where they were going.

"You don't know where the hotel is," said Sterghiades, surprised.

"Oh, I do," replied Emil. "It's there," he said, waving his hand in the general direction of the hotel. After climbing through steep, narrow alleys, he did indeed find the hotel, sitting cramped between buildings. He walked into the huge hall, decorated in Moorish style, past the mighty Albanian doorman who was dressed in traditional garments and held a rifle across his chest. Emil felt as though he were dreaming—somehow ending up in the very hotel that had seemed so fascinating to him as a young man. He heard Turkish, Greek and German being spoken amongst the guests, and knew he would have no trouble communicating. Marx arrived soon after and, feeling less comfortable in the strange setting, insisted on sharing a room with Emil.

"I don't trust the foreigners," he said as justification. A hydraulic lift carried them up to their spacious accommodation on the third floor. The view from their room, featuring the Golden Horn in the distance, was spectacular.

In the afternoon they went exploring, finding the streets to be full of international bustle and local soldiers in uniform. The fez was the predominating male head covering, and some women wore veils. There were no cars or streetcars, except for one tram from Galata to Pera. Masses of people thronged the bridge from Galata to Stambul, which trembled under the undulating human burden. Europeans, Asians, Turkmenians, Armenians, Greeks, Albanians, Jews, Arabs and Indians mingled in the streets speaking in their own languages. Constantinople was once the seat of sultans, and they saw a multitude of larger and smaller palaces. The harbor was alive with boats—commercial vessels of all sizes—and warships under various flags.

Emil and Max Marx stopped for lunch in a Greek garden restaurant on the Pera Road where Emil had no trouble finding a vegetarian meal and Marx enjoyed mutton, which was to be his constant standby as they traveled.

Emil wanted to visit historic sites, but Marx persuaded him to go see the modern town. So they went to visit the new train station, which had been designed by a Swabian and financed by a German syndicate. The station was impressive, and they saw a new train being touched up by a dozen workers wearing the fez. Suddenly Emil heard an idiom he knew from Württemberg: "*Do guck na, do isch au no net frisch aag'striche!*" (Hey look, that part isn't painted yet!) Hearing this familiar dialect in

Constantinople train station

the middle of Asia gave him goose bumps. He approached the speaker and learned that these men had been working for the eastern railway for twenty years and had helped build the line from Katakolon to Patras while Emil had been in Greece. They offered their countrymen a test run on the new train, but Marx thought it would take too long so they declined. Emil was proud of his people, realizing how cosmopolitan Swabians were, even while retaining their funny dialect.

The next day, the two friends took a carriage up to Bugurlu and the palace of the presumptive heir to the throne. They had lunch in a little café sitting next to some distinguished Turks, who were dressed in formal attire. Emil offered them a round of Turkish coffee, which sparked a polite conversation. The men belonged to the retinue of the Prince and were about to drive out with him, but before leaving they invited Marx and Emil to look around the palace grounds. The paths were bordered by hedges that had been artfully designed to both expose the views and give privacy to seating areas. A discreet door led to the women's quarters (the harem), which an intrigued Marx tried to get into, but was energetically barred from by a hefty guard. Emil found the view over the Bosporus to be stunning and the gardens exquisite.

Xanthi

That night they took the train to Xanthi with Sterghiades and Tassoudis to meet the Enfiezioglou family. In the morning, they passed Dedeagatsch and a large number of tobacco fields. To his disgrace, Emil did not recognize the tobacco plants, wondering out loud whether the passing fields might be planted with lettuce. His Greek friends were forbidden, on pain of death, ever to tell anyone that story.

Sterghiades' brother, Constantine, met them at the train station and took them to his family home, where they were warmly welcomed. Marx stayed with Constantine while Emil stayed at Sterghi's mother's house. The accommodations were simple but clean, and the entire family mobilized to look after Emil's every need. Xanthi was the center of the finest tobacco cultivation, and Emil's hosts hastened to offer him an exquisite, freshly cut and rolled sample. Emil's heart soared as he slowly savored it, and afterward he admired the aroma that lingered in the room like fine perfume. In his letters home, he recorded his impressions, sending detailed and affectionate accounts of the traditional hospitality extended to him and Marx.

Emil and Marx were taken to visit Omer Aga, a tobacco farmer and an old friend of the Enfiezioglou family, who invited his visitors into his best salon and offered them seats on two low divans. He served them Turkish coffee and sweets and had samples of his best tobacco ready to be rolled into cigarettes. A lively conversation ensued, with Constantine interpreting for the farmer who sat crossed-legged and full of animation. He showed the group his beautiful plantation, an estate large enough but no larger than his herd of sheep could fertilize. At the end of the visit, Omer Aga presented Marx with a side of roast mutton and Emil with a bottle of sheep yoghurt.

An Orthodox wedding

The next day was dedicated to the wedding of Sterghi (as Emil affectionately called his tobacco master, Sterghiades) with Rhodia Duka, whose father Emil had once met among tobacco salesmen in Berlin. Sterghi's mother's parlor was the wedding venue, and a venerable, bearded Orthodox priest with a melodious voice performed the ceremony. The family had planned the wedding to coincide with Emil's visit, and he was honored and delighted to say a few words in Greek. Afterward, the guests adjourned to laden tables in the garden, where the solemn atmosphere gave way to high spirits, wine and dance. Emil had a wonderful time, and even Marx took a few turns in the circle dance.

From Xanthi they traveled on by horse and carriage to Cavalla. As they rode in the heat of the sun, they watched eagles circle the air above them and saw turtles crawling in the dust as they passed. At the Karasu River, they boarded a ferry steered by two giant African men who took them across to Cavalla. The town was dominated by an old Venetian fortress and a Roman aqueduct, and tidy villas nestled in the hills

*Copper coffee dispenser with
100-year-old hand-rolled cigarettes*

surrounding the town. The most prominent tobacco companies were represented here, and the group toured warehouses and visited the manager of the German bank. In every place they were offered coffee in brass pots by the "cafetschis," or coffee men.

While chatting over coffee, business people got to know each other and had time to ponder their strategy instead of rushing in to trade. Marx, always impatient, could not understand the purpose of this custom, and Emil was hard put to prevent him from embarrassing them both by cutting the conversations short. Emil felt a great affinity for these reliable, forthright, and warm-hearted people who had such a deep bond with the land. As a Swabian, he felt he shared a similar soul constitution with them.

Passing through ancient lands

The friends traveled on, passing the ruins of Philippi and the spot where the Apostle Paul had been held prisoner. The trip was hot and they were glad to arrive in Saloniki, a small intellectual hub that was predominantly Turkish. It was here that the Young Turks started their revolt. It was also home to some 40,000 Jews who had been driven out of Spain centuries earlier. Some of them had converted to Islam, while others had remained Orthodox—the former gravitating toward business, finance and politics, the latter forced to work at the most menial jobs.

At a bazaar in the town's center, the friends bargained for silk shawls and other souvenirs to take home. In the evening, after the market stalls closed, the cafés on either side of the street moved their tables and chairs into the open space. On their last evening in Saloniki, bathed in the light of the evening sun, Emil and Marx sat in these chairs, enjoying the view of Mount Olympus.

From there, the train took them to Budapest, where they had planned to spend the night. But when Marx found out from the hotel porter that there was still a late connection to Berlin, he insisted on taking it. Emil felt compelled to go along, and thus their trip came to an end.

Souvenir tray

Tobacco culture

After this trip, Emil was able to tell his employees about how, in spring, tobacco farmers set the seedlings in their gardens, transplanting them to the tobacco fields when they are hardy enough. He described how farmers cropped leaf tips before sunrise to prevent the leaves from shooting too high and thus losing their strength and quality. Then, depending on the heat, harvesting begins at the end of August or the beginning of September. After the harvest, the leaves are sorted according to size before being bundled and hung to dry—first in the open air, then indoors where the leaves ripen and change color. Then, in early spring the leaves are packed in bales and taken to the dealers, whom the farmers know well and trust. The dealers sit cross-legged on the ground, usually with their apprentices, sorting the leaves and entering their details in a ledger. Emil explained that the leaves were then pressed in wood frames and packed in jute, after which fermentation began. This curing process was carefully supervised and the frames turned from side to side until early summer. Then the town mayor himself comes to inspect the tobacco, which is then classified and given quality numbers. Finally, in September or October, the tobacco is shipped to Dresden and from there to the Waldorf Astoria factory!

The knowledge Emil acquired on this trip with Marx gave him authority with his Hamburg colleagues, and they gave him more freedom in his decision-making as a result. Better yet, the memories of his travels remained vivid for months, adding romance to his work routine.

In his lifetime, Emil would see the industry move into rapid mass production with hundreds of workers replaced by a few technicians. Once cigarettes were standardized with the addition of aromas and other additives, their size and consumption increased while the price and the quality went down. Contemplative cigarette connoisseurs gave way to mundane chain smokers, and Emil would later reminisce about this trip with nostalgia and regret, grateful for the chance to have seen the industry at its best: "*Sic transit gloria mundi—et Xanthiae!*" (So passes the glory of the world, and of Xanthi!) he would muse with regret.

Refinement and elegance

In 1909 the desire for quality in all aspects of their lives became a preoccupation of the Molts. They rented a larger apartment and discarded sentimental knick-knacks, replacing them with artistic objects and elegant furnishings. They changed their clothing to reflect quality and style. Previously, Emil would appear at Hamburg Board meetings in sturdy South German Loden gear, hoping to exert a reforming influence on his "soft" northern colleagues and their refined ways. In time, though, he realized that they looked on him as provincial. On one of Emil's

Emil in hat

visits to Hamburg, Max Marx unexpectedly invited him to his birthday party, where Emil was mortified to find himself surrounded by elegant ladies and gentlemen in formal dress while he sat in his woolly broadcloth. First thing the next day, he went to town and bought himself a top hat. Back in Stuttgart, he had a fashionable tailor measure him for every kind of morning, afternoon and evening wear. With his new clothes, he felt equal to the best of society. It gave him tremendous satisfaction, later on, to learn that at one point Steiner had also succumbed to fashion pressure and had given his first lectures in tails to live up to his audience's expectations.

For women, the rigid Victorian bustles and corsets were gradually abandoned and hemlines inched higher. Berta had always detested corsets and, being slim, did not need them. She had an inborn sense of flair and began designing her own clothes in a more classical, flowing style with fine silks and beautiful colors.

Even Waldorf Astoria benefited from the Molts' quest for beauty and elegance. Emil organized a poster competition, offering 3000 Marks as a first prize. He arranged for a pool of leading artists to serve as judges. The entries were exhibited in a Hamburg hall open to the public. A poster fetched first prize, but the third prize went to some excellent sketches by Professor Kusche from Karlsruhe. Emil was impressed by his work and hired him for the company's graphic requirements. Kusche designed the wreath that became the classic look for Waldorf Astoria cigarettes.

Young Walter

When Walter was about three years old, he suffered from recurring dreams in which a demon chased him, threatening to crush him. These dreams turned him stiff with fear and were followed by a high fever. When Steiner came to supper, Berta brought Walter in to see him and asked for his help.

"You are quite a strong little man, aren't you?" Steiner said, looking at the boy kindly. "If that bad demon comes back again, just tell him, 'I am much stronger than you!'" Whenever

Little Walter

the nightmare returned, Walter only needed reminding and then would shout, "I-am-much-stronger-than-you!" The demon vanished and the child relaxed. In time the nightmare disappeared altogether.

Otherwise, Walter was a sunny child, smiling at everyone he met in the street. He was once overheard saying, *"Papa macht sein Gsäft immer grösser, aber wart' nur; wenn ichgross bin mach ich's Gsäftele wieder kleiner."* (Papa's making his business bigger and bigger. But just wait, when I'm grown up, I'll make it smaller again.) This childish career plan was probably motivated by his desire to spend more time with his busy father. Once, when Emil walked into Walter's nursery, the boy was so absorbed in what he was doing that he ignored his father. "Walter," said Emil, "you must greet me when I come in."

Walter gave him a long look. "Papa, 'must' is a hard word. If you said 'please,' it would be much easier." Emil was so unused to the world of the very young that he took refuge behind the mask of the serious adult. Father and son were to suffer years of edgy misunderstanding until, finally, they came to cherish a close relationship. Before that, Berta had to step in many times to mediate between her menfolk.

The Munich Summer Congress

In August 1910, Berta and Emil traveled to Munich for the annual Theosophical Summer Congress. Rudolf Steiner had written a drama, *The Portal of Initiation,* and rehearsed it with Society members. It was an esoteric play in a new style, merging outer events with inner experiences. It showed relationships evolving over lifetimes and portrayed heavenly

Scene from a Mystery Drama

beings standing behind the human protagonists trying to gain knowledge of higher worlds to bring it into practical life. The production with its lay performers was impressive. Watching it, Berta and Emil no longer felt themselves in the middle of a city; the noise and commotion faded away. The feeling of closeness among members was very strong; it was like a large family gathering, all feeling privileged to be at the vanguard of an extraordinary movement.

A meeting house in Stuttgart

The Stuttgart group of the Anthroposophical Society longed for a permanent space for their meetings—one that was large enough for lectures and other activities. One day Emil, treasurer of the Society, received the welcome news that a Swabian pharmacist friend of his had donated 50,000 Marks toward the purchase of a Society house in Stuttgart. Arenson, Unger, del Monte, the architect Schmidt Curtius, the builder Aisenpreis and Emil chose a site close to the Molts' apartment. They made plans for a three-story building that included an apartment for Rudolf Steiner on the top floor. A meeting room in the basement featured columns and artwork designed by Steiner. He laid the foundation stone on Sunday, January 1st, 1911, during the lecture cycle *Occult History,* and inaugurated the house on October 15th. It was the first building specifically designed for anthroposophical activities, and people came from all over the country to see it and hear lectures.

Early in 1911, Count Stauffenberg, a friend of Emil's, asked him why his firm never delivered cigarettes to the Court. "We can easily remedy that if the King so wishes," Emil said. Although the company was now producing in large batches, it was still flexible enough to create small special editions, and the workers loved these diversions. In no time, the designers and the tobacco master produced an elegant cigarette with a long,

King of Württemberg carton

gold mouthpiece, packed in a box labeled "King of Württemberg." So, on the occasion of the King of Württemberg's birthday, Waldorf Astoria was appointed royal supplier to His Majesty's Court. Other appointments to the courts of Hesse, Anhalt, Greece and Sweden followed and kept the factory buzzing.

A visit from Turkey

That summer Waldorf Astoria exhibited at the great East Prussian trade show and won a gold medal for excellence. Emil took the occasion to visit the northeast corner of Germany, which to him was almost like a foreign country. After his return, he helped the city of Stuttgart plan the visit of a hundred Turkish politicians, professors and students coming on a study holiday. All the local government ministers turned up for a banquet in their honor, and Emil sent individual sampler cases of Waldorf cigarettes, decorated with the Turkish crest, to the dinner guests. These gifts caused a sensation, and nobody—not even the Prime Minister— left the table without his little case under his arm. The next day, the guests were given a tour of the Waldorf factory. Emil, feeling himself to be a representative of the city and of Germany, was delighted to show the Turkish delegation the manufacturing end of Turkish tobacco and to reciprocate the hospitality he'd received during his magical time in their country. The visitors were exuberant in their praise.

"May we long be able to combine efforts," they said.

"Yes, nothing promotes prosperity and understanding better than working together," Emil replied. "May we long continue our relationship." Emil's comment reflected an anxiety borne out of newspaper reports of continual incendiary flare-ups between countries, especially those where tobacco fields flourished.

Worries about world volatility

"Why is everything so unstable?" Emil asked a government acquaintance. "It sounds as though a mere spark could cause a total explosion."

"There will always be flare-ups," said his contact. "But they will pass. Those people are volatile. Don't worry, Germany will never get involved. Your fields will always remain open to you. Those countries need your business."

But when, in April 1911, a rebellion broke out in Morocco against the Sultan Abdelhafid, France used the opportunity to dispatch troops. That, in turn, caused Germany to order its battleship, *Panther*, to Agadir in the assumption that German citizens in Morocco might be in danger and to safeguard its African colonies. At this point, Britain put pressure on Germany to back off, which it did unhappily to avoid escalation.

"Why do we fall into the overseas trap like the others? Aren't we happy and prosperous enough in our own country?" Emil asked Berta one morning, reading the news over breakfast.

"We don't want expansion but we don't run the country," Berta answered thoughtfully, while pouring milk for Walter. "It's the politicians and military men in Prussia who overestimate their strength and think they have to compete with their neighbors. When an army is built, it eventually wants to fight instead of parading and playing war games in which the Kaiser's side always wins."

"Greed for power and control blinds everyone. Where will it end?" Emil wondered. And indeed, these tensions continued to fester with the Balkan wars, which began October 1912.

Emil worried about his tobacco supply and also that the quality might be jeopardized by these wars. Greece had gained control of the Macedonian and Thracian tobacco lands, including Xanthi and Cavalla, and Turkey was much reduced as a European tobacco region. Its traditional growers were displaced and resettled elsewhere. Luckily, however, the Enfiezioglou family was allowed to remain as consultants and interpreters, and Emil relied on them for information and sources. His former host, Omer Aga, did not fare as well—his beautiful plantation was expropriated and he had to leave.

Royal heads of state protecting each other

The German Kaiser, while helping to negotiate a peace settlement in 1912, felt himself compelled to insure that tobacco lands remained in the hands of Greece under the rule of his brother-in-law, King Constantine. He may have thought he was doing domestic companies a favor, but it was not good news for Waldorf Astoria. The new Greek owners of the fields knew little of the art of tobacco cultivation, and quality suffered. To make the best of a bad situation and to bring attention to tobacco, Emil had a quantity of Xanthi and Cavalla cigarettes named "King of Greece" delivered to King Constantine when he came to Germany on holiday. Later, in the middle of the war, Emil was much surprised to receive a certificate from Athens that read, "Royal Purveyor to His Majesty."

Political flares

The animosities between countries worsened. Harold Nicolson[5] wrote: "Europe now found herself faced with the very crisis she had been dreading for years. It seemed inevitable that the hour had struck when Russia and Austria would decide their age-long conflict for supremacy in southeastern Europe." Foreign turmoil did not, however, impede Waldorf Astoria's continuing evolution into one of the most substantial enterprises in Stuttgart. Through his sources Emil managed to obtain enough tobacco to keep increasing amounts of raw material coming, and his warehouses were constantly packed. He leased buildings around town but worried about the company's becoming fragmented.

The wily builder Hausser

Some years earlier, Emil had met a wise old city councilor by the name of Hausser, who owned a large building firm that managed some of the finest private and commercial properties in Stuttgart. Hausser realized the potential of the cigarette trade and offered to build a factory

---

5 Harold Nicolson, *Portrait of a Diplomatist* (1913).

complex to Emil's specifications at his own expense and on his own land in the nearby Hackstrasse. In return, he wanted a ten-year lease amounting to a 5% interest on invested capital. Emil was excited about the prospect but knew that Marx was dead set against spending money on any kind of building and would be hard to win over. His lifestyle and that of the Abraham partners had become seriously opulent.

But Hausser had a deep understanding of human nature, and the next time Marx came to visit, he "happened by" the restaurant where Emil and Marx were having lunch. Marx knew and liked Hausser (they were both members of the same club) and was pleased when Emil asked him to join them. A relaxed conversation ensued, during which Hausser delicately mentioned Waldorf Astoria's need for expansion. As previously arranged, Emil voiced strong objections, which caused Marx, being a bit contrary, to argue. By the time they were all eating dessert, Marx had convinced himself and the others that a new building was absolutely necessary. This was on a Saturday, and the following Monday Hausser died suddenly of a heart attack. Although there had been no time for a written agreement between the businessmen, Hausser's son honored his father's wishes for the Waldorf Astoria project, and building began.

A landmark building

In 1913, the large extension to the factory was completed with no expense spared. The grand opening was like an artistic unveiling, presenting a new Stuttgart landmark that combined aesthetics with efficiency. Handmade wrought-iron gates and a wood and marble hall brought visitors into a beautiful reception room. Every detail was tastefully done—the doors were lined with black leather, and the tables and chairs were also black, with two large divans and two comfortable chairs upholstered in blue-green. The walls were covered in burgundy sacking. A large glass display cabinet inlaid in gold stood in one corner, and two gold-framed mirrors hung on the walls.

Emil's office was elegant yet comfortable, with oak paneling and oak furniture throughout. The work-rooms were clean and bright, each in

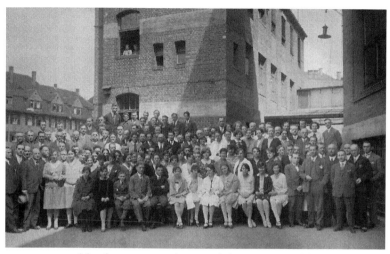

Waldorf Astoria workers and their new building

a different color. The Molts stood at the entrance with Hausser's son, receiving their guests, including members of the royal family and Emil's partners Abraham and Marx from Hamburg. Berta, who had overseen the decor, wore a sea-green silk dress and was charming and warm. Emil, in gray flannel, was in top form, engaging in conversation with the many people he knew and welcoming those he did not. Visitors strolled admiringly through offices and work stations, accepting a cigarette or pastry as they went. The staff from the different departments were on hand to guide the guests and answer questions. It was a festive, proud day for the company, for the builders, and for the city of Stuttgart.

At the end of the long opening day, Emil wanted to make one last round of the facility and proceeded to walk the entire length of the building. The only part of the new facility that was not yet finished was the lower basement, and when he got there, he had to feel his way along the wall in the dark in order to find a light. Suddenly, his foot lost contact with the floor and he fell down two meters into the open elevator shaft, one leg bent under him. Shocked and in pain, he was overwhelmed by the fright he'd experienced as a child locked into the pitch-dark storage closet. Astonished that such elemental fears lurked so close to the surface of his mind, he forced himself to be calm, lie

still, and wait for help. After a
while, Berta missed him and
sent Sterghiades to look for him.
Sterghiades came with a torch,
quickly fetched a ladder, and
helped Emil climb out. But Emil
shivered to see where he had
lain—the elevator shaft floor
was strewn with boards covered
in eight-inch- long rusty nails,
facing upwards like spears. Emil

Waldorf Astoria managers

knew his fall would have ended in catastrophe had his guardian angel
been busy elsewhere, but he'd somehow managed to fall into the one
small clear space. He escaped with a slight shock and a sprained foot
and was back at work the next day. But for the rest of his life Emil
experienced horror in the pit of his stomach whenever he remembered
that fall.

With his building project finished, Emil turned his attention to
moving the entire organization—offices, sales and marketing—from
Hamburg to Stuttgart. His partners were quite happy to let Emil manage
the business in Stuttgart as long as they had their steady income. This
move turned out to be just in time—had the company been managed
in two separate locations during the war, the company logistics, as well
as the social innovations Emil envisaged, would not have been possible.

Walter started school that September and did well, earning good
reports. But as he grew older he seemed to suffer a lack of confidence
and motivation. Although given extra lessons, he was called lazy by his
teachers. His parents knew that he was not genuinely lazy, but he was
unable to muster the attention required to sit on a school bench. *Perhaps*,
thought Emil later, *Walter might be suffering as an only child because he was
somewhat of a conference orphan, getting carted around by his parents and
left to his own devices while they participated in meetings.*

Walter, schoolboy (top, 3rd from left)

A center for anthroposophy

In 1911, 1912 and 1913, Steiner's Mystery Dramas[6] were performed during the Munich summer conferences. The plays were further enhanced by eurythmy, a form of movement also developed by Steiner and described as "visible speech and visible music." These events were powerful and unique, their only drawback being the inadequate and prosaic public theaters they were performed in. The Munich organizers longed for a hall of their own—a kind of Bayreuth, as Steiner pictured it, to be named "Johannesbau" after the Johannes Thomasius character of the Mystery Play. A group of people formed the Johannesbau Building Association to make this hope a reality.

However, both their prospective location and their architectural plans were contested by a leading local architect and by Catholic circles that were philosophically opposed to Steiner and his movement. Likewise, the members of the City Council were highly critical of plans that would put an unorthodox edifice with intersecting domes in a setting of traditional buildings. Permits were delayed and then denied in spite of

6 *The Portal of Initiation, The Soul's Probation, The Guardian of the Threshold, The Souls' Awakening.*

concessions by the group, which even offered to put the building largely underground. In 1913 the committee regretfully gave up on the idea of a cultural hall in Munich.

As luck would have it, though, a man named Emil Grosheintz and a group of friends donated a large tract of land above the village of Dornach, Switzerland, in the foothills of the Jura Mountains. This location proved to be beneficial on many levels, and when the war started, it became obvious that Dornach provided the anthroposophists with much-needed shelter.

Steiner sketched an outline of the building he envisioned, and plans to lay the foundation were set. Emil went to Switzerland to look at the land and found a beautiful, well-protected, green hill. Discreetly, friends gradually bought up small plots around the site, careful to avoid disturbing the sensibilities of locals and the wealthy Basel families who claimed the area as their own scenic retreat. Emil bought a small plot as well, but he sold it again later when the new building needed funds.

On September 20th, 1913, Steiner laid the foundation stone for the Dornach building—an impressive celebration, as Carl Unger later reported. Emil did not attend, even though he was on the same train as Unger traveling south to a business meeting. *Why,* he would later ask himself, *was I not aware of the importance of this event?*

Maria Vögele

At the beginning of 1914, Berta was having trouble with household help. One evening, on going down to the kitchen for a glass of water, she found her new housekeeper unconscious on the floor with the gas turned on. She revived the woman and listened to the housekeeper's tale of unrequited love. Then Berta found Maria Vögele, a lovely and bright young woman, who turned out to be a great all-round helper in the house.

Berta and Emil both feel ill

Later in the year, Berta felt poorly and went to a spa in the Black Forest. Lonely in the house without his wife, Emil decided to use the time for a business trip to Belgium and Holland with Marx. But on the morning of his departure, he suddenly came down with a severe throat infection and Dr. Stiegele prescribed bed rest. This was a blow to Emil, who always looked forward to his travels. Not wanting to worry Berta, he did not call her and allowed Maria Vögele to look after him instead. A few days later, Berta appeared at his bedside. Her well-developed instinct and the sudden lack of communication had made her feel something was amiss. She took over nursing him, then packed him up and brought him back with her to the spa. The resident physician there berated Berta for leaving the spa, saying her state of health was so bad that she could never again expect an active life.

"Don't worry," Emil told her. "Ask Dr. Steiner next time he's in Stuttgart. He'll know what to do." Meanwhile he entertained her by reading and drawing, and when they were both a little stronger, he took her on an evening jaunt to Stuttgart to hear the great tenor Caruso sing. All Württemberg seemed to be in attendance at the new Royal Theater.

Steiner's reassurance

The next time Steiner came to Stuttgart, Berta told him about the spa doctor's diagnosis. Steiner said she seemed to be suffering a pinched intestine, but told her that by following a careful diet and lifestyle she should have no cause for worry. "In fact," he predicted, "you will still be a very active woman." Looking back on this time in their lives, Emil and Berta recognized it as their happiest and freest period.

Death in Sarajevo

Whoever follows European history can easily believe that what the immediate future has in store is a general mass slaughter. The idea that true goodness can provide strength and a sense of human

dignity does not seem to coincide with our own and our neighbors'
enormous military preparations. It is one which I believe in and
which must enlighten us unless we prefer simply to do away with
human life by common consent and designate an official suicide day.[7]

One Sunday afternoon in late June of 1914, the Molts were on their way home from a long walk with Walter through the woods surrounding Stuttgart. The morning had brought beautiful weather, and they'd picnicked at a spot with a splendid view over the city. They had planned to visit an old cemetery in the forest, but as they approached it, the air became humid and oppressive and the sky darkened. Hearing thunder, they turned around and hurried toward home.

On their way back, an acquaintance stopped them to share the news that Archduke Franz Ferdinand had been assassinated in Sarajevo. The Molts were shocked, certain that this had been a staged event on a grand political scale with dreadful, intended consequences. They knew that political relationships in Europe had been volatile and often on the verge of explosion, with countries vying for territories and markets. "This time, Austria will not hold back," said Emil. "And, as an ally, it will mean war for Germany."

"It is unreal and perhaps it will pass," said Berta, her voice lacking conviction. "Why would a world that's doing well want to ruin itself?"

Together they recalled how normal things had been in recent months. The Waldorf Astoria representative in Belgium, M Kuhlen, had visited Stuttgart. The Molts had taken him on a tour of the city that included the newly built military barracks in Cannstatt, unaware at the time of how soon soldiers would be sent from there to Brussels. As recently as May 1st, the Waldorf Astoria company had exhibited at the large Baltic trade show in Malmö, Sweden, where Russians and Germans had met each other as cordial traders and peaceful competitors. Marx and Emil even had a sales trip to Russia planned for the summer, and an army

---

7 Hermann Grimm, *Fifteen Essays, The Last Five Years.*

officer friend—a member of the Supreme Command—had jokingly offered to come along as Emil's butler.

In the months leading up to this moment, the looming catastrophe had been far from most people's minds—even from the minds of diplomats and politicians, who felt that peace in Europe was secure. Few people had any idea of the tragedy facing them, humanly, politically and financially. Steiner had warned about a "social carcinoma" in April, but that was heard only in the smallest circles. "Today products are manufactured without considering consumption," he had said. "They are massed in warehouses or money markets in expectation of future sales. This tendency will increase until…it self-destructs."

Business as usual?

In late July, just a few days before declaring war, the Berlin government had discussed the "right relationship with France," and the military was complacent in the thought that it was ready for any eventuality. Later, Steiner described the principal international leaders as suffering from a kind of "darkened consciousness."

For a while after the news of Franz Ferdinand's assassination, it seemed that the conflict between Austria and its neighbor Serbia might be settled. People breathed a sigh of relief and the Molts decided to risk their planned July holiday. They took Walter, their young niece Lisa Dreher, Maria Vögele, and their cook to the picturesque village of Schwaz in the Austrian foothills, renting a large old country house at the edge of a forest. The village lay hidden behind rolling fields, and the tranquility there was broken only by the song of woodland birds. The group felt happy and secure. For a few days, Maria's brother, Wilhelm, joined them from Dornach, where he was working on the new anthroposophical building (the Vögele siblings had become students of Steiner). All were delighted to see him, unaware that four weeks later this gifted, handsome young man would become one of the first casualties of the war.

General von Moltke's assessment

On July 28th the Kaiser's General, Helmuth von Moltke, set out his thoughts on the situation in a prescient military memorandum. Emil received a copy through his Berlin-Stuttgart network:

> *It is without question, no European State would regard the conflict*
> *between Austria and Serbia with anything but human interest*
> *if it were not for the danger of a general political entanglement*
> *threatening a world war. For over five years Serbia has caused*
> *tensions in Europe…but Russia has taken sides with the renegade*
> *country and so the Austro-Serbian affair has become a storm cloud*
> *that could, at any moment, burst over Europe. Austria has declared*
> *that it makes no territorial or other claims on Serbia. It merely*
> *wishes to compel the unruly neighbor to accept the conditions that it*
> *feels are necessary for future cooperation…Russia assures it will not*
> *move against Germany but knows very well that Germany cannot*
> *stay idle if Russia clashes with its ally [Austria]. Germany will be*
> *forced to mobilize and then Russia can tell the world: "I did not*
> *want war but Germany caused it." This is what will happen unless a*
> *last-minute miracle occurs to prevent a war that will annihilate the*
> *culture of almost all of Europe for decades to come…*

Austria-Hungary declares war

On July 28th Austria-Hungary declared war on Serbia, and on July 29th Russia began mobilization, which was tantamount to a declaration of war. Meanwhile, in Berlin, Kaiser Wilhelm was in correspondence with his cousins, Czar Nicholas and King George, still trying to preserve peace. On July 31st, he summoned General von Moltke to a meeting with himself, his Chancellor, the Minister for War and several others. All were elated. The German Foreign Office had received a telegram from its ambassador in London, reporting on information said to have come from the British Foreign Office. It seemed to hold out hope for British neutrality and its ability to curb the French in the event of war.

False hope

The Kaiser, who had signed the mobilization order earlier, now demanded a halt to deployment in the west and a shift of all troops to the east, the seat of the trouble. Von Moltke protested vehemently. He did not believe the ambassador's report and felt the winds of war had been blowing for too long. For some time he had anticipated hostilities from both east and west and moreover did not believe his army to be invincible. He was determined to insure a quick and painless outcome by placing the bulk of his army in a defensive position in the east. In the west, instead of risking a frontal engagement he had planned to use the element of surprise, moving against France's flank before it had time to fully mobilize. In order to do this, however, he had to transport his troops through Belgium, a neutral country. He reckoned that he could negotiate with the Belgians, promising a quick transfer and indemnifying them for any damage caused.

However, von Moltke's protests were overruled. He was ordered to stop deployment to the west, which rendered him distraught. Shortly before midnight, the Kaiser received a telegram from the King of England stating that he knew nothing of a British guarantee preventing France from entering the war. The Kaiser recalled von Moltke: "Now you can do as you please," he told him, extremely upset. Von Moltke, in shock, with his orders reversed twice, could not prevent bloodshed in Belgium. This clash with the Kaiser, with whom he had been close, made him unwell. He was later reassigned to a humiliating position overseeing the home guard.

The nightmare of war

Meanwhile Emil, in Schwaz to do some shopping, observed that the local soldiers had begun to muster and were assembling at the train station. Highly disturbed, Emil cabled his office, announcing that he intended to return home with his family. Benkendoerfer, his comptroller, cabled back that Emil's apprehension was unfounded and advised against Emil's interrupting the vacation. The postmaster was also full of assurances. "Routine maneuvers, sir," he said. "Marianne [France] has no boots, and the Bear [Russia] has no teeth!" This did not reassure Emil. He returned to the family's lodgings and began packing. When a message from Benkendoerfer arrived late the following evening urging departure, they were ready. It was Friday, July 31st.

A frightful reality

On the morning of August 1st, the Molts boarded the last scheduled civilian train, which took them as far as Munich. Once there, they found themselves among crowds of confused vacationers vying for space on any train that might take them home. Most had to leave their luggage behind, but Emil went running for a porter and, tipping him handsomely, hung on to him until their baggage was safely on board the very last train scheduled for Stuttgart.

On the train, the adults sat close together, their children on their laps. Every seat was taken, with many travelers standing in the aisles. Tension marked every face. The air was laden with anxiety about what the next hours might bring, and passengers became more selfless, helpful and social in the face of inescapable catastrophe.

"Look," said Emil, pointing out the window when they reached Neu Ulm. "It's my old garrison town, and I can see them making preparations for war." Indeed, shortly after the family arrived in Stuttgart, war was announced and mobilization began.

Releasing his workers

Emil went directly to his factory and found his key workers waiting for him. They had just received their draft notices. Comptroller Benkendoerfer, no longer calm, was among the first to be called up, as well as the head bookkeeper, Braun, and many others who held crucial positions at the company. The only key member of Emil's staff who had not been drafted was his personal secretary, Otto Wagner. Emil sent them all home to prepare but asked them to return to the factory the next morning before reporting to their stations. That night, Emil prepared the salaries for his recruited workers in gold coin, and on Monday morning they assembled with their wives and children. Emil handed them their salaries, warmly bidding them farewell and wishing them a safe and speedy return. He promised to keep paying them for the duration of the war. To his astonishment and relief, many of the wives offered to stand in for their husbands at work. That day, he watched the first battalion march singing out of the local barracks and his heart was pierced by the profoundly serious look on the commander's face.

"How fine and courageous they looked," he told Berta sadly. "As though setting out on an adventure. How often Germany's army has set out only to return unharmed because tragedy was avoided at the last minute. This time is different. How many will return unscathed?"

Then Emil was left with a factory classed as "vital to the war," which meant it was to be kept going at all costs. He arranged training for the women and soon found them working well and enjoying it too.

Memoir of a Waldorf Astoria worker

Friedel Reik was one of the women who joined Waldorf Astoria to help keep the company running while the men were away. In her later years, she wrote about her experiences of this time:

I am writing down these memoirs for my grandniece and nephew because I don't want that good man, Emil Molt, to be forgotten. When war broke out in August of 1914, I lost my office job. The shoe factory I was working in had to close since half of its employees were sent off to war. A supervisor at the Waldorf Astoria factory, Mrs. Berta Moser, said to me, "Why don't you come to us. We always need help; right now there is a great demand for cigarettes!"

"What, do you work with all those Turks, Russians and Poles—and whatever else you have?" I answered.

"Ha ha, Stuttgart girl," she said. "Just come. It's really nice." So, in October I joined the handwork hall, working under the care of Miss Allmendinger for the first five years. The atmosphere there appealed

to me immediately. I heard the word "anthroposophy" for the first time and soon I was pricking my ears whenever Miss Allmendinger talked about it. Until then I had been very religious—church youth club and choir—and yet the outbreak of war shattered me inwardly. I didn't want to go to church anymore because the minister was more soldier than priest. There was no talk of all people being children of God. I wanted to hear the priests of every country saying: "Love thine enemies." I was still young, full of illusions, and was drawn to the universal and worldwide aspect of anthroposophy. Today it seems that it had to be like that: The vessel was empty and had to be filled.

I had my first personal experience of Mr. Molt at the beginning of 1915. The director of the machine hall, Mr. Schoeller, came in; soon he was surrounded by a group of supervisors: Mrs. Kaiser, Mrs. Meister, Mrs. Kleinfelder and Mr. Karschinierow. First the conversation was on technical matters, but then it became personal and merry. I had to ask Mr. Schoeller about casings and joined the group. Suddenly the door opened and Mr. Molt walked in. Everyone fluttered away except Mr. Schoeller and myself (I was there on business).

Mr. Molt said, "Oh dear, I was just looking forward to a fine business discussion and now it seems it's all over." Schoeller said, "No, nothing is over yet and I'm amazed at everyone's sudden departure, but (looking at me) youth has stayed with me." Mr. Molt put his hand on my shoulder: "Yes, I have the feeling that you are one of our loyal ones." Mr. Schoeller added: "Yes, Mr. Molt, we can count on her!" I was astonished that Mr. Molt knew my name and felt as though I had been knighted. Later I noticed that his kind heart knew hundreds of employees' names.

Trying to enlist

Emil himself had not been called up yet, but he belonged to a civil defense unit and was sure he would be needed before long. Wanting to stay close to his business rather than report to the more distant barracks he was assigned to, he went to the local military base to offer his services. There he was told they could not accept him because the base was reserved for people living outside city limits. Undeterred by such a minor detail, he gathered up Otto Wagner and drove to Echterdingen to rent a room. It was the closest village beyond the Stuttgart town limits. Fearful of espionage, the mayor of Echterdingen had posted an armed guard at the entrance of this tiny town: the local vicar dressed in morning coat and holding an ancient hunting flintlock. When they arrived, Emil and Wagner showed him identification and he graciously allowed them to pass. They rented a place, then went to have Emil's new address validated. In the town hall they found the mayor strutting up and down, armed with a saber and a revolver, rather suspecting the enemy in every stranger. On their way back, the vicar was gone, replaced by another civilian who shouted, "Halt," and raised his gun in a threatening manner. Emil rebuked him sharply, telling him to put his gun down. To which the good man replied, "Don't worry sir, it isn't loaded." (*Kei Sorg' mein Herr, s'isch jo net glade!*)

War psychosis was pervasive in those first days of the conflict. People suspected spies at every corner. A guard at the Stuttgart train station shot at some clouds, mistaking them for enemy aircraft. An elderly anthroposophical acquaintance of the Molts swore she had witnessed a pilot being shot down while cutting the wires on the main telegraph mast from his plane. In a streetcar, passengers attacked a reputable actor because he looked French. It was clear that the light of reason had been temporarily put out.

Emil's heart says "no"

Back at the local military unit with his new certificate of residence, Emil had to undergo a medical examination. But the doctor pronounced Emil's general condition, particularly his heart, so poor that at the age of 38 he was written off as permanently unfit for service. The doctor advised him to avoid exertion and alcohol, and above all, cigarettes. Devastated, Emil crawled home to Berta, imagining both of them henceforth no better than invalids. Berta, of course, was happy about his rejection, telling him that he would be of much more use to society as head of a company vital to the war than as a frail mortal with a shooting stick in his hand. Indeed, after moping for several days, Emil got bored and re-immersed himself in work.

The Waldorf van

First, acting on Berta's suggestion and with her help, Emil opened a small infirmary in one of the unused halls in the Waldorf factory. They did this in collaboration with the local hospital, and Berta co-opted friends with any kind of medical or nursing experience. A large cigarette delivery truck was fitted out with mattresses, and an orderly accompanied sales representative Hoerr as he drove the vehicle. The first wounded soldiers arrived at the Waldorf infirmary on Sunday, August 8th, following the Battle of Mulhouse. More soon followed, and the truck became popular with the military authorities. In a unique exception, the authorities gave Hoerr gasoline free of charge in exchange for his aid and his liberal gifts of cigarettes. No road was ever barred when that truck arrived. Indeed, Waldorf Astoria continually sent soldiers and their commanders gifts of cigarettes.

"It's the least we can do," said Emil. He couldn't send gifts to his beloved Greeks or any other "enemies," but he sent them to allied fighters in Austria, Bulgaria and Turkey. By the end of the war, he had a stack of thank-you letters and military decorations in his office, including a red garnet-encrusted half moon from the Sultan of Turkey.

Waldorf shops in occupied towns

When the war turned stationary, with soldiers stuck in ghastly trenches, Emil arranged for Waldorf shops to be opened in occupied towns such as Lille and Charleville. Wagonloads of cigarettes were delivered to these shops, and often enlisted Waldorf employees did the purchasing for their comrades, delighted to be able to stop in at

their "local" Waldorf outlet. The Waldorf Astoria's Blaupunkt and Walasco became the favorite army cigarettes, loved and serenaded by soldiers in the trenches. An officer even composed an elegy of how, at Verdun, a friend went to the canteen to buy Walascos for his mates and died by gunfire on his way back, cigarettes in hand.

One Alsacian widow had a lively trade going out of her shop in Zabern, phoning in a substantial order every day. But when the French took over the town, her orders suddenly ceased. Some time later, German military police visited the factory in Stuttgart because they had intercepted a large order from the widow in Zabern and were suspicious that "1000 Hockey" and "500 Chicago" might be code for "infantry" and "artillery." They had to be shown the price list before they believed that these were indeed the legitimate brand names of cigarettes.

Stocking up

The demand for Waldorf Astoria cigarettes meant that securing supplies was Emil's most pressing task. His instinct told him that raw material is worth far more than cash in wartime, and at the beginning of September he made a trip to Dresden with Marx. In Dresden they found deep gloom among tobacco people—nobody was buying and their warehouses were full of tobacco. Dealers were delighted to see their friends Marx and Emil buying thousands of kilos of Samsun and Trapezunt at excellent prices and lenient payment terms. The foresight exercised in this endeavor enabled Emil to sell cigarettes made with pure Orient tobacco for the duration of the war.

In October, Emil took Arenson to visit a group of Waldorf employees fighting in the Vosges Mountains. Their first stop was in Sennheim, where Arenson's son-in-law, Benkendoerfer, happened to be stationed.

Emil and Arenson were equipped with passes and were surprised at the ease with which they got through the Strassburg fortifications. Emil, Arenson and Benkendoerfer went to the outermost trenches—just a hundred meters away from the French—to hand out cigarettes, take photographs, and chat with soldiers trapped in those narrow holes.

A travel pass

Eight days later, Emil telephoned his friend Colonel Sproesser, who was stationed in a village down the road from Colmar. The colonel invited Emil to visit his regiment, which included a few Waldorf people. He even gave Emil's coworkers, Braun and Gutbrod, leave for a few hours so that Emil could take them to lunch at the famous Drei Ähren resort. Later, civilians would no longer be allowed anywhere near the battle lines, and this kind of visit would be unheard of.

Driving to Dornach with Steiner

In October, when life in Stuttgart had settled down a bit, Berta and Emil decided to go to Dornach. They wanted to see how the anthroposophical building was progressing. Steiner had been traveling in Germany and joined them for the trip. Emil mentioned his heart defect to Steiner, who said that Emil's etheric body (his vital force) was much larger than his physical body. Steiner said Napoleon had a similar constitution, being a large personality with huge energy compressed into a small body. He recommended a calming meditation and a few remedies, which he promised would do wonders. Subsequently, Emil no longer felt oppressed and his heart became so strong that at the end of his life it withstood the severe fever bouts of his last illness.

Arriving in Dornach they were astonished at the progress of the building. Emil soon left Dornach to return to Stuttgart, but Berta stayed on for another few weeks, carving the wooden interior of the hall with her friends, volunteers from seventeen nations, who worked together peaceably while their countries clashed. She was happy and started wishing for a house of their own, there on that spot, to which they could come at any time. Toward the end of her stay she received sad news. She wrote a postcard to Emil:

> *November 6th, 1914: My heart's love! Thank you for your dear letter... I sorrow that Maria's dear good brother succumbed to his wounds. My darling, we will think of him often, won't we?*

The war continues

> *The German spirit has not yet fulfilled*
> *The task the evolving universe has given it.*
> *With hope it lives in future care.*
> *Replete with life it hopes for future deeds,*
> *Deep in its being feeling strongly*
> *What, hidden, ripening still, will one day active be.*
> *How can the enemy's might, uncomprehending,*
> *Wish for its downfall and demise*
> *As long as life is there within*
> *That keeps it active in its depths?*
> — Rudolf Steiner, January 14th, 1915, in Berlin[8]

The war dragged on and expectations that it would be short faded. In the west, there was a stalemate—both sides bogged down by trench warfare—and by the end of the year, neither side had gained any advantage. By now it was truly a world war, for all England's colonies were obliged to join the fight.

---

8 Lecture: "The German Soul and the German Spirit" (*Die Germanische Seele und der Deutsche Geist*), January 14, 1915. German translation: *Der deutsche Geist hat nicht vollendet/Was er im Weltenwerden schaffen soll/Er lebt in Zukunftssorgen hoffnungsvoll/Er hofft auf Zukunftstaten lebensvoll/In seines Wesens Tiefen fühlt er mächtig/Verborgnes, das noch reifend wirken muss./Wie darf in Feindes Macht verständnislos/Der Wunsch nach seinem Ende sich beleben,/So lang das Leben sich ihm offenbart,/Das ihn in Wesenswurzeln schaffend hält!*

Books and booklets

Württembergers often found themselves at the front lines, and wounded soldiers who were brought to the Waldorf infirmary described long days of inaction in dismal surroundings. They were emotionally shattered and needed comfort as much as medical care—a need Berta tended to by bringing them books from her library.

"What a shame," she said to Emil. "Their comrades in the field have nothing worthwhile to read."

It set him thinking: "Yes, they would need mental stimulation," he said. "Cigarettes are not enough." With this problem on his mind, Emil noticed some miniature advertising booklets lying on a table in the company's bookbindery. "Herr Schmid," Emil asked the elderly binder, "can you do booklets like that for us, about ten or fifteen pages, thin enough to fit into cigarette boxes? I want something for our lads in the field, poems and stories and the like."

The binder, a man brought out of retirement due to staff shortages, beamed. "Of course," he said, overjoyed to have a new project. "We have small fonts and good cutting machines, and I'd be honored to do it." Emil imagined classical literature, but Berta recommended contemporary material.

"German poets and writers are suffering hardship too," she said. "No one considers them an industry vital to the war. And the material should be entertaining as well as inspirational."

"Perhaps," he thought, "we can do this on a grand scale. If other companies join forces with us, we can create a writers' fund." He duly sketched out a proposal and took it to the next Chamber of Commerce meeting. The members found the idea interesting, but it was vetoed by the chairman, who decided such a project should be organized by the Chamber and not by one company.

Hermann Hesse returns

Emil realized he would have to manage this project himself. He asked his secretary to locate as many authors as possible and to draft a letter to each, describing the project and offering remuneration for their best poems or short stories. One such request went out to his former school friend, Hermann Hesse, who was now living in Switzerland. Hesse replied cordially, enclosing some of his pieces.

"Your letter is signed by E. Molt," Hesse wrote at the bottom of his letter. "If this is my old schoolmate from Calw, please give him my regards." A short while later, he turned up in Stuttgart and the two friends, who hadn't seen each other in twenty years, had a delightful reunion. Hesse promised to write and edit for Emil, and he personally oversaw the first batch of booklets that went out to the soldiers.

Waldorf booklets

The booklets were a stunning success, becoming a trademark of Waldorf Astoria cigarettes—instant collectors' items. Each booklet had a theme—classical, adventure, poetry, ghost tales, romance—and was made up of three or four short stories printed on thin, illustrated paper with different colored covers. Eventually, they included material by Steiner: his *Calendar of the Soul* and more. For the troops, these booklets were points of light in a dark time, and their publication continued beyond the war.

At that time, casualties were rising on all sides, and Steiner started to preface his lectures with a supplication for those in danger.

*May our first thought be directed to those dear friends who were
with us and are now called to the battlefield where human destinies
and the destinies of nations are being fought for....*

He followed this with a plea for those who had already passed through the gate of death:

Spirits of your souls, guardian guides
On your wings may be borne
A prayer of love from our souls
To those whom you guard in the spheres
That, united with your might,
Our prayer may bring a ray of help
To the souls it seeks in love.

Maria Vögele's second brother, Theo, became one of those casualties. He had barely turned eighteen when he enlisted and was a handsome, lively youth who loved sports. Maria, mourning both of her brothers, took comfort from Steiner's thought that a young life lost might soon return to earth with unspent vigor.

People from 16 nations work on the building

Thanks to his connections in the military, Emil had access to travel passes and he frequently traveled to Dornach with Berta to follow the progress of the anthroposophical edifice. The activity at the building site was ceaseless—draft horses pulled cartloads of building materials through Dornach and up the hill, and volunteers from 16 nations worked

International volunteers and workers in Dornach

together to carve and chisel the columns for the interior. Berta was given a white smock and joined them. Anyone unable to carve contributed by sharpening knives. The sounds of wood and metal being hammered sounded like the percussion section in an orchestra.

When Steiner spread out his drawings of the building for Berta and Emil, they realized they were looking at a modern mystery center like the ancient school at Ephesus, but shaped in a way they'd never seen before. Steiner's plans called for a base consisting of two unequal bisecting circles covered by double intersecting domes. This was no easy task for the man supervising construction—a seasoned building engineer from Basel—and he had to invent as he went. Once the concrete foundation was poured, Steiner told him to find a way to anchor the two domes so they could support each other at their intersection. The engineer told Steiner that this was technically impossible, but Steiner made a few sketches for him further detailing the idea. A few days later, after studying the drawings, the engineer solved the problem and was able to raise the interlocking double roof.

Up until this point the Molts had known Steiner only as a lecturer, but now they saw him creating architectural forms, sculpting those ideas in clay, and inventing new technical methods. He invented a casein paste and plant colors for the ceiling frescoes of the two cupolas, and later painted half the small cupola himself. He designed large stained glass windows for the main hall and then designed an etching machine and a studio—called the Glass House—to make them with. He designed pillars for the great hall and began carving a colossal statue that would serve as a centerpiece for the stage, calling it *The Representative of Humanity.* He could often be seen striding through the construction area in long boots, encouraging and inspiring the artists and workers as they worked. Meanwhile, artillery thundered at the German-French border nearby and aircraft droned endlessly overhead.

"A strange juxtaposition," said Emil to Berta. "Ideal future hope, harmony and construction on one side, and an actual present war, hatred and destruction on the other."

For the most part the international volunteers worked together in perfect harmony, but once, during the 1915 Whitsun conference when Germany's erstwhile ally Italy declared war on Austria, some of the German members felt betrayed by their Italian friends. Relationships were further complicated when men were called away from Dornach

Steiner with his model

Arch

Scaffolding

Cupola

Inner scaffolding

Interior

Roof-raising celebration   Completed Goetheanum

to serve in the army. They always heeded the call, but knew that they might be fighting against the very friends they had been working with in Dornach.

While construction moved forward smoothly, there was also some jealousy. Berta, alone in Dornach, witnessed an unusual meeting called by Steiner. He and Marie von Sivers had married the previous Christmas, which had irked a certain group of devoted Dornach ladies, who went so far as to disparage Marie personally. In order to put an end to the ongoing gossip, Steiner and Marie held a special meeting in the carpentry shop. Steiner insisted that the gossip and small talk come into the open once and for all, after which, Berta later told Emil, the most dreadful, small-minded twaddle was aired. After listening, Steiner forbade, with great decisiveness, further interference in his private affairs. His followers were shattered, feeling rebuked, but he cracked a joke and told them all to lighten up. Berta, who hated small-mindedness, saved her notes and all the details for Emil back home.

Berta has a wish

Berta was upset for other reasons. She had been struggling to find lodgings in Dornach. When she brought Walter and Maria Vögele to the Whitsun conference in May of that year, she was forced to relocate because the landlady refused to let a messy child stay in the rooms Berta had rented. Impatient, Berta insisted to Emil that they build or buy an

Painting of Berta
by Karl Stockmeier

apartment of their own in Dornach to avoid such unpleasantness. He agreed, but kept putting it off—his visits were always too short and other things seemed to take precedence. At one point Berta wrote him a letter asking his permission to buy a place:

My darling…coming back to the question of the apartment in Dornach, I think it would be important for Walter to spend every vacation here; I feel he needs it. We should have something of our own so we don't always have to search. It is tiresome to be so dependent on others. If you would allow me, my heart, to take matters into my own hands, you would be satisfied. I would really like for you not even to be involved, and would definitely act in your best interest. So please, give me free rein… A thousand greetings and kisses, my love…

Although Emil exhibited much progressive thinking in his lifetime, he could not bring himself to let Berta proceed with finding an apartment on her own. Ultimately nothing came of her request, and they continued renting when they were there.

The building's name

Meanwhile, large gifts and loans from friends and supporters continued to finance the Dornach building project, with the money flowing in through the Johannes Building Association (*Johannesbau Verein*). Steiner was concerned by the fact that the fund's administrators were untrained volunteers, so he asked Emil to examine the handling of the funds. Emil agreed and quickly spotted vulnerabilities. Worried about record-keeping and lenders who might suddenly call in their loans or bequeath them to people unrelated to anthroposophy, he suggested turning the fund into a trust, which he offered to organize and administer with the help of his Stuttgart business friends. He also recommended a parallel Swiss branch and suggested changing the name of the building from "Johannesbau" to "Goetheanum"—a name Steiner himself sometimes used in honor of the beloved German poet and original thinker, Johann Wolfgang von Goethe. Emil felt sure the name would lend the project recognition and credibility.

Steiner accepted both of Emil's suggestions, but some anthroposophists in Dornach preferred the original name for the building and were upset that a German businessman was taking over the building's financial management. Steiner tried to appease the critics with a written endorsement:

> It gives me great joy to support Mr. Molt's initiative, the
> Goetheanum Trust,…which will give the building project a strong
> practical administration. Combining idealism and practical life
> is often difficult…I find it especially important that personalities
> active in the world are also able to find a social working space
> within our Society. An initiative such as this building will thrive only
> if it is placed fully in the world and not bashfully concealed, as some
> of our friends do with their affiliation to us… They enjoy coming to
> lectures but hide their involvement in the Anthroposophical Society
> from their work colleagues…There are practical reasons for the
> name "Goetheanum" instead of the more biblical "Johannesbau"…
> This is particularly important now since we are entering a time of
> extreme chaos…

His words were conciliatory, but the rancor over these changes was indicative of discord between some anthroposophists in Dornach and those in Stuttgart. However, the new trust fulfilled its function well and gave the Molts reason to travel to Dornach frequently. It was their first collaboration with Rudolf Steiner, and for them it forged a beautiful and valuable connection with the building and the artists and artisans working there.

In autumn, Emil fell ill with an intestinal infection that kept him at home for quite a while. His soul was suffering the strain of the war and his body was telling him to slow down. When he got a bit better, he spent time in the garden on the crest of the Uhlandshöhe hill, overlooking Stuttgart.

There, on warm afternoons, Emil could relax with his nine-year-old son and their black German Shepherd, Carex. This dog, named after a prickly wild sedge, was a gift to Walter from one of Emil's business associates and was very affectionate. When Emil packed his bag for a trip, the dog would lie down next to the luggage looking mournful, and when Emil returned, the dog's joy knew no

Walter with Carex

bounds. Once, Emil's secretary, Otto Wagner, took Carex with him to pick up Emil at the train station. When the dog saw Emil, he pulled free of his leash and jumped over the turnstile to meet his master on the platform. He was both guardian and companion, and the family always took him along on their holidays.

Belief in imminent peace

Around this time, as Emil was recovering, a few Stuttgart industrialists got together to draft negotiating points for the treaty they were expecting. In this second year of the war, most Germans and their leaders still believed in an imminent peace with victory. The group brought their proposal to the King. He, beset by doubts, took note of the fact that the delegation came without Emil—who was by now well known and trusted—and asked several of his cabinet ministers to get Emil's opinion. Emil told them that such plans were premature because the outcome of the war was still quite uncertain. Although the cabinet ministers maintained a diplomatic silence during this interview, Emil later learned that they had agreed with him and the subject had been closed.

By reading and rereading Steiner's printed material and attending his lectures whenever they could, the Molts kept discovering new elements of his teachings that related to issues of the day. These discoveries gave them strength and hope for the future. Conversely, each day a stack of newspapers arrived at Emil's office, and each day the news drove him to distraction. At Verdun, General Falkenhayn, who had replaced General von Moltke, would not stand his army back to join reinforcements and thousands died on both sides. At the battle of the Somme, Britain and France fought the Germans for months with thousands of casualties and no victor. Altogether, the German army was terribly scattered, with troops in Macedonia, the Dardanelles, Gallipoli, and even as far away as Syria and the Suez Canal. And still, the war raged on.

Tragic General von Moltke

The only voice that made sense to Emil during this time was his friend General von Moltke's, whose plan to quickly march through Belgium to France's flank had failed. On January 1st, 1916, von Moltke wrote a letter which appeared in the newspaper, *Die Tat*:

> …I was convinced that we [the German people] needed a renewal of our spiritual life long before…this war began, hoping with all my soul that we would be able for this…Only with spiritual weapons can the future be won. The souls of our people were full of ideals… [but] long suppressed by material life…and so divided by class and party that we hardly knew each other before the war…We wanted to take down the barriers that egotism had erected between us; bringing individuals together…[Now] it will depend on caring for the tiny plant trying to grow over the past few years and not to despair. If we fail this time, future generations will need to take up the ideas again. We must work for the future. We will soon be gone, but the people of the coming centuries should live upward: Every seed that is planted now will one day blossom. That is my hope and trust and my belief…

Why are good people shunted aside? Does no one hear what he has been saying? Emil thought after reading the article. That thought kept him awake again with indigestion, sorrowful for his friend.

On June 18th, 1916, General von Moltke died in Berlin of a broken heart, as his widow said. Ironically, he had just given a eulogy at the funeral of his old friend, General von der Goltz Pascha, the former instructor at the Turkish military school. Steiner spoke at von Moltke's funeral. He praised his character and honesty, saying that in future years the world would recognize how faithfully he had carried out his obligation to his country. Emil happened to be in Berlin and was able to attend the eulogy.

A case of Swabian wit

During that summer, Emil had been given the draft of a new company contract, which contained improvements only for the Abrahams and Marx and otherwise was detrimental to Emil. He made up his mind very quickly that this was not the time to bargain for scraps—he would have to take a larger view if he wanted a decisive role as business manager. When June 30th rolled around, Emil simply canceled his contract. Marx responded to this move in a light-hearted manner, as did the Abrahams, but they worried about what stood behind this theatrical gesture. After Emil returned from the Black Forest, Marx came to Stuttgart to hear what Emil had to say. Emil demanded a contract that corresponded to his position, presenting Marx with a new draft that he'd prepared with the help of an attorney. After some negotiation and minor changes, this version of the contract was approved. It took effect on December 31st. The success of this Swabian coup (*Schwabenstreich*) marked Emil's entry into his 40th year. An entry from Friedel Reik's memoir touches on life at the company during that time:

> *One evening Mr. Molt walked into the handwork hall and asked*
> *why there was so often light on in the evenings. Miss Allmendinger*
> *said that we had started a "Soldier's Delight Station" and were*
> *already taking care of 500 soldiers. Cigarettes were always popular*

and workers could buy 100 seconds for 1 Mark. Every payday,
I collected money from the workers, each of whom brought the
address of a needy soldier. Fräulein Allmendinger wrote letters and
I packed the parcels from 1914 until the end of the war.

Friedrich Bauer, an old friend from Patras, knocked on Emil's office door one day in search of work. He described how, after Greece had been drawn into siding with the Allies, all German people—the Hamburger family included—were forced to leave and allowed to take only one suitcase with them.

"Stay with me," Emil said without hesitation. "I don't know what you can do yet, but opportunities will arise. Meanwhile I shall pay you as much as you need to live." A short while later, when the Germans and the Bulgarians moved into Cavalla, where Waldorf Astoria warehoused 100,000 kilos of the finest Xanthi tobacco, Bauer stepped in to help.

"For you," he said in Greek, using the familiar form of address, "I will go." He was able to rescue the invaluable merchandise and return unscathed, even as typhoid fever raged among the beleaguered townspeople of Cavalla.

Air attacks

Emil was on his way home from Dornach when enemy aircraft began bombing Stuttgart. When he heard the news, it filled him with fear for his home and his workers—his house was on the crest of a hill and his factory was in a large and conspicuous building. Luckily, neither suffered damage, but the bombing continued. During one onslaught, Berta lay ill in bed, unable to get into the cellar. Maria ran downstairs with Walter, and Emil stayed with Berta, expecting the worst. They were unharmed, but the following Sunday, while they were on the way to visit Berta's mother and sister Paule in Weilimdorf, low-flying craft started strafing the road. They sped up, arriving just in time to see a live shell fall to the ground, barely missing Berta's mother who had walked out to meet them. They scooped her up and sped into the village.

Such aerial raids to Württemberg became more frequent as the war went on, and during one week, planes attacked three nights in a row, obliging people to seek shelter. These attacks were especially hard on Walter—being ripped out of sleep by the sound of aircraft and howling sirens in the stillness of the night remained etched in many children's memories.

Waldorf Astoria in Switzerland

Although many people still believed in an imminent, victorious end to the war, Emil and Berta were very aware of the danger of Germany's downward spiral. With access to Dornach and raw materials for the company in mind, they thought it wise to start a branch of Waldorf Astoria in neutral Switzerland. So, in 1916 and with a number of business acquaintances, Emil set about incorporating the Swiss Waldorf Astoria branch in Zürich and transferred his skilled assistant, Sophie Kaiser, there as personnel manager.

This maneuver made many things possible that Emil could otherwise not have achieved. He had no difficulty obtaining clearance for travel to Switzerland and was able to watch the progress of the Dornach building, freely buy tobacco, and borrow money from solid Swiss banks. After a while, Zürich even became the new center for the international tobacco trade, while nearby Romanshorn and Geneva served as stockpile hubs. In Zürich, the Café Huguenin blossomed as a meeting place for Turkish tobacco dealers, and Emil loved the atmosphere there—almost like Cavalla, with strong coffee, wreaths of smoke and lively bartering.

One day, the Ministry of War invited Emil to a meeting in Berlin. The politicians and military officers sitting around the table at the meeting knew of Emil's international connections and travel, and they asked him to provide them with information.

"You won't be required to spy, but simply to report what is common knowledge abroad," they told him, promising he would not be compromised. Emil agreed to this, seeing it as an opportunity to be an ambassador for more peaceful relationships.

Part Three

Transformation

1916 - 1936

By late 1916, what with trench warfare, mounting casualties and serious food rationing, German enthusiasm for the war dropped dramatically. The Molts experienced a surge of hope when, in December, they heard that Kaiser Wilhelm had issued a peace proposal directed at the warring powers. They thought U.S. President Woodrow Wilson, whose pro-peace campaign had recently helped him get re-elected, would help broker peace with the Entente powers. Moderate German newspapers were full of expectation, but the Entente quickly rejected the proposal, pronouncing it an ill-disguised effort to reach a separate peace with some while freeing up forces for action against others. The failure of the peace initiative was dreadfully disappointing. President Wilson, although he berated the European nations' continuation of the war, authorized America's intervention soon after. To build support for the war in a highly reluctant nation, he signed off on a new propaganda initiative[9] that sparked an international campaign to portray Germans as barbarians and the Kaiser as a beast.

These news items soon found their way into the German news and further demoralized and confused the general public, already bombarded by propaganda from their own censored press.

Time out for health

The next time Emil, still in poor health, was in Dornach, Steiner advised him to visit a specialist in Basel, who urgently recommended

---

9 The Committee on Public Information, also known as the CPI or the Creel Committee, was an independent, U.S. government agency created to influence public opinion regarding American participation in World War I.

an extended period of rest. By now Emil and Berta were able to afford leaving their smoothly running Waldorf Astoria for an extended stay in the high Alps of Switzerland. They chose a spa hotel called Chantarella.[10] Since they were to stay there for a significant amount of time, the Molts took Walter along and enrolled him in a nearby boarding school.

The Chantarella lay just above the village of St. Moritz, with a funicular that shuttled passengers to and from town. The wintry views were spectacular and the Molts' south-facing rooms included a balcony that allowed for almost continuous sun. The days were surprisingly warm and calm, and although the resort was modern, guests were scarce due to the war.

Walter loved his new school and the brisk mountain air. He spent weekends with his parents, who were always happy to see him. The hotel had everything Berta and Emil needed—including a large library, vegetarian food, a tailor, and a messenger boy.

Berta and Emil skating at St. Moritz

They took their exercise in the form of skating on the lake, Berta swirling and looping around her husband on the ice. Beyond that, they spent most of their time inside, reading, talking and reminiscing.

"Can you believe it," said Emil, "that it's been twenty years since I went to Greece and eighteen years since I started working with Georgii? I wonder how he is getting on. So much has happened!"

Karma of Untruthfulness

Early in 1917, the Molts' friend, Camilla Wandrey, came from Dornach to visit them at the Chantarella. She brought along extensive notes she'd taken during a lecture series Steiner had given called "Karma of Untruthfulness."

---

10 The Chantarella Hotel still exists as of 2019.

"We weren't supposed to take private notes, you know…but I did," she confessed. This lecture series was the culmination of a prodigious amount of research Steiner had done in an effort to provide his friends and followers with an explanation of world events. Before this, he had focused his full attention on building the Goetheanum, but as the war continued, the people he worked with became ever more troubled, begging him to explain what was happening. His research led him to identify numerous threads that connected seemingly disparate world events, and he delivered his findings to a small, intimate circle of friends at the Goetheanum. In this lecture he described some triggers of the war and predicted great instability unless the killing stopped:

> People say that the murders will not cease until there is a prospect of eternal peace. It is virtually impossible to imagine anything crazier than the notion that murder must continue until, through murder, a situation has been created in which there will be no more war. It is hardly necessary to have knowledge of spiritual matters today to know that, once this war in Europe has ceased, only a few years will pass before a far more furious and devastating war will shake the earth.

The Molts spent long evenings going over Camilla Wandrey's notes, and they were astonished at the level of detail. The lectures had included a history of people in control, but it also presented the infinitely larger spiritual causes behind the events. These notes put heretofore inexplicable happenings into an understandable perspective. "The world should know about this!" Emil said brashly, frightening the women. Berta disagreed. "If this is published, Steiner could be in great peril. I hope it stays among ourselves," she said. Emil, however, decided he would at least try to persuade Steiner to let him share the parts relevant to the war with leading military circles.[11]

The next visitor to the Chantarella was Hermann Hesse, who stayed with the Molts until they left at the end of March. Hesse, when in a

---

11 Rudolf Steiner, *The Karma of Untruthfulness*, lecture series, December 1916 in Dornach.

good mood, was full of humor and energy. He raced across the lake on skates, climbed the hills and went skiing. When he was not in a good mood, he was irritable, exhausted by the war and terrified he might still be drafted. He, whose writings were to influence generations, was suffering writer's block at the time. To calm his nerves and help with his insomnia, he started painting, taking lessons from the painter Ernst Kreidolf who lived

St. Moritz, with Hermann Hesse

down the hill. The Molts found Hesse's presence enriching, but his frequent depressions were a trial, especially for Berta. Emil found that the only effective remedy was reminiscing with Hesse about their youth in Calw. It pained both Berta and Emil that Hesse was not able to find a

Hesse painting

relationship to anthroposophy. He had read some books by Steiner, including *How to Know Higher Worlds*, but his long-standing affinity with Eastern philosophies perhaps hindered a relationship to a Western philosophical outlook. Still, the Molts' friendship with him remained close, and it was a special pleasure for them to receive a small folder with poems handwritten and illustrated by Hesse, as a thank-you gift for his stay. Later he dedicated one of his fairy tales "To Berta and Emil Molt."

An unexpected honor

One day, a dispatch embossed with the seal of the King of Württemberg[12] arrived for Emil at the Chantarella. The King made a practice of handing out awards to his worthiest subjects on the occasion of his birthday, and Emil was surprised to find he had been awarded the title *Kommerzienrat*: Royal Württemberg Councilor of Commerce. This title was usually reserved for outstanding businessmen in their later dotage, and it had not been easy for the King to give the award to Emil. He had to send his chief of staff to persuade the interior minister that Molt was the best choice.

At first Emil was embarrassed and did not want to talk about his elevation. At dinner the very evening before he received the award, a group of Swiss hotel guests had made fun of the German penchant for titles, especially ridiculing the title of *Kommerzienrat*. For a while, he kept it a secret, hiding the dispatch in his pocket and not even sharing it with his wife. But eventually he became resigned to the honor, merely begging his acquaintances not to address him by it. Emil was among the last to get such a title, as they were abolished after the war.

During his long convalescence at the Chantarella, Emil let go of preoccupations. He left his daily mail unopened and put it into a drawer. Shutting out the war was harder for him, however—the daily papers were full of disturbing news about a revolt in Russia and the abdication of Czar Nicholas. However, as March 1917 came to a close, the snow at the Chantarella began to melt and the spring air made the Molts restless. Suddenly, they found they'd had enough of their cold mountain perch. Not ready to return to war-torn Germany, they decided to complete their cure in southern Switzerland, in the Italian-speaking canton of Tessin (Ticino).

Hermann Hesse came with them, and on the way they spent a day in Zürich. Then they sped away by train, zigzagging higher and higher

---

12 King Wilhelm, born on February 25, 1848, in Stuttgart, successor to King Karl who died in 1890. His wife Olga died the following year.

toward the great Gotthard Tunnel. The Gotthard mountain range allows for spectacular changes in climate—on the north side snow often lies thick, while the sun shines bright and warm on the south side. Down in the flatlands of Ascona, bordering the Lago Maggiore, the Molts found exuberant spring. Berta, Emil and Walter stayed at the Esplanade Hotel, but Hesse protested, saying that in the Ticino one should live as the Ticinese do and not in an urban super-hotel. He found what he deemed a "real" place to live, with good Italian cooking.

The lovely Ticino

In those days, Ascona was a very small village, although its beauty and climate made it a popular tourist attraction. Colorful houses nestled together surrounded by azaleas and palm trees. Ascona was home to artists and an early version of hippies. On the Monte Verità above Ascona, colorful vegetarian theosophists strolled about in flimsy garments and long hair. Gusto Graeser, a well-known eccentric in buckskin attire, preferred living in a wigwam pitched on the mountain.

The war seemed far away in that idyllic neutral corner of Europe, but still, the Molts spotted fortifications on the hills across the lake and occasionally heard the rat-tat-tat of artillery near the Italian border. Ascona was host to brigades of German-speaking Swiss militia, while the local Ticinese militia was stationed in the north, near Dornach and Arlesheim. Locals said that in spite of Switzerland's tiny size, many northern German Swiss and southern Italian Swiss met each other for the first time thanks to these cross-postings.

The Ticinese inhabitants worried that one day the Italians would invade and force a passage through their land. Happily, that never happened, although weapon smuggling flourished on the steep, wild paths of the uninhabited hills high above the lake. If a border patrol came too close to the smugglers, they simply heaved their contraband into one of the ravines to be collected early the next morning.

Returning to Stuttgart

After Easter, Berta and Walter went home so that Walter could return to school. Emil stayed on in Ascona with some anthroposophical friends, spending several quiet weeks reading Steiner's *The Philosophy of Freedom* and taking long walks. The Canton of Ticino showed Emil that there are people who live their whole lives far from the commotion of the world. He couldn't continue such a way of life in the long run, but he savored it for a while. Then, feeling strengthened, he returned to Stuttgart and resumed his tasks with vigor. In the factory, nobody begrudged him his leave. With its good organization and his friend Bauer's stewardship, the business was doing fine.

Emil tries to enlighten the War Ministry

Back in Stuttgart, Emil prepared a summary of the "Karma of Untruthfulness," in which Steiner had addressed the hidden intentions leading to the war. When Steiner came to Stuttgart, Emil explained that he would like to make this material accessible to influential people in the War Ministry.

"I have an army contact who can circulate it in the highest military circles," he said, expecting Steiner's opposition. But Steiner surprised him by approving, and Emil realized that Steiner very much wanted to serve the public with his spiritual and scientific insights. In fact, Steiner had even made himself available to the military authorities once, offering to create a kind of news bureau in Switzerland to inform the wider international public about the truth of the origins of the war. He wished to counter the Entente's endless propaganda, which put the blame for the war on Germany. He felt that, in the face of the devastating effect this propaganda had on German citizens, the project was of the highest urgency. In Berlin, military officials were in favor of the plan until they discovered that Steiner was not a German but an Austrian citizen, at which point they rejected it.

"Should we pass this material around in political circles as well?" Emil now asked. "As long as the current people are in power, there is nothing we can do," Steiner replied. The next day proved him right when the mayor of Stuttgart summoned Emil to his office to revisit the idea of building warehouses for reparations streaming in from the defeated foe. "When we have won the war," the mayor asserted, "we will need plenty of space to store the goods." "Are we quite sure of victory and of merchandise streaming in?" Emil asked. This question astonished the mayor, rendering him speechless.

Emil knew that sending the "Karma of Untruthfulness" material to the military could open Steiner to attack, but he trusted that Steiner wanted it done. He gave several copies to Major Fessman, an acquaintance of his in the Stuttgart War Ministry, who promised to forward the manuscript to the General Staff in Berlin. Emil stopped by a few days later to see if there had been any interest. Fessman shook his head. "I'm sorry," he said. "The gentlemen would have preferred reading a document about the movement of troops. They showed no interest in larger connections."

Despite this initial response, the material did in fact circulate. One copy was returned from General Headquarters shortly after this meeting, surprising Hans Kühn, a friend of Emil's and a committed young intern in Fessman's office. The document had been annotated by the German Secretary of State for Foreign Affairs and was eventually taken along to the peace negotiations in Brest Litovsk, although it did not gain mention. Another copy reached the Austrian Emperor's Chef de Cabinet, Count Arthur Polzer Hoditz, through his brother Ludwig, one of Steiner's close adherents. The brothers were impressed by the content and amazed to know it had gone through official channels. Count Polzer told Emperor Karl about it, but could not get the actual document into his hands because protocol required that every communication addressed to the Emperor first be read and approved by his cabinet. Whatever held it up, the Emperor never saw it. The political landscape did not improve, and the Brest-Litovsk peace treaty, signed by Austria, Germany, the Ottoman Empire and Russia on December 22nd, 1917, did not prevent the Entente powers from fighting on.

Deprivation

On the war front, a certain quiet prevailed during the early part of 1918. On January 7th His Excellency, Hans-Adolf von Moltke, nephew of the deceased General Helmuth von Moltke, arranged a meeting between Steiner and Prince Max of Baden in Karlsruhe. The purpose was to acquaint this political aristocrat with certain insights into the catastrophic world situation, and to suggest possibilities for its resolution. Prince Max was a liberal and seemed open to spiritual matters. Steiner revised his lecture cycle, *The Mission of the Folk Souls,* with a special foreword and presented it to Prince Max during an hour-long conversation. Although the Prince listened, he did not take Steiner's suggestions further.

Paper was becoming scarce, either requisitioned by the army or simply unavailable. While Emil's printer managed the tiny booklets, very few regular-size books were published. One day, while checking inventory in the storehouse, Emil discovered reams of unused paper, mostly obsolete advertisements and uncut brochures printed on just

Newsprint in bound book

one side. "Put them to use," said Berta. "Raise them to lofty heights by printing Steiner lectures on their blank sides." "Won't some of our more devoted members be shocked, seeing Steiner's words next to Charlie Chaplin and boot polish ads?" asked Emil, and they both started laughing. "They will say that you're just a crass businessman, but they'll devour the material," she said. He found it delightful that he was the only one privileged to see the frivolous and roguish side of Berta.

The printer assembled a large number of these books and sold them quickly, the proceeds going directly to Steiner. When Emil met him in Berlin to discuss a reprint of his groundbreaking book, *The Philosophy* of *Freedom*, Steiner thought a thousand copies would be more than enough. "No one will read it," he said, but his librarian and Emil insisted on a run of four thousand, and these quickly sold out. This work was later translated into many languages and has become a classic.

A foster son

When the school year began, the Molts made room for their nieces, Lisa and Dora, to stay with them, and they took in a 9-year-old boy named Felix Goll. Felix was a difficult child, the son of a well-known, widower artist who was unable to care for his children. Felix spent his early childhood in several foster homes, where he was ill-treated and certainly not loved. Walter immediately accepted him as a brother, and Berta lavished affection on him. Her care transformed the boy, who was very devoted to his new family and eventually became a fine artist. The Molt apartment now became lively with the four children and their games.

The deadly Spanish flu

That spring the Spanish flu spread through the depleted military and civilian populations of Europe and eventually the world. For a while, Waldorf Astoria closed down, but the Molt family and most workers were spared.

The military leadership looked forward with hope to a big spring offensive following the cessation of war with Russia.[13] In June, the long-expected offensive began. Battles raged on the western front. There were a few successes but nothing was decisive. In spite of the obvious failures, the German public remained optimistic. In August official reports were still favorable, claiming a slow retreat but continuing German freedom of movement. In reality, the Allies were victors all along the line.

---

13 On March 3, 1918, in Brest-Litovsk, a city in today's Belarus, Russia signed a treaty with the Central Powers (Germany, Austria-Hungary, Ottoman Empire, Bulgaria) in the hope of ending their participation in World War I.

Ersatz and a cow

Week by week food became scarcer and less palatable, especially in northern Germany. Homemakers were inventive with substitutes, using mainly root vegetables. Mock marmalade, milk and eggs were cobbled together from beets. Bread was scarce and often contained harmful ingredients. Even the best hotels were not exempt from deprivation, since most of the available food was requisitioned by the troops. Early on, all kitchen and domestic utensils were surrendered to the army because imports had ceased. People resorted to makeshift, ersatz, or substitute materials—bicycles had wooden wheels, clothing was made of paper. The remaining men were drafted and women replaced them as field workers and machinists as well as streetcar conductors, taxi drivers and barbershop staff.

A number of the younger Waldorf workers began suffering from symptoms of malnutrition, such as bronchial catarrh. Emil realized he would have to supplement their diet in some way. The factory had free warehouse space and, on impulse, he bought a couple of cows and hired a milkmaid, providing his employees with enough milk for the duration of the war. He also kept an open account with his homeopathic doctor friend Stiegele for employees who really needed him.

At the time I had a bronchial catarrh. Mr. Molt asked me about my cough and I said, "I've had it for a year and can't get rid of it." Miss Allmendinger explained, "The young people lack milk." Mr. Molt asked, "Am I supposed to have cows carting cigarettes to the post office?" I laughed and said, "I suppose the cigarettes wouldn't mind if they heard 'giddyup, Brindle, giddyup.'" We laughed, but then Mr. Molt got serious and said: "Miss Allmendinger, make an appointment for Miss Schott with Dr. Stiegele first thing in the morning and charge it to my account. That cough should be seen to." Dr. Stiegele examined me and said, "I can still help you, but only just," and he gave me a little bottle. "If it works, you'll be fine; otherwise come back to see me."

It was a miracle bottle! A few weeks later there was a phone call: "Miss Schott, the cows will be arriving tomorrow. Please search for a dairy maid among the workers to take care of them. I insist you drink milk every morning so you don't cough anymore." "Oh, Mr. Molt, I am fine. Dr. Stiegele gave me wonder drops." "Well, well, I'll have to talk to him. It's not nice that he didn't keep a few of those for me!" The two cows remained in a warehouse until milk became plentiful again. – Emil's employee, Friedel Reik

Berta had trouble digesting food, although she tried to be careful with her diet. When summer came, she took Walter, a friend of his, and her nieces, Lisa and Dora, to the country in an effort to improve her health. They stayed in the Bavarian resort town of Garmisch Partenkirchen in a region relatively untouched by war. She thought Emil would be unable to join them, but he said he would simply bring along his secretary, Rosalie Schollian, and work remotely. Rosalie, he said, was too thin and too pale and the air and fresh vegetables would do her good. Dora recalled that trip: "In the summer of 1918, Uncle Emil and Aunt Berta took Lisa and me on a family vacation—our first time in the Alps. It was wonderful, playing barefoot in the grass, wading in the stream and Uncle reading to us. That was in the last months before the collapse of Germany."

When Berta returned home, her health was improved but she found their apartment too noisy—the street they lived on had become a thoroughfare. Knowing this, their friend del Monte offered them a beautiful apartment in his house, with seven rooms, a glass veranda and modern heating. The Molts moved in, bought an adjacent garden, and hired a gardener. Soon the family had abundant fresh vegetables and fruit to spare for friends and factory workers. Walter was at odds with the energetic Mrs. del Monte, but he loved the garden with its jungle gym and rotating swing.

Defeat under harshest terms

In September 1918, Emil heard rumors that Austria was falling. Bulgaria deserted the alliance. In October, Prince Max of Baden was appointed Chancellor of Germany and given the task of forming a new government. Karl, the Emperor of Austria, recognized imminent defeat and asked Steiner to come to Vienna to present his ideas. But Steiner refused, deeming it too late to change the course of events. Under pressure from General Hindenburg and General Ludendorff, Prince Max dispatched a request for an armistice negotiation to President Wilson. To the great disappointment of the anthroposophists, this request did not include any of Steiner's suggestions. Kaiser Wilhelm went into exile in the Netherlands and the military relinquished its authority. Prince Max gave over the office of Chancellor to Friedrich Ebert, leader of the Social Democrats.

On November 8th, civilian representatives of the newly formed government were presented with the harsh terms of the armistice. On November 11th they signed the armistice with the Allies, ending World War I. *How was it in reality?* Emil wrote in his memoirs.

On one side, a coalition aided by thousands of fresh, well-nourished and well-equipped American soldiers. They possessed every conceivable source of raw material and supplies and had access to munitions factories. On the other side a weary and undernourished army with worn-out equipment. The civilian population was emaciated after four years of being sealed in. And finally, Germany's allies no longer could, or would, help.

All this went beyond what a people could bear, mentally and physically. Surely, it wasn't dishonorable to admit this to the world which could see the unprecedented effort with which the army and the people had waged this unequal battle for so long. Should it not have been possible for a judicious, prudent political leadership to come to an honorable peace? Rudolf Steiner certainly provided materials to refute the accusation that Germany was solely responsible for the war. These materials could have been used at the deliberations in Versailles. Alas, nobody dared to present them.

Revolution, Dornach and resolve

On Saturday, November 9th, while on business in Zürich, Emil heard the news of revolution in Germany bursting into the streets. He heard that kings and princes were being deposed—that one ruler after another, even the popular Württemberg monarch, was forced to abdicate and a republic had been declared. Emil could not believe his ears. Zürich, a town full of socialist radicals and foreigners, caught the revolution fever, and bank buildings had to be secured by guards wielding machine guns while armed police patrolled public gathering places.

Emil immediately packed his bags to go home, but he decided to get Steiner's view on the situation first. He took the next available train to Dornach and arrived in time for the evening lecture in which Steiner, interrupting his regular series, talked about social renewal as a way out of the crisis.[14] Emil listened intently, wondering what he himself could do about the situation. As if in response, Steiner said, "And if someone were to ask me what to do now, I would advise being alert to what the situation demands."

Yes, thought Emil. *I will take these thoughts on social renewal back to Stuttgart and see what I can do to implement them.* It seemed to him as if his destiny had brought him to Steiner at this decisive moment.

After the lecture, Steiner greeted him warmly and wished him well for his trip home. Emil returned to Basel from Dornach, spending the night near the railway station. Early the next morning he heard the sound of drums and, going out, saw Swiss guards marching to contain what was by now an uprising in Switzerland as well. Although the train station was about to close, Emil caught the last train to Zürich. While he was on board, the government declared a general strike, including all public transportation. Emil became agitated, thinking his trip to Dornach may have prevented his return to Germany. But in Zürich his friend and Waldorf Astoria manager, Römer, located a man with a car willing to drive Emil as far as Lake Constance. In the Swiss town of

---

14 Lecture: "A Historical Foundation for the Formation of Judgment on the Social Question."

Winterthur they encountered crowds massed in the streets. The driver managed to get through but, when they arrived at Lake Constance, Emil learned that all ferries had been canceled. "You won't get across into Germany before Monday afternoon at the earliest," he was told. "A train to Constance on the Swiss side of the lake is uncertain too, and besides, the town is in flames."

Traveling home with some luck

Emil, not one to remain passive, managed to get himself on the single train to Constance. He climbed aboard, almost the only passenger, and arrived at midnight. The town lay peacefully asleep without a hint of flames. He asked to be taken to the stationmaster since his pass was for Friedrichshafen and not Constance.

"Are you Mr. Molt of Waldorf Astoria?" the stationmaster asked cordially when he saw Emil's name on the passport. When Emil said yes, the stationmaster told him he was engaged to one of the secretaries in Emil's office. Then, calming him down and encouraging him not to worry, he arranged for a hotel room and gave Emil a soldier as escort and to carry his luggage. Emil, considerably heartened, relaxed into an undisturbed sleep. The next morning, he boarded the ferry across Lake Constance to Friedrichshafen. On deck, he was amused to observe his first revolutionary soldier—a florid, freckled country boy with red hair and a red armband. He was harmless, but very much admired by the other passengers.

Arriving in Stuttgart, Emil was met by his porter, Gutbrod, who assured him that family and factory were fine but urged Emil to go to the town hall where Mayor Lautenschlager was presiding over an emergency meeting with industrialists. Walking the short distance from the station to the town hall, they passed groups of angry rioters milling about. Emil was glad to have Gutbrod with him.

"What has happened to my Stuttgart?" Emil asked.

"I don't know," Gutbrod answered. "It began as a peaceful workers' demonstration, organized by the Social Democrats. They marched past the palace. Suddenly, quite against the will of the organizers, a radical group of sailors from Kiel took over the march and attacked the palace. The palace guard had strict orders to avoid bloodshed and so, in spite of their resistance, the rowdies broke in and demanded the King's sword. For a short time, they succeeded in hoisting a red flag. The King took it so much to heart that he left Stuttgart, vowing never to return. They say he even stipulated that in case of his death his funeral cortège should not go through the city."

Now Emil deeply regretted that his destiny had placed him far away at the time of the uprising. He felt sure he could have done something, or at the very least taken his leave of the King properly. He was appalled to see a group of young boys attacking two passing officers and pulling epaulets and medals off their uniforms. The officers seemed lamed, making no resistance—almost an unbelievable reaction from soldiers who had faced the enemy for so long. Emil, furious at this disgraceful behavior, and in utter disregard for his own safety, stormed toward the harassers, brandishing his umbrella. He demanded the medals back and threatened the youths, who were instantly cowed by the force of his authority. This dressing down gave Emil a small measure of satisfaction, as though he had in some way avenged the deposed monarch.

Chaos and back to old ways

When he arrived at the town hall, Emil found that the civic leaders had no idea how to bring order into the chaos, especially considering the hordes of famished and desperate soldiers streaming back into the city from the front. Emil suggested diverting the soldiers from town by disarming them at outlying stations and giving them money to return directly to their own homes where they were urgently needed. His suggestion was ignored and the meeting ended abruptly when news came through that the onerous armistice had been ratified. Once again Emil realized that if he wanted to be effective, he would have to act independently.

In the following days, the revolutionaries caused further havoc, and chaos prevailed. Finally two Stuttgart regiments returned from the battlefield, marched into town in perfect formation and restored order. Soon the government adopted a constitution for Württemberg, drafted by a professor of civil law from Tübingen—a Steiner admirer named Wilhelm von Blume.

In Stuttgart, the revolutionaries made an alliance with the old Imperial order, deciding in favor of a republic and parliamentary democracy. The result was that new heads of government were quickly installed, but the lower echelons of administration remained with all their old ideas and set ways. So instead of a fresh, new wind and clear direction, things remained the same, and these revolutionary Social Democrats quickly transformed themselves into comfortable middle-class folk, thanks to their new-found positions in life.

The threadbare Minister

A few days after order was restored in Stuttgart, Emil tried to make a sizable donation in support of returning soldiers but learned that such a donation required the approval of the Minister of War. He went to the Ministry and found it in the hands of revolutionaries. A wispy-looking young soldier in shabby uniform presented himself and went hunting for the Minister, who was nowhere to be found. The soldier then informed Emil that he was the Deputy Minister of War, so Emil negotiated the donation with him. At the end of the interview, and because the Deputy Minister's outfit looked so very threadbare, Emil invited him to his house where he offered him a pair of new gray trousers, a jacket and a pair of good boots. Everything fit perfectly. The soldier insisted on changing into the clothes immediately, asking only for a piece of brown paper for his old uniform. Thrilled, he departed with the package under his arm.

Shortly after that, one of the better men's clothing shops in Stuttgart sent Emil a bill for a coat that had been delivered to a certain Mr. X. Emil's soldier had apparently found that a good suit deserved a matching outer covering, and whether Emil liked it or not, he had to honor the soldier's purchase. Emil reported the little scam to his friend, Hans Kühn, in the Ministry, and he never heard of nor saw the fellow again. Kühn was high in Emil's estimation for having freed a large number of French prisoners after wiring Berlin asking for instructions on what to do with them. On receiving no reply, he had simply sent them home.

During the first days of the new government, Emil looked for ways to promote Steiner's social ideas. He introduced himself to the new Minister of Commerce, Dr. Hugo Lindemann. "I assume," he said politely, "that you will be looking for experienced business advisors. I am placing myself at your service." Dr. Lindemann gazed at him uncomprehendingly with no idea why he had come. Just then, Emil's colleague, Julius Baumann, walked in. He was the former secretary of Württemberg's tobacco association and the new Minister for Food.

"You can see, Mr. Baumann," remarked Emil, "what a hard time I have, offering my services here."

"Just come with me," answered Baumann. "I always need people like you." He gave Emil an office and a young staff member.

Four projects

While in that office, Emil took on four projects: an attempt to start a Württemberg Industrial Credit Union; purchasing food in Switzerland; introducing Steiner's social and political views to leading government personalities in view of the approaching peace negotiations; and working in the Commission for Social Reform. Two of these projects failed, two were moderately successful. But Emil pursued all four. It is said that nothing done in the world is ever lost, it may just hibernate until the climate is right.

The attempt to create a credit union

Initially Emil tried to encourage all Württemberg industries to pool money into a trust to facilitate members' capital needs and help the transition from wartime to peacetime production. He hoped for three things: to protect struggling companies from being taken over by the victors, to protect financially needy members from the usury of capitalist banks, and to provide a social framework where stronger and weaker companies could work together in the interest of the total economy. The plan found a cordial reception in the Ministry of Commerce. The Finance Minister was inclined to authorize State funding, and the central bank was willing to invest, providing the industrialists endorsed the plan. Ministerial Councilor Dr. Wilhelm Schall called a gathering of leading industrialists and presented them with the project in great detail, but despite the early momentum, this group did not endorse the project. They were not ready or willing to cooperate with their competitors and the project collapsed.

Later Emil had occasion to meet with Dr. Schall, who told him confidentially, "Your plan was really good and it is a pity it wasn't implemented. But you committed the gravest error by involving so many of your fellow [anthroposophical] believers."

Obtaining food

Emil's next project involved obtaining food from Switzerland to feed the starving people of Germany. Emil asked the banks to begin stockpiling 1000-Mark bank notes, as these were still traded at a fair exchange. He then traveled to see Swiss President Felix Calonder, who said that food was in short supply in his country too. The only thing he could offer was chestnut meal that had been stockpiled in Swiss army mountain recesses, but that turned out to be worm-ridden and unusable. A short while later, Emil succeeded in negotiating a freight carload of Tobler chocolate at a cost of 1.2 million francs. He stuffed a suitcase with 1000-Mark bills and took a train to Zürich, accompanied and protected by his muscular machinist, Herr Schoeller. Traveling across borders with so much cash was a risky undertaking, but they safely brought back a heavenly treat instead of a basic food staple. After more than four years of privation, nobody complained.

Around that time, Emil traveled to Switzerland again, this time in an official capacity and in a military car with Herr von Thuena, the director of Daimler Aerospace. The German government, concerned that it might be obliged to turn over its airplanes to the Entente, was interested in selling or leasing them abroad. Emil introduced von Thuena to his friend, Dr. Frey-Zamboni, and the famous pilot, Alfred Comte. The Swiss, planning to launch a national airline company, were interested. The Ad Astra Aero company, later Swissair, was founded several months later with German Junker planes.

The Threefold Social Order

During one of his visits to Dornach, Emil asked Steiner for his views on social renewal. In response, Steiner gave him a short, written treatise describing a "threefold social order." In this document, Steiner reinterpreted and revitalized the French revolutionary principles of liberty, equality, and fraternity. He paired liberty with free cultural and spiritual life, equality with human rights, and fraternity with economic life, explaining how to integrate these ideals into society. The concept made sense to Emil and he shared it with some of the government ministers he was in contact with.

On January, 9th, 1919, a few radical youths led another rebellion in Stuttgart, and the government fled to the train station tower. From there they rang Emil and asked him to please come and explain Steiner's Threefold Social Order to the group of government officials. Although these gentlemen had become somewhat more attentive due to their circumstances, when the rebellion subsided a few days later, their interest in the Threefold Social Order evaporated.

A workers' council

The new government in Württemberg tried to meet the demands of protesters by creating "workers' councils" that were loosely modeled along Bolshevik lines. Emil realized that such councils had potential use within a company to communicate with management about basic workplace issues and needs.

"The task of the employer, blessed with experience and knowledge," he mused over dinner with Berta, "is to share as much as possible of his own experience with his employees. Through such a council, workers could collaborate more and become invested in their work, not only for the purpose of making money but for an understanding of the larger whole." Berta knew about the traditional chasm between workers and management and she loved the idea. Knowing the Waldorf workers, she was sure the concept would succeed and promised to help.

The next day Emil called an all-factory meeting and presented the idea of a Waldorf Astoria workers' council, inviting his employees to choose representatives who would regularly meet with management. "I will teach you everything I know," he offered. The plan was enthusiastically endorsed.

Berta laughed when he told her what he had done. He had acted impulsively in creating the council, without using a model—it was natural for him to trust his intuition, taking action first, and developing the idea as he went along. "You don't hang about when you get an idea," Berta said.

"When business people are asked how they come to decisions, they answer, 'We just try it,'" Emil replied peevishly. "After all, God did his creating in the first six days and only contemplated it on the seventh." Berta laughed again.

"Yes, my darling, that's all very fine for God, but don't forget that you and all good business people like you have gone through years of trial and error to come to those intuitions."

Waldorf Astoria was the only company in Württemberg to have this kind of workers' council in which matters concerning the firm were discussed and resolved. It remained an island of tranquility in a city full of companies dealing with rebellious workforces in a charged atmosphere.

Education for workers

At the start of the war, Emil had promised to keep jobs open for his employees who had gone to fight, and now those workers were returning home, many wounded and severely demoralized. As a result, Emil had many double placements in the factory, and workers' hours were cut down to half days so that everyone could be accommodated without anyone losing their job.

Herbert Hahn

To facilitate a return to normal life, and because workers had time on their hands, Emil decided to launch an educational program at the factory. For this purpose, he installed a works library and hired Dr. Herbert Hahn—a highly talented secondary school teacher with an interest in anthroposophy—to coordinate the program. Hahn developed courses in history, language, painting and geography, as well as an introductory course on the broader questions of life. Berta was an active participant in this program.

Every week a guest speaker gave a special lecture in one of the work halls. Groups from the company's various departments visited each other, listening to colleagues describe their work. Through these visits, the women sorting tobacco, for example, soon began to learn about processes in the machine hall. Emil lectured on tobacco cultivation, purchasing, sales, and advertising. Rudolf Steiner became a frequent and welcome guest lecturer as well. To ensure everyone's participation in these activities, the courses were held within paid working hours. With the help of these educational efforts, workers at the company regained interest in life and work, posing many questions and offering thoughtful comments during these sessions.

"Your tobacco is good, Mr. Molt," one hand worker told Emil, "but for the cigarettes to taste really special more is needed. They have to be made with love, and we supply that."

Visitors to the factory often remarked on the bright eyes and positive demeanor of the workers in contrast to those in other enterprises. When Emil told them about the educational activities, the visitors understood what they were seeing.

The Waldorf News

Emil also started publishing a bimonthly in-house journal called the *Waldorf News*. Although this publication was initially an employee newsletter, it soon enjoyed a much wider readership. Employees and salesmen received *Waldorf News* free of charge, and doctors, lawyers, hotels, and public libraries subscribed to it for waiting room and lobby reading material. It proved to be an important

Waldorf News

showcase for the factory, but it also contained articles by Steiner and other anthroposophical writers, and therefore garnered attention from the spiritual scientific movement as well. A few people told Emil that they joined the anthroposophical movement because of it.

The Kingdom

A short essay by Hermann Hesse appeared in the *Waldorf News*, January 15th, 1919, Issue No 2.

> *Once there was a large and beautiful land inhabited by a modest yet strong people content with their lot though not all that rich or opulent or elegant. Wealthier neighbors sometimes looked on them with disdain, or at least pity tinged with mockery.*
>
> *All that ceased in the great war that so dreadfully devastated the world and in whose ruins we still stand, deafened by its sound, embittered by its senselessness and ill from the rivers of blood that run through our dreams.*

The war ended and this young, blossoming realm, whose sons had gone to battle with such high spirits and enthusiasm, collapsed. It was terribly defeated. The conquerers demanded a heavy tribute even before there was talk of peace, so day after day the soldiers streaming back were met by long trainloads of goods, symbols of their possessions, on their way out to the victorious enemy.

Meanwhile, in their moment of greatest need, the people took stock and felt they had come of age. They chased away their rulers and royalty and formed councils, proclaiming their willingness to deal with their own misfortune.

This folk, though matured by heavy trial, does not yet know where their way will lead, and who will be their helper, but the hosts in heaven know. They know why they sent the sorrow of this war over the people and all the world and have provided a shining way out of the darkness that this conquered folk must go.

It cannot return to childhood. It cannot just give away its cannons, its machines and its money and start making poems and playing sonatas in its peaceful little towns again. But it can walk the path that every individual takes when his life has led him into error and deepest pain. It can remember its heritage and childhood, its growing, its brightness and its decline and by remembering find the strength at its core. It must turn inward to find its own being, and when it does so, this being will accept its destiny willingly, saying yes to it, and beginning anew.

If this beaten folk can accept the path of its destiny and walk it with assurance, some of what once was will renew itself like a steady stream, and flow out into the world. Then those who now are still its enemies will hear this quiet stream and be moved by it.

Recreation and rehabilitation for workers

With Berta's encouragement, Emil looked for recreational possibilities as a means of helping workers and their children recover from the war. Taking advantage of a depressed real estate market, he bought a large

Workers' holiday

property in Schorndorf, east of Stuttgart. The old estate, named Villa Sunshine, was situated in a beautiful park with a little dairy attached, which provided milk for the guests. Emil had the main building refurbished into a cozy and popular retreat, run by a manager whose wife did the cooking. Employees contributed a very modest sum toward room and board. The workers loved the place and used it for years. Later, Waldorf teachers and their families enjoyed staying there too.

The Molts only stayed at Villa Sunshine once, taking Walter, Felix and two of their friends along. They drove through the clean and peaceful town of Schorndorf, noting its picturesque houses untouched by the war. A long driveway surrounded by tall trees, meadows and gardens led to the villa, and the Molts saw a vacationer on an upstairs balcony. He welcomed the Molt party, telling them to be sure to read both signs before entering. The first sign read:

Villa Sunshine welcomes you.
Forget your cares, your troubles too.
Take your ease, your soul renew
With apple cake and coffee brew.

The second read:
Terms and Conditions:
Whoever mentions business here will be thrown out the door.

Frau Pelargus offered her guests an excellent afternoon coffee with fresh milk and generous portions of whipped cream, currant cake and cheesecake. They walked through the tastefully furnished house that the architect had turned from prosaic to modern. Each room had its own color scheme and was decorated with fresh-cut flowers. Although this was their first time seeing the house in its new and improved form, it didn't seem strange to them, but rather more like home. The well-appointed kitchen offered the Molts three meals a day, along with morning and afternoon tea, announced by a gong. Frau Pelargus had cows in the barn, chickens in the yard, and a large vegetable garden out back. She was therefore able to provide tasty and abundant dishes in spite of a national shortage of supplies.

The Molts were delighted by their stay at Villa Sunshine, and promised to come back often, although they never managed to revisit.

Mr. Molt wanted me to have my voice trained. It was at the Villa Sunshine. Every evening after supper we adjourned to the drawing room and I sang a few songs while one of the gentlemen played the piano. One evening Mr. and Mrs. Molt arrived unexpectedly and were upstairs. Suddenly a voice called down, "Another song, please!" Next morning, Mr. Molt wanted to know who the singer was and said, "My wife says this voice should be trained. You should be a singer." I shook my head, and he said, "Oh, you never want anything I suggest." "Mr. Molt," I replied, "I want nothing else than to stay at Waldorf!" He looked at me and gave me his hand. "Yes, do stay! I don't want my best people to leave!" – Friedel Reik

Because of the number of requests for respite, Emil bought another vacation place near Rietenau. It was a medieval monastery. In the 18th and 19th century it was converted to a popular spa with a mineral spring. It included a bathhouse and eight cabins set in a nice little forest.

In a further effort to improve the working conditions and well-being of his employees, Emil opened a canteen at the factory, as well as an in-company savings bank that returned 5% interest.

Outing to Rietenau

Around that time, Emil's workers affectionately began calling him Father Molt—Vater Molt—behind his back. Although he was only 43, he had a fatherly quality.

The idea of a school

One day toward the end of the year the Waldorf Astoria's machinist, Herr Speidel, told Emil that one of his sons had been recommended for higher education based on his excellent grades, but that the family would not be able to afford the education. Emil saw the simultaneous pride and disappointment in the father's face. At that moment, the idea of a school for his workers' children flashed through his mind and he realized that he could create such an initiative without any outside help. The thought fired his heart so completely that he left his office and rushed home to Berta.

"Will we start a beautiful school together?" he asked, describing his vision. Berta was intrigued by the idea and the two of them discussed it for a long time. But for once Emil held back, sharing it only with her and giving the idea time to mature.

1919: Threefold and the Waldorf School

At the beginning of 1919, a new government and the fading revolutionary mood seemed to promise a more democratic future. Emil and his friends longed for another opportunity to bring Steiner's ideas to the public before this hopeful mood evaporated. When the local government established a cultural workers' council, several anthroposophists joined in the hopes of influencing its direction. As a business director, Emil could not join the council, but

The 'Father'

after every meeting his friends adjourned to the Molt house to plan their course of action. Together, they helped publish a pamphlet that included some of Steiner's social ideas.

On January 25th, 1919, Emil, Hans Kühn, and a Swiss anthroposophist in Stuttgart named Roman Boos traveled to Dornach to present this pamphlet to Steiner, wanting his commentary and guidance for something they felt had political potential. They had several long meetings with him, which ended by him saying: "We cannot rely on old forms any more. We need something completely new. I will give you a document. If you approve of it, then we should have it endorsed by the signatures of at least 100 publicly known personalities. If you can get their support, I will have a mandate and will begin by holding a series of lectures in Zürich which should reach a wider public there and abroad."

The idea of a tripartite society

On February 2nd, Steiner presented the three friends with a beautifully handwritten document titled *An Appeal to the German Nation and to the Civilized World.* In it, using a classical cadence and rhythm reminiscent of the German literary greats, Steiner described his idea of a tripartite social form.[15] It divides society into three distinct but interactive branches: the spiritual-cultural, the economic, and the rights domains. These ideas expressed the basis for the Threefold Social Order.

The friends were moved by this Appeal and promised to do their best. With this document in hand, Roman Boos set out to canvass for signatures in Switzerland, while Hans Kühn and Emil undertook the project of gathering signatures in Germany. Steiner suggested they ask Walter Johannes Stein for help canvassing in Austria.

"He is sitting around in Dornach, waiting for something to do," Steiner said. Emil went to see Stein, finding a young Viennese person almost bursting with intensity who immediately declared himself willing to help. Emil stood by as Stein threw a toothbrush and a shirt into an ancient knapsack, after which Emil drove him to the train station in Basel. Emil stuck an extra 100 Swiss francs in Stein's pocket because of his rather threadbare appearance, and Stein set off for Austria.

In Germany, Emil, Kühn and Boos created an action committee that included Dr. Unger and Professor von Blume, the man who had helped draft the new Württemberg constitution. They decided to memorize and absorb the contents of Steiner's new Appeal, the better to become its public proponents. One of the first signatures Emil obtained was that of Dr. Lautenschlager, the mayor of Stuttgart, after which he traveled to Munich and other cities, successfully collecting signatures. Emil Leinhas, an intense but somewhat melancholy businessman from Mannheim, was also invited to collect signatures, but when he received copies of the Appeal and a list of people, he was unable to absorb the content and so failed to collect his allotted signatures. However, after having enough time to review the Appeal thoroughly, he steeped himself in the ideas and soon wished for nothing more fervently than to become active in the Threefold movement.

---

15 "An Appeal to the German Nation and to the Civilized World," 1919, printed as an appendix in: *The Renewal of the Social Organism*, Rudolf Steiner (Anthroposophic Press, Spring Valley, NY, 1985). It is reprinted in the Appendix of this book.

Before long, the group had collected 250 significant signatures, and Emil brought them to Steiner who was lecturing in Zürich. Far from being idle in his spare time, Steiner had written a book in his hotel room that contained the essential ideas of a proposed new threefolded social form. Emil immediately took the manuscript to a typesetter in Zürich and carried the typeset sheets back to Stuttgart to be printed.

In the first year of publication, 50,000 copies of the Appeal were distributed—not just in Germany but abroad, even as far away as India. Every major newspaper in Germany, Austria and Switzerland published Steiner's *An Appeal to the German Nation and to the Civilized World*, and most included a copy of all the signatures. The Waldorf Astoria workers noticed Emil's signature in the papers and wanted to know more, so he presented them with his first lecture on the topic. The employees endorsed the ideas, and from then on the Waldorf Astoria crew became a kind of vanguard for the Threefold movement.

"Basic Issues of the Social Question in Life Necessities of the Present and Future"

Leinhas

Emil's comptroller, Benkendoerfer, decided to leave Waldorf Astoria to work part-time for del Monte and to concentrate on developing the Threefold idea. When del Monte's partner came to negotiate for Benkendoerfer and asked Emil how soon he could spare him, Emil, annoyed that Benkendoerfer had chosen to leave at such a critical time, brusquely answered, "This afternoon at 2 pm." Emil's preferred choice for a replacement could not join him because of a prior commitment, so he considered Emil Leinhas, whom he knew from occasional anthroposophical gatherings. He remembered someone describing Leinhas as a "business powerhouse, experienced at organizing a sales force and marketing branded products."

Although Leinhas had dreams of being a writer, he had gone into business instead and had worked for a cocoa butter company for years. Early in his life he became attracted to spiritism and theosophy, and in 1908 he heard Steiner speak for the first time. Emil knew Leinhas was now a devoted follower of Steiner's and thought it would be fine to employ someone who was both a dedicated anthroposophist and seasoned businessman. Emil did have some doubts about Leinhas, though, so he wrote to Steiner telling him of his need for a comptroller and asking for a reference on Leinhas.

On February 16th Steiner wrote back with a somewhat ambiguous recommendation:

> *My dear Herr Molt! …Regarding your question about Leinhas, I believe him to be astute and a talented initiator and think he would suit your business needs well. I am less able to judge how Leinhas would behave humanly in such a setting, which is also an important factor. You will understand that I have less opportunity to say something in that direction, since people dealing with me don't always act the way they would in other circumstances. However, given this caution, I would still expect the very best of Herr Leinhas and would say he is a good acquisition in every way. That we would have needed him here is balanced by the thought that it will be good for you to have him in Stuttgart…*

Emil took Steiner's words positively and, without further inquiry, offered Leinhas the job, engaging him at a salary close to his own. In his memoir, Leinhas wrote:

> *When I arrived in Stuttgart in mid-April, Mr. Molt was away, having gone to Dornach to collect Rudolf Steiner. I had a few days to orient myself as to the conditions in Stuttgart and Waldorf Astoria. Actually, I had no great inclination to join the management of a cigarette factory. As a non-smoker, I had no relationship to that branch of industry, and conditions in the firm seemed to me, in contrast to my previous sphere of activity, somewhat narrow and patriarchal… I very much wished, on the other hand, to connect*

myself to the Threefold work and for that reason finally decided to accept the offered position…

Interestingly, given his own struggle to understand Steiner's Appeal, Leinhas was quick to pass judgment on Emil's ability to interpret Steiner's teachings: "Molt relates to Threefold through his feelings; he isn't so concerned about understanding it conceptually," he wrote.

Initially, Emil experienced Leinhas as a great relief, but the relationship with him soon became a soul burden. Leinhas's low opinion of products and business soon became evident, especially in comparison with his high opinions of lecturers and authors.

The Threefold Social Order

On March 23, 1919, the Stuttgart Threefold proponents—now formally associated—addressed a packed audience in one of the largest halls in the city. After this event, requests for lectures poured in from Stuttgart and across the country. Emil, realizing they would all have to rush to keep up with the demand, went shopping for additional transportation. The Daimler motor corporation had a number of slightly used limousines that had belonged to high-ranking military officials during the war. The cars were in top condition and available at bargain prices, so Emil bought several. One, an eight-passenger, high-quality Mercedes, came with a chauffeur named Herr Stahl. This car, fast for its time, was mostly used for transporting Rudolf Steiner, and it served Emil faithfully for a long time.

The country was still volatile with continuing civil unrest, and on March 31st, radical right-wing rowdies forced a general, week-long strike in Württemberg. Factories closed, mail remained undelivered, trains stopped running, and street lighting failed. In the dark of night, wild shooting broke out between citizens and radicals, especially in the Molts' part of town, with bullets flying over their house. For some reason, Emil's hotheaded young friend, Hans Kühn, contacted the leader of the "Radikalinskis" and tried to appease the rabble by instructing them in Steiner's social ideas. When the strike ended, he was convinced his intervention had helped defuse the crisis, but his friends, including Emil and Berta, shook their heads at his escapade, glad he had come to no harm.

When Steiner arrived in Stuttgart on Easter Sunday, April 20th, 1919, Emil was able to present him with copies of his text in book form. At this stage, everyone was sure of public success. Two mornings later, a committee of twelve people including Emil met with Steiner and discussed formally organizing the Threefold initiative into an international association spanning Germany, Austria and Switzerland. In the evening, in one of the largest Stuttgart halls, Steiner lectured on the theme to a full house. A question and answer period followed and copies of Steiner's book and the Appeal were given out.

Emil presents the idea of a school

The next day, April 23rd, Emil invited Steiner to speak about the Threefold Order to his 1200 Waldorf Astoria employees. His words touched their hearts and they applauded warmly. Afterward, Emil introduced Steiner to the members of his workers' council and they discussed ways to develop the threefold model within the factory. In this small circle, Emil shyly presented the idea he and Berta had been living with all winter—his desire to create a school for the children of his workers. The council members showed surprise, but Steiner's face lit up; he had been hoping for this. Emil, delighted, asked whether Steiner would consider overseeing such a school and was overwhelmed when Steiner agreed. Immediately, Emil went over to practicalities.

"I have planned for this project and set aside 100,000 Marks from the profits of last year," he said confidently. "It should be more than enough." He was somewhat taken aback when Steiner remarked, "That's quite a nice sum to begin with."

"Berta," Emil exclaimed when he got home, "this is the best day of our lives. We may not be able to change politicians, but our children will one day change the world. Yet, why does Dr. Steiner need so much money for a little factory school?"

"Perhaps," said Berta, "he has a larger vision and foresees a proper school, accessible to all and in its own building." She was right. Over the next weeks the project expanded like bread in an oven.

The first teachers and the curriculum

On April 25th, 1919, Steiner and Emil met with the Waldorf Astoria's in-house teacher, Herbert Hahn, as well as Ernst August Karl Stockmeyer, a handsome young educator from Malsch whose father had once painted portraits of the Molts. Steiner suggested guidelines for the form and management of the new school. He emphasized the importance of teaching foreign languages (especially English), mathematics and physics—with special emphasis on mechanics, history, drawing, painting, singing and gymnastics. Latin he dismissed as a mere remnant of convent schools, saying Greek would be preferable.

In a conversation with Emil and Berta a few weeks later, Steiner developed the curriculum further, talking about the eight primary classes. Every three to four days, he said, the morning should start with singing; otherwise mornings should begin with drawing. Arithmetic and other main subjects should be taught in blocks of three weeks, two hours every morning. School was not to begin before 8 am, nor go beyond 12 noon. He thought that the upper grades should have fewer classroom lessons and more practical and field work.

Berta worried about children whose families did not attend church but who, she felt, needed to experience a measure of devotion. She asked Steiner about a children's service. He came back with a beautiful non-denominational service that teachers or parents themselves could hold.

Searching for teachers and the Cultural Minister's consent

Stockmeyer traveled here and there looking for suitable teachers in time for Steiner's pedagogical training course. By August he had assembled a provisional faculty. Meanwhile, mindful of the necessary State approvals, Emil, Stockmeyer and Steiner went to see the Minister of Culture, Berthold Heymann. This official, a Social Democrat, was delighted that an industrialist—in other words, a capitalist—was founding a school accessible to all. He gave his formal consent, promising his support, especially in the matter of allowing teachers to retain full autonomy over the curriculum. The only thing he wished to control were the "hygienic facilities." Emil left with a signed permit mandating a new form of independent school.

Hopes and failure of Threefold

In April there was much public excitement in Stuttgart around the idea of the Threefold Social Order, so much so that the organizers thought it would be established by the time school started in September. They imagined the new school as a perfect representation of the "cultural realm" of the Threefold Social Order, and it gave them added impetus.

They needed all their strength—with Steiner in Stuttgart, the days passed in a whirlwind. In the mornings and afternoons, Emil brought Steiner to a succession of large companies to talk to the workers. Venues included the Dinkelacker brewery, del Monte's box factory, the Robert Bosch Works, Daimler Works, Werner and Pfleiderer, the zoo, the railway, and the Union Hall. Emil lectured as well—at the Walter Rau soap factory, Eckhardt, Lauser, Staehl and Friedel, and to the Stuttgart streetcar employees. He spoke in Heilbronn and in Ulm. Steiner's books always came along with Emil, and every listener received a copy of the Appeal.

Despite this momentum, the Threefold group never noticed that a large segment of the population was either uninvolved or deeply resistant to their ideas, including the broader middle class, politicians, government officials and those generally on the conservative right. Having lost their Kaiser and their honor in defeat, these segments of society feared communism and mistook "social order" for "socialism." Indeed, socialists and communists were looking for converts among the very workers Steiner and his friends addressed. On one memorable occasion, Emil spoke to a workers' group on the subject of workers' councils. He was one of three speakers, and after a while he noticed his fellow lecturers turning the event into a kind of election campaign for the German Socialist Party. When it came his turn, he spoke to his theme, and the audience loved it. Thereupon the organizers shook his hand and begged him to come back the next day for another rally, calling him "Comrade Molt." He declined politely, letting them know that he did not share their political views.

Resistance among contemporaries and a lack of understanding proved far stronger than anyone anticipated and in the end they failed. The tasks they set themselves were too large. Neither the audiences nor they themselves, could envisage Steiner's Threefold principles through to their practical application. Lectures continued, but in time listeners became bored and, when the general political situation stabilized, workers were drawn back into the union fold with bosses who looked to bread-and-butter issues.

Finding a building

Meanwhile Emil began his search for a suitable building for the school. Initially he thought of renting a public facility, but when that failed he realized he would have to buy a property with his own money—such a burden could not be put on the company. The need had become pressing, since the school was to open in September, but nothing Emil saw seemed suitable. Then one day a realtor showed Emil a site near his house: a former hunting lodge turned restaurant. It was right below the garden he and Berta had once rented and where, as a schoolboy, he had played with his friends. The asking price was 450,000 Marks, which seemed an impossible amount. Yet the property intrigued him.

May 1, 1919, the "Casino" (our recreation office) planned an outing to the Restaurant Uhlandshöhe to celebrate May Day. It was a lovely day and great fun—with dancing and singing. Dr. Hahn confided that he had wanted to give a little lecture on the poet

Uhland, but he didn't get a chance to say a word. Late in the day we walked arm in arm, past the Molts' house. The gentlemen wanted to serenade them but we ladies were shy, so it became a "pianissimo serenade." Next day, when I arrived at work a colleague called out, "Here comes the dancer!" Herr Molt came up and said, "Yes, and she can sing too! Fräulein Schott, one phone call and I would have come up to celebrate with you!" Then he sat down next to my desk and we discussed the day. I praised the restaurant and its large hall, so suited for dancing, and the splendid view over Stuttgart. Herr Molt shut his eyes in a gesture I noticed before when he was thinking. Then he looked at me and said, "That would be an ideal place for a school!" I had no notion of the decision to start a school, and therefore said uncomprehendingly, "Oh, but we want to go up there often to dance." Yet this site for the first Waldorf School was decided at that moment. – From the memoirs of Friedel Reik

On May 30th Emil brought Steiner to view the Uhlandshöhe property and Steiner pronounced it quite adequate. He seemed untroubled by money considerations. The impossible happened: A few days later Emil closed the deal with the owner. It was a lucky move. A few years later, the other sites he looked at would have been too small for the rapidly growing school.

One day all the "Waldorfians" were called into the tobacco hall. First, Dr. Rudolf Steiner gave a lecture about what could be learned at a Waldorf School. Then Herr Molt said he would be pleased for the parents to entrust their children to him; they would learn the same as his own son, Walter. There would be no slapping children in the Waldorf School; other pedagogical means would be employed. Finally he said, "Of course there is a young lady present who would rather dance in the place we have in mind, but I especially invite her to come to the Waldorf School often."
– From the memoirs of Friedel Reik

The news of the purchase hit Stuttgart like a bombshell, more so after Emil published an article describing what was to happen at that site and who was responsible for its direction. Those with misgivings about the Threefold Social Order found the idea of an independent school for workers' children highly dangerous in a society where everyone should know their station in life. Some among Minister Heymann's colleagues questioned his judgment in allowing what they considered an unproven experiment by an Austrian esotericist whose writings were incomprehensible to them. They were somewhat relieved that Emil supported the venture, knowing him as a solid and generous member of society.

Uhlandshöhe Restaurant

The hardest direct confrontation happened with the local diocesan priest, who informed the Catholic Waldorf Astoria workers that their children would not receive communion if they attended the Waldorf School. Two Waldorf parents, both Catholic, requested an interview with the priest to hear his reasons for this decision, and they brought Emil along to the meeting. At first, the priest tried to label the school as sectarian. Emil opposed this energetically, saying that every religion would be respected. At last the Waldorf parents said firmly, "We will send our children to the Waldorf School even if the Bishop denies them communion." As a result, permission was granted for the Catholic children to attend.

A story about the Uhlandshöhe by Emil's friend, Walter Rau:

In the middle ages this small mountain was a strategic pass with a gallows at its crest. In my childhood, salutes were fired from there whenever a new little prince or princess was born to the royal house. The restaurant was a favorite destination for hikers walking up through the vineyards. After the war, we heard the restaurant would close because the industrialist Molt planned to make an independent school there, open to children of all social classes, boys and girls. I witnessed the development of the school as a neighbor and participated in several courses for adults. When my own children were of school age I sent them there and was delighted at the closeness of teachers, children and parents. Over the course of time, I became friends with Molt and treasured his fiery will. His generous ways as an entrepreneur awakened similar feelings in my soul. He combined great ideas with exact implementation, but the strength of sacrifice he brought the school, jeopardizing his industrial life to keep it going in post-inflationary times, filled me with awe and admiration.

In June, Steiner and his friends were forced to acknowledge that the Threefold Social Order ideas were not accepted by the greater public and that their initiatives would be limited to what their small group could achieve within the cultural-educational domain. This was a significant shift—no longer could the planned school hope for a comprehensive social organism to carry it; rather it would have to exist in an environment of old educational and legal forms, possibly having to fight for its rights and for its existence.

When Emil traveled to Switzerland for business, he would often stop in Dornach for one of Steiner's lectures and a meeting of the Goetheanum Trust. Steiner always had time for him, often inviting him to dinner at his house where he constantly talked about rebutting the Entente's claim that Germany bore sole responsibility for the war. He pointed repeatedly to the Kaiser's last-minute efforts to prevent war and wanted the international community to know about the events that had actually taken place during those fateful days. Emil begged him to write something that could be distributed to every member of the German delegation planning to attend the upcoming peace treaty negotiations in Versailles, and Steiner agreed. A most fortuitous opportunity presented itself when the late General von Moltke's wife, Eliza, showed Steiner the General's extensive diaries. With Eliza's permission, Steiner prepared a brochure based on these diaries, arguing the case against sole German culpability.

This brochure, intended for the German delegation, was printed in Stuttgart, but von Moltke's nephew kept it from distribution at the last moment because the family felt the material to be too compromising to the principal individuals, the Kaiser in particular. Emil was sure the content would have made a difference to the outcome of the negotiations, but the pamphlets were destroyed. Emil did manage to send a salvaged copy to the representative of Württemberg, but to no effect.[16]

On June 28th,1919, the Treaty of Versailles was signed. The German delegation had been barred from the negotiations until the very end of the meetings. Then Germany was presented with conditions that required years of reparation payments, occupation by the Allies and the United States, and forfeiture of many national resources and privileges. Thousands of German planes, trains, trucks, stores of coal, and other natural resources were relinquished. Germany's borders were closed, merchant ships were blockaded, and the treaty of Brest-Litovsk was renounced.[17]

Planning and building

Meanwhile, preparations to open the new Waldorf school continued unabated during the summer months. Emil's architect friend, Weippert, remodeled the building, working closely with Steiner who visited frequently, driven in the Waldorf Astoria car. In August, on the first of these trips, Emil took Steiner and his wife back to Switzerland, taking Walter and Felix along. They took a route through some of Emil's

---

16 When, a few years later, the von Moltke diaries were published, the material was old history and garnered little interest.

17 The economist and member of the British delegation, John Maynard Keynes, resigned in protest and wrote his insightful book, *The Economic Consequences of the Peace*.

favorite landscapes, but he wasn't sure what to expect 'of his revered fellow travelers. Were they in a hurry? Would they like to stop for a rest at a scenic spot or have a bite to eat?

"As you wish," Steiner would reply calmly whenever Emil asked. Emil thought this meant he should bring them to Dornach as quickly as possible, and he drove nonstop to the border, where they were obliged to wait for hours. They arrived at their destination exhausted and hungry, and 13-year-old Walter got sick with a fever. Later, Emil realized that Marie Steiner loved sightseeing, and he scolded himself for having been such a simpleton. He also discovered that liberal cigarette offerings opened most border gates quickly and prevented the long wait they'd been forced to endure.

On August 10th, during that same trip, Emil met Steiner and the members of the Swiss Goetheanum Trust, leaving Walter and Felix in the care of the landlady. Steiner showed them the new Goetheanum building—the small cupola was almost finished and the large cupola only needed its supports removed. The expenditures to date totaled one million Swiss francs, with at least another 450,000–500,000SFr estimated for completion. Those figures didn't even begin to include the expenses for special materials such as the roofing tiles from Norway and the fine wood. In contrast was the incredibly modest labor fee of 35,000SFr over the course of six months—a number that showed just how much volunteer work was rendered.

In Emil's eyes, these were huge sums, and the sudden outlays both in Germany and Switzerland worried him greatly. He did not doubt, however, that the movement's potential justified the elegant building, which he hoped would pay for itself over time through public events. He spent the next ten days looking for additional responsible people for the Goetheanum Board. He had the balance sheet audited and organized a regular newsletter and donation appeal for members and friends of anthroposophy. Walter recovered from his fever, and Emil put him and Felix to work helping the builders, but left them enough free time to explore the hills and the nearby limestone caves.

The following week Emil took the boys and the Steiners back to Stuttgart, this time driving the scenic route with rest stops along the way. Later, he often had the good fortune to take this route with Steiner, but he never again experienced him as happy and light-hearted as on this trip—his joy at the impending school inauguration was palpable. That evening, Steiner welcomed the participants of the pedagogical training course.

On Thursday, August 21st, 1919, teachers and guests gathered in the morning for Steiner's opening address, in which he called the creation of the school "a festive act of the world order." It was an auspicious moment that took place in the grace period before the dire consequences of the peace treaty became truly felt in Germany. The course was three weeks long, and both Molts attended from beginning to end, marveling at Steiner's universal knowledge of philology, natural science, mathematics and history.

On September 9th, the last day of the course, everyone noticed two of the teachers, Paul Baumann and Elisabeth Dollfuss, looking expectant. Around 11am, they disappeared only to reappear again an hour later as a married couple. Everyone was delighted, and lunch turned into a celebratory wedding reception. That afternoon Steiner chose the teachers of special subjects and appointed class teachers.

Considering how quickly the 100,000 Marks Emil had put aside had been spent, he worried about the number of teachers Steiner planned to hire, for he was responsible for the teachers' contracts and salaries, as they were all employees of the Waldorf Astoria Company. He tried to avoid set salaries, instead paying each according to their need, a practice which later could not be sustained. Eventually, he managed to cover the costs and salaries for the school, which proved to him the importance of proceeding one step at a time when starting a grand initiative, so as not to become frightened or overwhelmed by his own daring.

Emil's business partners in Hamburg did not even know about the school until they were invited to the opening—a fact that illustrates Emil's freedom in the administration of the business.

"At the Ringing of the Bells," the Waldorf School morning verse:

To wonder at beauty
Stand guard over truth
Look up to the noble
Decide for the good,
This leads us truly
To purpose in living,
To right in our doing,
To peace in our feeling,
To light in our thinking
And teaches us trust
In the working of God
In all that there is
In the widths of the world,
In the depths of the soul.

— Rudolf Steiner

The festive inauguration day

On Sunday, September 7th, 1919, a beautiful sunlit day, the festive inauguration of the Waldorf School took place in the large auditorium of the municipal park. Steiner would have liked to draw attention to the importance of the event by having teachers, parents, and children walk through the city in a long procession. Although that was not possible, the event itself caused enough stir with over 1000 people packing the hall. Emil greeted them. He mentioned the spirit imbuing the school, the responsibility toward it, and the joys awaiting the children. "We ourselves were not able to enjoy this education and we thank our destiny that we can make it available for others today," he said. Steiner gave the keynote address: "[I]sn't the service of education a consecration in the highest sense, helping develop the divine-spiritual that lives in every child?" Stockmeyer spoke on behalf of the teachers, and Mr. Saria, a workers' council member, spoke for the Waldorf Astoria factory. The children, including Walter Molt, gave a little eurythmy performance. Walter did his part very solemnly while the other young performers

180

Emil and Berta and the teachers

held in their laughter. They were all dressed in loose-fitting white shifts, but Walter's had an extra pocket, sewn on by him. An attentive observer might have noticed the pocket moving because Walter had brought along his pet mouse.

After the ceremony, Berta and Emil invited the Steiners and the teachers to their house for a gala lunch. Concerned that he might be obliged to make a speech, Emil consulted his friend, the physician Dr. Noll, who said no, he would not have to make a speech—their circle was not so bourgeois. Yet, right after the soup, Steiner became thoughtful, tapped his glass, and gave a wonderful speech.

"That here warmth is added to light," he said of Emil and Berta, and raised his glass to their good health. That meant that Emil, unprepared as he was, had to reciprocate and express his gratitude with a few impromptu words. Walter, Felix, Lisa and Dora, with the dog Carex at their side, watched the proceedings from their table in the side room and were delighted when Steiner, in exceedingly good humor, brought over two apples. They looked whole, but he had cleverly cut them into a puzzle form. With a flourish and a small twist, he opened them into four perfect halves, presenting each youngster with one. Emil, looking over from the main table, smiled, thinking back to his own childhood and how incredibly fortunate these children were.

In the afternoon, the Molts hosted the families in the school garden where there was much lively activity. Each teacher gathered his or her new class and played games with them. Every child received a box of chocolates with the words "Welcome to the Waldorf School" printed on the lid. A new spirit of trust and love had entered the Uhlandshöhe, and the parents and children were given a taste of it on that first afternoon. To end this most festive of days, the Molts invited the Steiners and the teachers to a performance of Mozart's *Magic Flute* in the Stuttgart opera house.

Eight days later, classes began for 256 children in eight grades with twelve teachers[18] and from then on the otherwise peaceful Uhlandshöhe became populated with flocks of lively children.

News of the school spread quickly among educators and parents involved with anthroposophy, who wanted their children to have the benefit of such a school. Soon schools opened in Berlin, Hamburg, Hannover, Kassel, Breslau, Dresden, and further afield in Basel, Zürich, The Hague, London, Oslo and New York. The French Ministry for Culture sent students to Waldorf schools at state expense, and courses for parents and educators became popular. Emil and Berta saw the significance of the school as a transformative cultural element and imagined it spreading across the world.

Berta discovered her vocation as a handwork teacher, using her needlework and felting skills. She worked with Helene Rommel, sister

---

18 The teachers and staff on opening day were: Rudolf Steiner, director; Marie Steiner, director of eurythmy; Berta and Emil Molt, school founders. In the Collegium: Elisabeth Baumann (eurythmy), Paul Baumann (music and gymnastics), Johannes Geyer (class teacher), Herbert Hahn (German, history, French, and religion), Caroline von Heydebrand (5th grade and foreign language), Hertha Koegel (4th grade), Hannah Lang (3rd grade), Leonie von Mirbach (1st grade), Friedrich Oehlschlegel (6th grade), Walter Johannes Stein (administration, literature, and history), E.A. Karl Stockmeyer (7th and 8th grade) and Rudolf Treichler (7th and 8th grade). During the first year the following teachers joined: Elisabeth von Grunelius (kindergarten), Eugen Kolisko (school doctor, English, Naturkunde), Berta Molt (handwork and bookbinding), Edith Röhrle (eurythmy), Helene Rommel (handwork), Karl Schubert (Förderklasse) and Nora Stein (eurythmy).

An early class with teachers Bettina Mellinger, Helene Rommel, Elisabeth Baumann and Nora Stein

of the notorious "Desert Fox," Field Marshall Erwin Rommel, and with Olga Leinhas, the wife of Emil's comptroller.

Both Molts continued to attend the faculty meetings whenever Steiner was in town. They felt privileged, like students in a very unusual university. Steiner was at his best during these sessions—relaxed and entertaining. He seemed to know all the children in the school, describing their individual needs with uncanny precision. Emil loved to accompany him on his classroom visits.

"Do you love your teachers?" Steiner always asked.

"Yeeeeessss," the students would shout in unison, a sound that always thrilled Emil.

Once only a reversal to old habits took place. At a Waldorf Astoria assembly Emil addressed the workers: "My dear Waldorf people, I promised you too much when I said there would be no corporal punishment in the Waldorf School. Blows have been administered"—(shouts of "hear, hear" and "let 'em have it")—"and here is what happened: A group of boys insisted on playing catch right under the teachers' meeting room windows. One of the teachers came out and asked them to stop but they ignored him. He asked them again, then finally grabbed the nearest boy, put him over his knee and spanked him. When he set him back on his feet, rather ungently, he saw that it was… Walter Molt!" A thousand voices roared—it was a regular orchestra of laughter—and Emil laughed as well!

At this point, one could conclude that Emil's star had guided him unerringly to fulfillment of his destiny. But this stage in his life marked the beginning of a search for his true self. In the years to come, trial and sorrow would reform his life, and he would be subjected to the whims of others while trying to hold fast to his own ideals.

Conversation with Dr. Noll

Emil's friend, Ludwig Noll, was a physician and longtime follower of Steiner's. His strength was inventing remedies prepared for his patients. Noll stayed with the Molts for three months during the preparation for the school and the teachers' course, and he was present at the festive school opening. At the end of September 1919, Emil and Noll went to Dornach for a Michaelmas conference together, and during their journey they talked about the Threefold movement.

"We can't let it die," said Emil. "It should be possible to spread these ideas internationally. I could imagine people in America and England finding them of interest since both countries are more advanced in modern ideas than we are." Noll agreed.

"Roman Boos wants to launch a newspaper in Zürich called *The Social Future*," he said. "It could be translated into English."

"That is a fine idea," said Emil. "But we don't even have the funds to finish the Goetheanum." Despite voicing his doubts, Emil was already visualizing the newspaper on every English-speaking newsstand.

"One thing is a real pity," said Noll at an inn in the Black Forest where they stopped for lunch. "We only write and talk about Threefold but haven't applied it anywhere ourselves. The English and the Americans need practical examples."

"We do have one example where the Threefold Social Order is working," replied Emil. "It is well-developed within the Waldorf Astoria factory. Our rights sphere is represented by the workers' council, our cultural sphere by the educational initiatives, and we are, after all, as a business, in the economic sphere. We work in association with other firms obtaining the raw materials and sending out the finished product."

"Everything we create," Noll remarked, "should be arranged like that. I have been asked to direct a clinic and research center, and I can imagine it being threefolded. My remedies would be the economic branch, with the proceeds supporting the clinic and perhaps the Goetheanum. The way the clinic is set up would be within the rights branch, and our research would fall within the cultural branch." Emil agreed.

"Still," he said, looking out of the restaurant window at the autumn woods, "the question remains, where will the money come from for everything we envision? We need as much as there are leaves on those trees."

When the two friends arrived in Dornach, they climbed the hill to the Goetheanum with other conference-goers and found the unfinished building shimmering in the late afternoon sun. Steiner's lecture was held in the wood workshop behind the Goetheanum, and, as always, Emil felt Steiner's discussions had a direct relevance to his preoccupations. Steiner seemed to be describing the very topic Noll and Emil had just discussed.

The need for funds

After the lecture, Emil stepped before the audience and pointed out the necessity of completing the Goetheanum and the serious lack of funds. "Individual donations are not enough," he said, "and there is no help from the State. Perhaps proceeds from various enterprises could cover the shortfall." He mentioned the medical work and the publishing company as examples. Leinhas, Unger, and an engineer from Stockholm named Ruths found this idea interesting, and decided to pursue it further. They invited Emil and Noll to join them.

On October 3rd, the discussion continued with Steiner. The idea was expanded to include lectures and books to spread the idea of three-folding to an international audience. Emil was keen to continue with

185

this endeavor, but his own question—how to threefold the existing enterprises and institutions—was never addressed again. This is an important point because when Steiner was asked later about his biggest contribution to society, he said without hesitation: the Threefold Social Order.

Envisioning a bank-like institution

Emil returned to Stuttgart, but Leinhas, Unger, Noll and Ruths remained in Dornach and continued their discussion. They wanted:
~ completion of the Goetheanum by the end of December
~ an international publishing house
~ a scientific research institute
~ widespread advertisements for Threefold on an international basis
~ acquisition of existing businesses able to support Threefold enterprises out of their surplus.

How were they going to do all this? By creating a community bank, they thought, and harnessing businesses which would allow them to raise at least two to three million Swiss francs. Perhaps the group was carried away by a remark Steiner had made to the effect that wealth should be put to use immediately because of the devaluation he foresaw.

"One would need to do something real with the available capital," he had said. They asked Steiner to write a flyer describing the vision of a banking institution fed by businesses that would offer investment opportunities.

"Where will you find the capable people to run this?" Steiner asked. But never one to block the initiatives of others, he obliged the group with the following memorandum:

On founding a bank-like institution (abbreviated):

A bank-like institution is necessary to serve economic and cultural enterprises. It will be oriented, in its goals and way of working, to promoting anthroposophical ideas. It will be different from usual banking institutions in that it will serve not just financial needs but advise the initiatives it supports. Thus the banker is less an outside lender and more a businessman fully versed in the conditions and needs of the enterprise to be financed. Preferred businesses are those able to work associatively, allowing people with legitimate talents to find their optimum positions. It will be essential to sign successful businesses that are able to help fledgling initiatives whose efforts are to bear fruit at a later date. The bank personnel must be able to insure that the anthroposophical view of life can translate into healthy productivity.

In our case, anthroposophical initiatives are to be supported, such as the Goetheanum building which cannot yet support itself but will produce a good income stream in times to come. Initiatives endowed with healthy thinking and social sensitivity, able to cooperate in a really fruitful way within their community, are those our bank will support…

Looking after one's money today means supporting enterprises oriented to the future, since these alone can withstand the devastating forces of our times…the future depends on a new spirit carrying a variety of ventures.

Grand ideas and Futurum

By October 15th, Leinhas, Boos and Noll, with a few others (but without Emil) had completed a business plan describing a banking trust that would buy up established enterprises, compensating their owners with shares and paying them salaries as managers of their former businesses. Additional income would be obtained by issuing bank shares to individuals and by bringing the fundraising Goetheanum Trust back to Dornach from Stuttgart. The group hoped to co-opt a Bern banker named Hirter. Steiner suggested a name for the enterprise: *Futurum*.

In his memorandum Steiner didn't exactly say that the bank should acquire existing businesses. He merely talked about association. The planning group, however, made two wrong assumptions: 1. that private ownership must be eliminated to "neutralize capital," and 2. that businesses should exist, not primarily to provide goods or services but rather to provide funds for cultural endeavors.

The group began by going abroad to win support and shares for their new project. They co-opted a willing Emil to help raise money. He did not question them, assuming Steiner had sanctioned the idea. He traveled extensively in the last months of 1919 to promote the project.

Emil berates himself for "blind spots"

"Why was I so carried away?" Emil asked himself bitterly later on. "Why didn't I advise Steiner better, given the circumstances and the people involved? I read his memorandum on founding a bank-like institution and it made perfect sense, but I didn't stop to examine the group's interpretation of it, simply assuming his approval."

"You were under pressure to find money and you weren't present at the planning," Berta said in an effort to comfort him.

When Steiner was asked later why he did not veto the undertaking at the outset, he said one might then have accused him of suppressing a good idea that could have worked out under better circumstances. He held Emil responsible, though, perhaps because the others were not as suited to developing such undertakings: Unger had distanced himself from his business to teach, Leinhas disliked business, Ruths was an engineer, and Noll was a physician. Emil later recalled Steiner telling him about blind spots in consciousness, and he felt he had succumbed to one of those.

For the moment, though, Emil was riding high on the success of the school and eager to take on a new project for Steiner and the Goetheanum.

On December 14th Steiner gave a prophetic talk in which he stated,

If people continue thinking in the same way…if they cannot become aware of the relationship between this world and the spiritual world, we will, within thirty years, have a devastated Europe. If people can't relearn and rethink, a moral Noah's Flood will come over Europe…

The New Year's Eve decision

On New Year's Eve, 1919, at a late night meeting, Emil and others met with Steiner in Stuttgart to discuss the formation of a German banking trust, similar to the one planned in Dornach. Steiner seemed to be in favor of the idea and even suggested it be called "The Coming Day Shareholding Company for the Promotion of Economic and Spiritual Values" [*Kommende Tag Aktiengesellschaft zur Förderung Wirtschaftlicher und Geistiger Werte*]. It was to be a beacon for the future, and Emil asked Steiner whether he would consider heading this venture as Chairman of the Board. The story goes that, as midnight struck, the New Year's church bells began to ring and Steiner gave his assent. Emil was emotional and the group was in a celebratory mood.

1920: The pivotal challenge year

In 1920 new teachers joined the school. Three of the most gifted came from Vienna. Dr. Eugen Kolisko was a young medical doctor with a flair for art and science. Dr. Karl Schubert had studied literature, philosophy and languages at the Sorbonne in Paris; he came to Stuttgart as a language teacher, but Steiner soon asked him to take on the extra lesson work for slow learners. Alexander Strakosch, a philosophy and

Waldorf teachers, including Strakosch, Wilke, Kolisko, Stein and Bindel

Young Waldorf teachers, including Hermann von Baravalle

Classic Greek scholar, was a railway engineer. He became friends with the artist, Kandinsky, and then discovered anthroposophy. Strakosch and his wife moved to Stuttgart and he became a class teacher.

Verbal and written attacks

The Threefold Association continued its weekly newspaper, the *Threefold Commonwealth,* and continued giving public anthroposophic lectures. The lecturers shifted focus to scientific and philosophical themes rather than political and economic issues in the hopes of avoiding the verbal and written abuses of 1919. But the strategy didn't work—once unleashed, public criticism continued. German politicians felt that Steiner's ideas threatened their power and their standing in the next election, and the churches, both Protestant and Catholic, condemned any talk of a spiritual world that didn't come from them. The corporations, for their part, opposed ideas that might give more rights to workers and limit stockholder authority. They hated Steiner's statements that a person who works solely for money is treated like a commodity to be bought and sold, and that everyone should have the right to advance in a company.

*This person [Steiner] is still considered the great man in
Württemberg where his friend Hyman [Heymann who facilitated
the school] is Minister of the Interior, and his blood relation, Hieber,
is Minister of Culture. His associates Unger and Arenson are
preparing the great Hosanna in Stuttgart with which they want to
greet this Jewish neo-Cagliostro. Supported by Jewish professors,
he portrays himself as Germany's savior…millions of Marks have
already flowed into his bottomless pockets…*

– Excerpt from the *Münchener Beobachter* newspaper in Munich

Steiner did not fight back against this kind of invective, but his friends
did. One young man, Sigismund von Gleich, even felt compelled to
issue a pamphlet called *Truth against Untruth* in which he refuted his
own father's attacks on Steiner.

On January 31st, Emil lectured in Stuttgart's state museum,
countering slander point for point even while being heckled by a female
politician who was a member of the Württemberg Assembly.

Many trips to Dornach

By his own count, Emil spent 115 days in Dornach during the year
1920. The Waldorf limousine, driven by the chauffeur, Herr Stahl,
provided transportation for the Steiners and many others back and forth
between Stuttgart and Dornach. Occasionally, the overused car broke
down. One of the more memorable car trouble days began when Emil
learned that his car needed repairs, but that del Monte's car, parked in
Zürich, was available. Emil sent Herr Stahl to take del Monte's car to
Dornach to pick up Steiner and his wife. Stahl returned to Dornach with
the car late in the afternoon and was rather put out when he learned he
had to drive Emil and the Steiners straight on to Stuttgart. Shortly after
leaving Switzerland, in the middle of nowhere in the gathering dusk,
this car broke down too. Emil, worried about delaying the Steiners,
looked in vain for the problem by the light of a dim streetlight.

After two hours, he found a mechanic who was able to get the
car running again, and they drove on. Then, on a country road near

Freiburg, they found themselves in the middle of a wild snowstorm, with Stahl dodging broken telephone poles and wires draped over the dark road. It was midnight by the time they finally reached their hotel in Freiburg. The next day, the car broke down again—this time it had run out of gasoline. Emil trudged through the snow in his new shoes to the nearest village and returned with a gas can and a runny nose. The group eventually arrived in Stuttgart, just in time for Steiner's evening lecture, the first of a two-week series.

Expending much energy

Whenever he arrived in Stuttgart, Steiner would have a quick cup of coffee, then deliver the first lecture of a lecture cycle. After it he answered questions and met with students. On each of the following days, he gave lectures, met with initiative groups, visited classrooms, advised teachers, and received individuals who wanted to see him about their personal problems. He held appointments with government officials and spoke with notable people from all over Europe. He advised doctors on methods of healing, showed children tricks, and told jokes at lunch—because, as he said, food is easier digested with humor. After supper every night, he met with the core anthroposophical group—Emil, Unger, Arenson, del Monte and Leinhas—and then wrote deep into the night, emerging looking refreshed and prepared every morning. He never seemed to need more than three or four hours of sleep.

These lectures and meetings sometimes saw Emil and friends working from six in the morning until three the next morning, often at Emil's house. Under these circumstances, tempers frayed and emotional reactions to small issues (which, at a more leisurely pace, could have been dealt with easily) were inflated.

"The Coming Day" is registered and enterprises gathered

On February 13th, 1920, Emil and Steiner registered the name "The Coming Day Trust" [*Der Kommender Tag*] in Stuttgart. The Board of Directors consisted of Steiner as chairman and Emil as vice chairman, with Leinhas serving as Secretary. José del Monte and Carl Unger completed the Board. A few weeks later, The Coming Day Trust obtained legal status.

This organization was to be a beacon for social initiatives, but getting it off the ground proved extremely difficult. Preliminary work included interviewing staff and planning projects, of which there was no shortage. Steiner wanted a clinic where doctors and therapists could treat patients according to anthroposophical medical insights. Emil, Steiner, and some of the physicians looked at potential venues for this clinic in outlying areas—a sanatorium, several resorts, and even a castle near Ludwigsburg. They finally settled on a building complex in a scenic location in Stuttgart named "Wildermuth," which had enough space for a clinic and a laboratory.

Shortly after that, on a field trip to his birth town, Schwäbisch Gmünd, Emil and his group found a former mill next to a stream. The property was suitable for producing larger quantities of Dr. Noll's medicines and personal care products and included plenty of land for growing medicinal plants. The group bought this site at the favorable price of 43,000 Marks; this complex on the Möhlerstrasse later became the Weleda company.

Steiner also suggested a scientific research laboratory and a publishing house (he kept talking about needing a newspaper or some other "organ of communication"). Wolfgang Wachsmuth undertook to set up this initiative, while Lily Kolisko, whose husband taught at the Waldorf School, agreed to run the laboratory. One of her ideas was to develop radiation-resistant cloth by weaving peat moss fibers into cotton or wool thread. Another was a veterinary preparation made from a coffee extract for treating bovine hoof and mouth disease. On the financial side of things, a Darmstadt bank manager (a dedicated "threefolder") offered to manage the fledgling bank. All these ventures required massive capital and organization.

The commercial judge

Compared with the intensity of this constantly charged atmosphere, Emil's duties as commercial judge for Stuttgart were refreshingly simple. His appointment to this post came as a result of the time spent in the Department of Enterprise, where he was known for his integrity. The court sessions were infrequent, but each one required at least a day of preparation and one for the hearings. He enjoyed the job, getting satisfaction out of finding solutions to tangled personal and business situations.

Fortunately the Waldorf factory continued to function efficiently while Emil's attention was on The Coming Day. The employees were engaged in their work and the various sections interacted well with each other. Salary questions were resolved without the need for a union, and on their own initiative employees called themselves "work providers" [*Arbeitsleister*] and "work managers" [*Arbeitsleiter*]. Emil invited students and professors from the University in Tübingen and elsewhere to seminars at Waldorf Astoria, and he lectured in his warm and lively manner about the working methods at the factory and its connection to the school.

Three helpers lost

During 1920 Emil lost three of his staunchest supporters under tragic circumstances—all three while he was away from Stuttgart. These three represented the threefold pillars of his business—production, administration and rights.

On July 21st, Emil's foreman, Hermann Schoeller, who had once accompanied Emil to Switzerland with a suitcase containing one million Marks, was fatally struck by a train while crossing the tracks on his motorcycle. An hour before his death, Emil had passed him on the road. He had wanted to stop and greet him, but only waved because his chauffeur was in a hurry. Later, he grieved at the thought that, had he stopped to chat with Schoeller, he might have prevented his death.

Later that summer, Emil's personal secretary, Maria Kraus, died of complications following a ruptured appendix. August Rentschler rushed her to hospital during a general strike—there was no electricity and the doctors had to operate by candlelight. She would have needed ice packs, but none were available.

"If Herr Molt were here, he could get some," she said in the hospital. Later, her mother mentioned how conscious Maria was at the moment of death. She recounted that Maria had spoken with awe of the great experience awaiting her. Emil was devastated, having been stuck in Switzerland because of another strike.

In October, the Waldorf's attorney, Dr. Hugo Elsas, suffered a fatal stroke after chairing a meeting of the Goethe Association. Emil and Marx were in Freiburg at the time on their way back to Stuttgart. Both men were close friends of Elsas, who had served the company as shareholder and member of the Board since its founding. Elsas had been a skilled negotiator and a shrewd problem solver, who knew the Waldorf's legal requirements inside and out.

Sales threats

While the working atmosphere at Waldorf Astoria was healthy, cigarette sales were down. Supplies were becoming harder to get. Imports and exports were threatened by the beginnings of inflation. Germany's reduced size after forfeiture of significant industries and territories to the Allies—combined with ruptured international relations— exacerbated these issues. Emil made several trips to Holland, hoping to open branches of the company there, but he found there was too much postwar antipathy toward Germany. He and Marx also traveled to Copenhagen to gauge opportunities, as Waldorf cigarettes had been popular in Denmark before the war. But the prospects in Copenhagen were too uncertain and the costs too high to pursue business there.

A scam in Holland

On his last trip to Holland, Emil found an agent willing to distribute Waldorf cigarettes that were made in neutral Switzerland, and for a while this agent's sales seemed to be going well. Then Emil noticed the man was paying Swiss invoices with increasingly devalued German currency. Emil immediately traveled to Holland, where he discovered his agent conducting a thriving black market business, smuggling cigarettes back into Germany at cut-rate prices through a border house with the front door in Holland and a back door in Germany. This meant, of course, that Waldorf cigarettes were competing with themselves. Emil put a stop to this scam, but in so doing had to sell off the large stock at a reduced price.

Although success was difficult to find during these business trips out of the country, Emil did use his time abroad to make friends with leading industrialists and other individuals interested in anthroposophy and the threefold idea. He formed ties with the fuel works in Delft, the Verkade biscuit factory, Hengel's cotton mill in Utrecht, De Mouchy, the machine factory Storck, and the Twende industrial center. The Haarlem printing press Ensched excited Emil more than all the rest—this old publishing house had a wonderful collection of first editions, where Emil indulged his passion for acquiring rare books.

Walter suffers from his parents' pace

Walter suffered during his father's long absences from home. At 14, he was a slender, gangling youth, and as the owner's boy, he found life in the new school difficult. Listening to ongoing anthroposophical talk over dinner was tedious for him, and although he was obedient by nature, he vacillated between withdrawing and getting into scrapes. Berta, always lenient, insisted Emil take his son hiking or to the new roller skating rink whenever possible, and when Walter pleaded with his father to be allowed driving lessons, she supported that as well.

The teachers' decision

One day in May 1920, Herr Stockmeyer delivered a memorandum from the school collegium to Steiner in Dornach. In it were recommended changes to the school's organization and Emil's position. The teachers, as bearers of the free spiritual life, no longer wished to be regarded as employees of a cigarette factory, and they did not think that Emil, as a non-teacher, should be in their collegium. Emil, unaware of this memorandum, was also in Dornach at the time and happened to run into Stockmeyer. The men greeted each other, but Stockmeyer didn't tell Emil of the school collegium's proposal.

Just before Emil left to return to Stuttgart, Steiner handed him the memorandum. Emil was indignant and hurt by what he read, but erred in not stopping to talk it over with Steiner. Instead, he traveled back to Stuttgart.

Why did I not know about this? he asked himself in the car. *Does Berta know? Why did they do this behind my back?* Over the next few hours, he struggled to contain his emotions. *Take hold, practice equanimity*, he told himself, but the more he tried, the less he was able to do this. His chauffeur Stahl knew something was amiss, but couldn't engage Emil in conversation. By the time they reached Stuttgart, Emil was fuming. He asked Stahl to drive him straight to the school, and when he arrived, he walked in to the teachers' meeting, put the memo on the table, and demanded answers. The teachers looked flustered and embarrassed. Hahn, Emil's former Waldorf Astoria educational coordinator, remained silent. Stockmeyer got up and escorted Emil out.

"Could you not have included me in this?" asked Emil, angrily. "I thought we were colleagues. I have a good mind to fire the lot of you, and I certainly won't attend your collegiate meetings any more." With that he stormed away home, leaving the teachers in a state of panic.

"Did you know about this?" Emil asked Berta.

"I found out yesterday through Olga Leinhas," she answered. "The collegium called in her husband for a financial meeting, and the discussion turned to the appropriateness of a school dependent on a cigarette factory. I thought you'd come home first so we could talk it over."

"Why didn't they have the common decency to discuss this directly with me?" he asked.

"They didn't know how to talk to you," she said. "They really like and admire you, but perhaps they feel your problem-solving style is too businesslike. After all, they are members of the cultural sphere, which, as Steiner says, needs autonomy without interference from the political or economic domains." By now Emil was crushed. He had enjoyed being with the teachers, and by acting irrationally he had jeopardized that relationship. Berta tried to ease his distress.

"You don't really want to be seen as their boss," she said.

"I will talk it over with Leinhas," said Emil, still feeling ashamed. "But I wish he had warned me. And I will ask Steiner for help. He is, after all, the director of the school."

Ideally, in this situation, the Threefold Association would have served as the entity through which the teachers, who represented the cultural life, could meet Emil, who represented the economic domain, to resolve the issue. But a mediating body would have been necessary, and in The Coming Day organization, the political/rights domain had never been developed. It therefore could not serve as mediator to that little community and Emil had to work things out for himself.

A new constitution

Berta helped him understand that what the school was asking for was a new constitution. He knew his company would not be able to carry the robustly expanding school's financial burden much longer, especially since children from outside already far outnumbered the "Waldorf" children. Eventually Emil relented and apologized to the teachers for his behavior. He urged the creation of a Waldorf School Association, composed of parents, teachers and friends, to oversee and protect the school, care for its finances, and help spread its educational ideas. He said he would miss the collegium meetings, but would stop attending.

The teachers, in turn, assured him that both he and Berta were the true patrons of the school and that he should continue accompanying Steiner on his rounds through the classrooms. Steiner further helped heal the wound by his continuous warm recognition of Emil's founding impulse. After that, and until the end of his life, Emil and the teachers shared a relationship of friendship and trust.

The first Waldorf School Association meeting took place on May 19th, 1920, marking a new relationship between the Waldorf factory and the school. In a five-year contract, the factory committed to paying full tuition for all factory workers' children and children of the workers' relatives.

Another difficult situation

Although Emil had resolved his struggle with the teachers, his self-confidence suffered, and he soon found himself in another difficult situation. Steiner had become concerned that, with all the energy in Stuttgart going into new ventures, the central spiritual-philosophical focus of the anthroposophical movement might get lost. He suggested creating a circle of representatives from these new ventures to nurture commonality through anthroposophical ideas. The aim was to prevent initiative groups from becoming estranged from one another. However, trouble arose when the younger anthroposophists, including some doctors, wished to change from the old way of studying, wanting more dynamic and experiential gatherings. They considered the older approach, such as the Unger-Arenson group, too intellectual and theoretical.

Leinhas put himself in the middle, trying to be a mediator. One day he brought Ernst Uehli, the Swiss editor of the Stuttgart newsletter *Threefold Social Order,* to Emil. Uehli was a year older than Emil but he supported the younger crowd's desire for a livelier

Ernst Uehli

199

format. Emil's affinity for members of the younger set was growing, but he told Uehli that he and Berta derived benefit from the Arenson-Unger group and would never want to cross them. Knowing Emil was about to drive to Dornach, Uehli then asked whether Emil might take a letter from the young group to Steiner. Emil reluctantly agreed to serve as mailman but said he would not take sides. Coincidentally, both Unger and the rather hot-headed young Dr. Otto Palmer asked Emil for a lift to Dornach. Emil sat in the car, the letter burning a hole in his pocket, and didn't know what to say. He had become cautious in the aftermath of his encounter with the teachers. The three men arrived in Dornach and dropped Unger off at his lodgings. Emil introduced Dr. Palmer to Steiner and handed over the letter. The next day, Steiner called Emil in to a meeting with a very upset Unger, who felt betrayed by Emil, thinking him one of the party opposed to his methods. Emil tried to explain himself but could not undo the clumsy situation.

When Steiner finally met with the new circle of representatives, Emil went gladly, believing everyone would meet on an elevated plane, resolving issues and seeing each other's good intentions. He was dreadfully taken aback when Arenson, Benkendoerfer and Unger collectively accused him of having incited the teachers and the younger group—particularly Dr. Palmer—against them. Uehli and Leinhas, who were in attendance and could have defended Emil by explaining what had happened, remained silent. Emil was shocked and upset, and left the meeting early.

A significant meeting

When Emil saw Steiner again in Dornach, Steiner rebuked him for his emotional reaction at the meeting. He said Emil should become more sensitive to other people's feelings and that, in the case of Unger and Arenson, antagonisms remained from a previous lifetime. Since they were on the topic, Emil asked Steiner about Leinhas. Between Leinhas and Emil, said Steiner, there was no past karma.

"Well, there is now," remarked Emil. "It's hard working with him, although the finances have never been in better shape."

"Trust, trust, trust," said Steiner.

"More warmth, more temperament, more humor," sighed Emil wistfully. Then Steiner began to talk to Emil in a very intimate fashion, sketching out Emil's past lives and the achievements, trials and debts that had carried over into this incarnation.[19] During this intimate interview with Steiner, which took place over two beautiful June days in Dornach, Emil realized how much he still had to learn. Steiner gave him a meditation to help him overcome his feelings of constraint and gave him a task which he hoped would help the struggling Threefold idea so dear to Emil's heart. He appointed him "Curator" of the Threefold Association, telling Emil how, once, years before, he'd given Marie Steiner the same designation, hoping she and a few others in his esoteric class would become custodians for new art forms. It was a designation more suited for a person caring for an art exhibit, and Emil understood that he was meant to open as many hearts as possible for the Threefold Social Order in the world. This meeting was a great comfort to Emil, who felt highly honored by it.

The Curator

On returning to Stuttgart, Emil described his interview with Steiner to Berta. She understood the responsibilities of his new position as Curator, but he was unable to explain it to anyone else. In fact, it provoked feelings of jealousy in others. Walter Kuehne, the new director of the Threefold Association, later wrote in his memoirs that he went to Leinhas asking him to explain Emil's elevation in station. Leinhas, instead of supporting Emil, said, "I suppose it means that there is now a Curator and we are two sub-curators standing half a step below him."

---

19 See Frans Lutters, *An Exploration into the Destiny of the Waldorf School Movement*, Ghent, NY: AWSNA Publications, 2011.

Making connections

Emil didn't campaign anymore. Rather he turned his attention to leading personalities, business people and politicians, explaining the nuances and attributes of the Threefold Social Order. He had tea with Baron Neurath, who had facilitated Emil's title to "Councilor of Commerce," and Neurath became an interested supporter. He also met with the German Foreign Minister, Walther Simons, who was familiar with the Threefold concept. He had heard from a French journalist that there would be order in the world when Rudolf Steiner's Threefold ideas were implemented. A warm friendship developed between these two men.

Not long afterward, and as a result of this first meeting, Dr. Simons gave a great political speech in Stuttgart in which he outlined the moderate suggestions he planned to bring to the coming war reparations negotiation in London. After his speech, he had lunch with the Molts, meeting Steiner at their house and visiting the school. The next day, the local left wing newspaper ran a malicious article about the "opulent meal" that the diplomat enjoyed in the house of the capitalist.

Courage to speak—an unseen help

Emil's trouble with his friends made him extremely nervous, and when he was asked to give a presentation to the anthroposophical circle of responsible people, he was petrified, spending hours preparing. When the day arrived, Berta was sick in bed and could not accompany him, which exacerbated Emil's anxiety and gave him heart palpitations. He lay down in the afternoon, the fear of failure and criticism giving him a cramp in his heart. He remembered the terror of his Confirmation, how at fourteen years old he had forgotten his Bible quote while facing the congregation. He appealed to his higher self and to his angel, and became calmer, but then became despondent again, feeling he'd forgotten everything he'd ever learned.

"Your knowledge is not lost. It's in you," Berta said gently. "Take a walk in the evening air and you'll find it again." He went out along the Kanonenweg, trying to look at himself objectively. He wondered if antipathies were affecting him.

It is not for me I'm doing this. It's for Dr. Steiner, he said to himself. Then he stopped at the parapet across from the school, looking down over the city and willing his fearful heart to be strong. Suddenly, he felt, standing behind or beside him, a spiritual being, instructing him. He became calm, and that evening his presentation went well and the applause was overwhelming. Unger told him his speech had been first-rate, and Uehli was exceedingly cordial. Emil went home feeling ecstatic— it had been a magical day, and he wanted to share the end of it with Berta.

"You are my helper and guardian angel," he told her, "with whom I shall be united beyond the grave. Without you, I could not have done this tonight." He promised her everlasting love and gratitude for her support and more time spent together.

The Swiss Futurum…

On May 16th, 1920, a small group launched the Swiss holding company Futurum with a capital of 650,000 Swiss francs. The Board included Dr. Steiner and the Swiss banker, Hirter. It was a troubled venture from the start. The first hurdle was finding a general manager, as no one was prepared to take the job. Finally Steiner's personal assistant, Roman Boos, agreed to take on the position, although he was an attorney by training and had no business experience.

Futurum was based on the abstract notion that businesses bought on the open market could become income sources for the Goetheanum. Among the businesses bought were some with directors suspicious of or opposed to Futurum principles, and others with logistical and management issues. More successfully, Futurum acquired a small cane and pipe factory and a small glue factory run by Dr. Lagoutte, the same factory that had manufactured the paste Steiner used for the Goetheanum's cupola paintings.

One of the ventures needing Futurum's support was Dr. Ita Wegman's clinic and laboratory in Arlesheim, near Dornach. Steiner was very involved with this medical work—he even designed logos and packaging for the products made in the laboratory by the pharmacist, Dr. Oskar Schmiedel.

...and ventures arising in Stuttgart

Meanwhile, in Stuttgart The Coming Day organization developed organically, with businesses and farms run by anthroposophical friends eager to work together. The preparations took longer than expected, and Emil sometimes lost heart seeing people taxed beyond their ability— especially when reality fell short of the ideal. But Steiner pushed them all onward. *He probably is aware of urgencies we know nothing about*, thought Emil, who wrote in his diary:

> *Not just Kuehn and Leinhas, we all are at the end of our strength. We wanted to get up early today but couldn't manage it, while Dr. Steiner was up and doing some of our work as well as his own. What enormous energy he has – it can only come from spiritual sources.*

The official inauguration of The Coming Day took place on September 16th, 1920, with Steiner as chairman of the Board, Emil as vice chairman, and Hans Kuehn as general director. Participating business owners willingly exchanged their private shares for shares in the Trust, receiving a salary instead of dividends. They were trying to avoid conventional capitalistic practices and to create a model for what Steiner described as the future age of brotherhood. It was an untried paradigm, run by a very small group, pushed into being in only 36 months, and during the worst financial upheaval in the history of Germany.

Dr. Rudolf Maier and his brothers joined with their flour mill and lumber company, and Carl Unger brought in his factory of precision instruments. The Maiers wanted to increase the scope of their business, and Unger hoped to free himself from financial concerns in order to devote more time to anthroposophical pursuits. José del Monte joined with his box factory, the young doctors Palmer and Wallach joined, and Ernst Uehli also became involved. Stock in the holding company was issued to members and friends of the Anthroposophical Society. Within an incredibly short time, one million Marks had been raised—people were delighted to invest in such a worthwhile cause.

The Stuttgart Waldorf School outgrew its premises in the first year and Emil managed, through The Coming Day, to buy a large adjacent piece of land. It was an old quarry that had to be filled in. A smaller piece of land on the school's southwest border came up for sale and Emil purchased that with his own money. Later, he gifted it to the school.

Inauguration of the Goetheanum

On September 26th, 1920, the Goetheanum building was opened. Two weeks of celebrations, lectures, presentations and performances by well-known members of the movement were held in the great hall of columns and etched windows. The only thing still missing was the centerpiece—Steiner's unfinished sculpture, *The Representative of Humanity*.

The unfinished sculpture

The Molts attended the opening and were in awe of the atmosphere and the international personalities gathered together for the celebration. Emil was familiar with every detail of the building and marveled at how much had been achieved. Steiner asked him at the last minute whether he wouldn't mind giving three lectures, as one of the scheduled speakers had canceled. Steiner suggested speaking about entrepreneurs in the context of the past, present and future. Emil managed the first two sessions well enough, but at the end of his last presentation, Steiner commented kindly that the subject was a difficult one and he would have needed more time to prepare.

A number of listeners, especially young ones, warmly applauded Emil, but afterward in the canteen his former comptroller, Benkendoerfer, criticized him roundly, and when Emil turned red, loudly called over to him, "Don't be so emotional." That was a trial made even worse when Emil happened to hear that Unger was preparing a world economic congress in Vienna without inviting or consulting him. It was odd that the one who administered the money for the new building was made to feel so small in it.

Emil was relieved to return to Stuttgart with Berta. "Don't be upset," she said. "What do they matter?" "I think they just see me as a crude capitalist," he replied. She told him he was feeling inadequate because he was overstrained. "It will take time," he said. "What we are all doing is so intense that emotions are bound to flare up."

Still, he began to feel vulnerable again, wondering whether he might be viewed as an outsider by his peers unless he gave his company over to The Coming Day Trust. With that in mind he set off to convince his business partners to join The Coming Day. He started with Marx, who was having a lovely time in the spa town of Baden Baden. Marx, ever the pragmatist, told Emil that the idea was foolish, and that he would not hear of such a thing. In vain Emil regaled Marx with glory tales of the wonderful Coming Day enterprises that were thriving in spite of the worsening economy, but Marx remained adamantly opposed.

Upper Silesia

Once more the Threefold idea was presented to the public: Upper Silesia was a resource-rich area in eastern Germany, populated by a mix of Germans and Poles. After the war, these two ethnic groups were at each other's throats. The Entente debated whether it should remain in Germany or be given to Poland, and decided to settle the ownership by a plebiscite. The likelihood was that, whatever the outcome, the conflict would continue since neither group was willing to be subjugated by the other.

In November 1920, Moritz Bartsch, an anthroposophist from Breslau, asked Steiner whether one could implement a Threefold Commonwealth in the region. It would allow the two groups to coexist independent of ties to either country. With Steiner's consent, a great effort was made to realize this goal. The majority of the population voted in favor of it, but the Entente split the region nonetheless, awarding most of the coal-rich territory to Poland. The animosity between the two ethnic groups continued but, what was worse, now Steiner was branded a traitor by conservative Germans for plotting to make Upper Silesia independent.

The Coming Day ventures

These were the ventures in The Coming Day by the end of 1920, and more were to join the following year:

The Head Office, Champignystrasse 17
The Publishing Division
The Book Sales Mail Order Division
Press and Offset Press
Dr. Unger Machine Factory in Hedelfingen
Slate Manufacturing in Sondelfingen
Del Monte Box Factory, Stuttgart, with branches in Zuffenhausen
    and Weil Im Dorf.
Ruethling Boarding House, Stuttgart
The Coming Day Branch, Hamburg
The Maiers' Grain Mill, Saw Mill and Agricultural Estate in
    Dischingen
Five large agricultural estates in different townships
Clinic Therapeutic Institute
Clinic Therapeutic Institute Production, Schwäbisch Gmünd
Scientific Research Institute, Stuttgart
Scientific Research Institute, Biological Division, Stuttgart

From The Coming Day's prospectus:

…In future…people will have to learn to care for the earth again with intuition based on a love of nature and its vital forces, and not just strive for the highest yield. People today are not aware of the great dangers facing farming. The instinctive ability to care for the life of the land is being lost as the older generation dies out; animals and plants are becoming weaker. Modern methods based on the materialistic model cannot counter this degeneration…

The Coming Day spent its startup money in less than a year, and Emil found it hard to contain its sheer diversity of initiatives. The Waldorf School was expanding fast and needed a building; the Guldesmill had unsold wood; Dr. Husemann had to find doctors and staff for his new clinic; and how would Noll's remedies be sold?

The Threefold Association still drew a surprising number of people to its lectures, but it needed cash infusions as well. The publishing company wanted an offset press and a prospectus, and Marie Steiner needed a lending library for the books from Steiner's old headquarters in Berlin. Furthermore, sales in Carl Unger's machine factory were down due to the recession.

Meanwhile, Dr. Lili Kolisko's foot-and-mouth remedy, tested on infected animals on one particular farm, had restored them all to health. She and her colleagues dreamed of an international academy for experimental scientific work, including sections for chemistry, geology, astronomy, embryology, botany, meteorology and zoology. There was talk of new, light-resistant plant colors and a machine to activate forces similar to magnetism and electricity. Steiner predicted that this, if successful, would surpass Einstein's discoveries, and energy was poured into pursuing these projects.

All this, while wonderful and inspiring, was completely unwieldy and made Emil feel helpless. Steiner himself was critical of what he termed "the Stuttgart System"—the bureaucracy put in place by office staff lacking expertise who were trying to oversee everything and getting bogged down in details. Making things more difficult for Emil, the Administrative Council (Steiner, Leinhas, del Monte and Unger) often appointed him to the unenviable task of chastising or firing people.

Emil worries about financing the endeavors

"How long will it take for these new initiatives to pay for themselves?" Emil worried, thinking back to how long it took to build his own company in the best of times. "A mill, a machine company, and a box company can't finance them all. I feel beaten," he told his wife, "with no peace, no rest, and long work-days."

"I must say," said Berta, "you brought it on yourself. You didn't allow time to recover between the effort of the school founding and the next big venture."

"What could I do?" he asked. "The money question was too urgent."

"You could have let others take it further," she said. "But that would have been against your nature. Let's talk to our friend del Monte. He may help you to see the situation more clearly." Del Monte was glad to oblige, and together he and Emil tallied up the positives of The Coming Day: terrific people such as Dr. Werr, the veterinarian, the Maiers with their grain mill and lumber company—all projects that were expected to yield results over time. On the negative side, financial conditions in the country were deteriorating and moving toward inflation. Neither del Monte nor Emil thought they had the means necessary to carry the projects through, and they decided that adding the Waldorf Astoria company to The Coming Day would solve most of their problems.

Dr. Steiner has a headache

The next time in Dornach, Marie Steiner asked Emil to drive her and a friend to a scenic area of Switzerland for a few days. He booked the Grand Hotel at the wintry Lake of Lucerne for them, from where they made excursions. After a few days Steiner joined them and they drove to Bern to visit the Futurum cane factory in Boeningen. Before returning to

Dornach, Emil had a glimpse of Steiner as a fragile human being when, during a tea break, he caught Steiner whispering to Marie that he had a terrible headache. *How strange*, thought Emil. *No one ever wonders how Steiner is feeling and always assumes him to be well.*

Supporting The Coming Day

Emil worried about the possible destabilization that moving Waldorf Astoria to The Coming Day might cause, but he desperately wanted his business to be truly representative of anthroposophy. Berta encouraged him. She thought it would be a good thing for the firm to be sheltered under The Coming Day leadership and for Emil to move on to new projects such as helping develop Dr. Noll's medicines. She believed this move would allow her husband to breathe again.

At the end of January 1921, Emil traveled to Hamburg to talk with Marx and the Abraham brothers about the transfer. Marx's son, Hans, came to meet him at the train station, looking dapper in tweeds. Hans had wanted to join Waldorf Astoria for a long time, and Emil had promised to find him a position. In an effort to include Hans, Emil told him about the planned merger with The Coming Day and then took him to sit in on the meeting with Marx and the Abrahams. In the meeting, Emil described in detail some of the interesting projects of The Coming Day, explaining that they all had the potential to withstand a fluctuating market. He brought gifts—samples of hair lotion from the laboratory, small knife sharpeners from Unger's factory, and cheese from the farm. His partners listened with interest but said they preferred Waldorf Astoria to stay as it was. "It is doing well," they said, and besides they did not believe in any long-range problem with the economy. Emil argued on, frustrated and wondering how astute business people could have such unreal hopes of peace and prosperity. Then he stopped, deciding to continue another time, and joined the Abrahams for dinner at their villa, helping them celebrate a children's birthday ball.

Threefold "dead and buried"

That same month, Emil met with his friend, Foreign Minister Simons, who wanted to know how The Coming Day project was developing since their last conversation. Simons asked how much Steiner was involved in the project, describing Steiner as a deeply thoughtful and knowledgeable man of high morals and a love for humanity.

"The Threefold social question is dead and buried in Berlin," Simons said. "They only talk about the economy now. In a few days I'm off to London for the final reparation negotiations, but I wonder whether I even belong in those circles anymore." He promised his assistance and took his leave.

Later, Emil came home furious, with a newspaper under his arm. He showed Berta a scathing article by Adolf Hitler regarding Simons and his negotiations in England. In it, Hitler described the Threefold Social Order as a "Jewish method of destroying peoples' normal state of mind" and asked, "What is the driving force behind all this? The Jews, friends of Dr. Rudolf Steiner, who is a friend of the mindless Simons."

Taking a break in Holland

"We need a break," Berta said toward the end of February 1921. "Why don't we join Dr. Steiner on his lecture tour to Holland? You've been instrumental in promoting him to your Netherland friends; you will be a good help."

Emil was glad to get away, and glad to meet his business colleagues in Amsterdam and Utrecht. Berta was in great form, charming everyone, while Steiner lectured in The Hague, in Utrecht, and to students and professors at Delft. They went to Leyden and Rotterdam. Emil intended on returning home, but Steiner and some of his other friends urged the Molts to stay on, and they were glad to do so. Emil promoted the Waldorf School, talking about expansion plans and the need for an international Waldorf School Association independent of state and business control.

A group from The Hague distributed leaflets put out by the Stuttgart Waldorf School Association.[20]

Meanwhile, Berta mentioned Steiner's 60th birthday to a few of the ladies, and together they organized a splendid celebration for him. Steiner reciprocated with an extra lecture in which he described spiritual research as an extension of modern scientific research. He discussed education as a field of research, as art, and as moral force. Then, perhaps because he was among the internationally minded Dutch, he expanded on Emil's theme, dwelling on the necessity of an international school association. He said that true spiritual life needs social forms and can be created only by people interested in community.

"Let us move toward the future," he said, "where freedom in education is striven for; …where the powers of the State are limited to what lies in the scope of each person of voting age; and a future in which economic life is structured according to the principles of association: freedom, equality and brotherhood… The source of misunderstanding is the tacit assumption that the State must be given sole determination in matters pertaining to all three spheres of society…" Much lively discussion followed his talk, both on how to start an international association and how to develop a training for teachers.

Discussing Waldorf Astoria transfer to The Coming Day

Early in March, Marx came to Stuttgart from Hamburg. Steiner was there, and Emil invited them both to lunch with Berta to discuss the possible transfer of Waldorf Astoria shares to The Coming Day Trust. At first, Steiner was rather stiff in the company of this Hamburg business executive, but after an excellent soup made by Berta's cook, he warmed to Marx's good nature. He said it would be fine if Waldorf Astoria were in The Coming Day although he feared the Trust would not be able to hold it for very long. He spoke of the necessity of having one's money in a stable situation independent of market fluctuations and of enterprises

---

20 Within two years The Hague had its own Waldorf school up and running.

working together—and that a group of companies could achieve much more than a single venture. To Emil, this was Georgii's idea of the United Cigarette Works taken to a higher level. Marx looked thoughtful and was not opposed. When they parted, Marx shook Steiner's hand warmly and sent greetings to his wife. However, when Emil went to Hamburg a few weeks later to once again broach the topic of the transfer with Marx and the Abrahams, he achieved nothing except for a pleasant social evening.

Hans Marx

While there, he talked with young Hans Marx about his future position at Waldorf Astoria, and invited him to come back with him to spend the Easter holiday in Stuttgart. Hans was delighted, and they enjoyed a pleasant train ride together.

"When your father and the others decide on the transfer you can join the company," Emil told him. "This weekend I'll take you on a tour of The Coming Day enterprises." Hans was delighted. When they arrived in Stuttgart, they were met by not-quite-fifteen-year-old Walter who, to impress Hans, had driven the family car to the station. "Does your mother know about this?" Emil asked severely. Of course she did not, and Emil almost walked home in protest. Walter cajoled and pleaded, saying his driving instructor was very happy with him and allowed him to take the car all over town. In the end, Emil relented and Walter drove them flawlessly up the winding road to their house, making his father grin in spite of himself.

Easter that year was an extended family affair. Walter and his cousin, Lisa, went to the youth service in the morning. Lisa's mother, Paula, came for lunch. Berta organized an Easter egg hunt in the garden for the neighbor's children, and Lisa, Hans Marx and Walter hid the eggs, with the dog Carex on sentry watch. The next afternoon the family went to a matinee of Wagner's *Parsifal*. Hans did not attend, as he had received a letter from Frankfurt over breakfast that had transformed him entirely (it was obviously from a young lady).

"I won't be able to stay for the tour," he told Emil. "I'm urgently needed in Frankfurt, but I promise to come back soon." Walter teased him mercilessly, but Hans could not be deterred—he thanked everyone and dashed off to catch the next train.

The agreement to merge

A few days later, Emil took Walter with him on a business trip to Dresden and Leipzig, and after their return to Stuttgart, Marx phoned, saying he and the Abrahams had talked things over and were ready to negotiate the transfer of their shares to The Coming Day. Heartened by this development, Emil redoubled his efforts to win financial support for The Coming Day and the school. He went to the annual Frankfurt trade show where he gave a presentation about The Coming Day, showed a short film, and handed out pamphlets. Back in Stuttgart, he took a visiting official from the Ministry of Foreign Affairs around the factory, saying it would soon be part of an exciting new consortium. He met with the Minister for Food about The Coming Day farms and renegotiated loans with the banks. Then he and Berta went back to Holland, where he lectured about The Coming Day to the Industry Club in Amsterdam in the hopes of finding someone willing to make a one-time donation of 500,000 Marks. This time, the Molts spent a few days enjoying museums and a leisurely afternoon on the windy beach at Scheveningen.

Back in Stuttgart, Emil found Leinhas poring over The Coming Day books and sat down with him to help. The two of them worked on the numbers until three in the morning. They were concerned that the contributions from Waldorf Astoria might not be enough to cover the deficits. Compounding Emil's worries, The Coming Day's new general manager, Benkendoerfer, came to him privately asking for help to deal with the complexities of the enterprise. Emil, not one to hold a grudge, arranged a meeting with Unger, del Monte and Leinhas, and the group agreed to support and regularly advise Benkendoerfer in his decision-making. Emil in particular worked at organizing Berkendoerfer's office more efficiently.

On May 18th, 1921, the Executive Council of The Coming Day, Emil, Benkendoerfer and Leinhas, met with Marx, the Abrahams, and their associates, Stern and Asten, to negotiate the transfer of Waldorf Astoria shares into The Coming Day. The bargaining was critical, with both sides giving up several times before they finally came to an agreement. The Waldorf shares were exchanged for The Coming Day shares, with Marx serving as a new member of the Board. Emil was happy that Marx would now be supervising the factory, but disappointed because Leinhas was opposed to taking Marx's son Hans into the company. "I promised him the job, and it was probably thanks to his persuasion that his father decided on the transaction," Emil told Berta. "You're not the decision-maker anymore," she said. "Let his father work it out."

Helping Futurum

With The Coming Day stable for the moment, Emil turned his attention to Switzerland to help facilitate a replacement for the Futurum director and editor, Roman Boos, who was suffering a nervous breakdown due to strain. Emil drove Boos and his wife (the niece of his former Hamburger bosses in Patras) to the Waldorf Astoria spa at Rietenau. They checked the patient in and got him medical care. Emil found replacements for Boos's editing work in two dynamic people— Willy Storrer and Edgar Dürler, both in their mid-twenties. Storrer, a former editor of a Stuttgart daily paper, had a large circle of friends, including the famed Bauhaus artists, Willy Baumeister and Oskar Schlemmer. Edgar Dürler, a young Swiss from St. Gallen, had inherited a textile business and made a success of it. Dürler loved anthroposophy. Like Emil, however, he'd had to overcome doubts before joining the movement.

"I wondered whether I should join the Anthroposophical Society but was plagued by conflicting inner voices. The one said, 'Concentrate on the books about threefolding; then you won't need the Society.' The other voice said, 'To understand social threefolding, you need a comprehensive study of anthroposophy in all its diversity. And look at the amazing people you've already met, even though you are just a beginner.'"

The new editors set up office and living quarters at the Friedwart, a charming chalet in anthroposophical style halfway up the Goetheanum hill, and this location became a social magnet for anthroposophists.[21]

Walter's proposal

In July 1921, during a Sunday walk through the fields east of Stuttgart, Walter told his father that he did not want to continue school. "It's too difficult," Walter said, "and besides you left school at fourteen, and I'm already fifteen."

At first, Emil would not hear of it. "I did not leave school at fourteen. I left Stuttgart at fourteen and went to the Lyceum in Calw, the best schooling I ever had."

His son drove the bargain harder. "It's not that I've given up on school," Walter said. "I am willing to go back, but now I want a break and I'd rather be working with you. You don't have to pay me. But if I do well, perhaps you can buy me a car. Wouldn't it be nice," he added quickly, "if we had our own family car, since yours is mostly gone with Mr. Stahl?"

Oh, the blackguard, thought Emil. *I wonder how often I'd get to see that car!* He told Walter he would think about this during the holidays. That Sunday walk was a rare occasion—for once Emil had no meetings or obligations.

That night, Emil spent a quiet evening with Berta. "I love our busy life and the tasks we are given," he said, thinking about his conversation with Walter. "But sometimes I wish we could run off and sell Dr. Noll's flu medicine in America!"

"So does Walter," Berta said, thinking of how often Walter had been asked to "be good" and how good he really was. "He's a late developer but now he's in the middle of puberty and needs his father."

---

21 The Friedwart still exists today and is a bed and breakfast for visitors to the Goetheanum. It has an inimitable mystique.

Emil was touched by Walter's request and decided to take him in as an intern at the company on a trial basis. Temperatures were unusually high in Stuttgart that summer, and Emil was happy to spend the days in his cool office with Walter. After work, they often collected Berta and Felix for a walk in the woods or by the river. When the evenings became intolerably hot, the Molts decided to go to the mountains for a few weeks. Emil took Steiner with Dr. Palmer to visit Boos, who still needed care; then his chauffeur dropped them off in Freiburg, leaving Emil to meet Berta, Walter and Felix. They arrived in the new Hanomag car that Walter had persuaded Emil to buy. Hanomag automobiles did not survive for many years, but they were small, affordable, and nicknamed "bread loaf" because of their shape.

The family drove through Munich to the scenic Tegernsee, a lake nestled in a ring of mountains. Walter and Felix spent the days exploring on bicycles; their parents used the open car. The Molts remained undisturbed there, apart for one incident when a Russian intelligence agent was looking for a Citizen Molt, who had absconded from Russia. Somehow he tracked down Emil, believing him to be related to the absconder. Emil told him roundly to get lost—he wanted nothing to do with Bolshevism.

Otherwise the Molts enjoyed a relaxing holiday. They attended rural theatre performances and village dances, and savored freshly harvested fruits and vegetables. Berta especially loved visiting with other families vacationing there—the neighbors played parlor games in the evening together, took moonlit boat rides on the lake, and one rosy morning, climbed a hill to watch the sunrise. Walter promised Emil he would go back to complete school the following year.

Leinhas takes over

A fortnight later, Emil returned to Stuttgart alone, leaving the others to enjoy themselves for a few days more. During an evening lecture by Steiner in September, Emil was surprised to learn that Leinhas had been appointed as Co-Chairman of the Board of the German Anthroposophical

Society, joining Unger and Uehli in that position. What an interesting combination, Emil thought—Unger, proponent of the "old guard" and Uehli, champion of the "young crowd," working together with Leinhas. Perhaps, he speculated, this was a final attempt to bring all members together, but he had trouble understanding how Leinhas would function in the middle. At supper with Steiner, Emil once again mentioned his own difficulty working with Leinhas, who by now was openly critical of Emil. Steiner told him again to trust the man for his sorely-needed abilities.

"Remember his willingness to go where he is asked," Steiner said. "And I do need him. The leadership of the German Anthroposophical Society is now no longer in my hands."

Of course, thought Emil. *I must not fault Leinhas's apparent coldness. If our methods differ, our ventures are as one, and I must learn to cherish his abilities.* But Emil doubted that bringing in Leinhas would be enough to hold the Society together.

A short time after this, Benkendoerfer asked Emil to accompany him to a meeting with Steiner, who explained that it would be best if Leinhas took over Benkendoerfer's job as general manager of The Coming Day. He asked whether Emil could release Leinhas from his position at Waldorf Astoria. Emil and Benkendoerfer were unprepared for the news. Emil, certain that Leinhas had initiated this plan and was not simply "going where he was asked," wished Leinhas had discussed it with him first. But he realized the work experience he had at Waldorf Astoria would help him now in this new capacity. He was sure The Coming Day was where Leinhas had wanted to be all along.

"Of course I'll release him from the factory," he told Steiner. Concerned about how the sudden transition would impact Benkendoerfer, Emil offered to assist him with his next steps, and advised taking a short vacation to clear his head.

Appointing Leinhas

On September 22nd, 11 o'clock in the morning, Steiner appointed Leinhas as managing director of The Coming Day. "Have trust in one another, trust, trust, trust, and recognize one another's worth; otherwise the work will fail," Steiner said to The Coming Day staff. "Don't ask yourselves whether your coworkers have trust in you but rather whether you have trust in them." He then praised Leinhas as the one who could make The Coming Day work.

"Releasing Herr Leinhas from Waldorf Astoria to The Coming Day was not easy. Besides, I was looking forward to stepping back a bit, but in difficult times, personal wishes should not play a role. It is more important to work for the larger whole." He wished Leinhas well in his new position.

> *It was no easy thing to reach the stage at which I was able to introduce Leinhas personally to his office at The Coming Day…*
> Steiner wrote in a letter to his wife, who was in Berlin.
> *Benkendoerfer, for whom the whole affair became very difficult, has returned to del Monte…although still a member of the supervisory board and delegate of the Board of Directors of The Coming Day. The matter was arranged this way by del Monte, insisting he needed Benkendoerfer in his firm for the successful development of his company…*

Leinhas's new colleagues at The Coming Day had mixed reactions to this sudden news. They complained to Emil that the regular flow of work would be interrupted once again by the transition and said they had been happy having Emil, del Monte and Unger guiding their affairs with Benkendoerfer. Emil assured them that he and his colleagues would continue to help and that Leinhas would ensure a smooth transition.

By taking over at The Coming Day, Leinhas became Emil's boss. He also took over some of Emil's tasks, including traveling to anthroposophical and school meetings, while Emil retained the lead role in tobacco meetings and negotiations. Emil promoted his old school friend, August Rentschler, to be his second in command in Leinhas' place and introduced Rentschler in his new position during a company-wide assembly. Emil and Rentschler understood and trusted each other, and Emil felt he now had three protectors in Berta, August Rentschler, and his trusted secretary, Otto Wagner.

Leinhas worked hard to prove himself in his new role, and the Waldorf Astoria financial reserves allowed him to be liberal with the projects he knew to be close to Steiner's heart—the laboratory and clinic, and the agricultural and publishing work. The timing for focusing on these projects was good, considering that even just a year later inflation would have prevented their completion. The factory in Schwäbisch Gmünd began producing larger quantities of remedies under the name "International Laboratories, AG." Leinhas was serving as the new director for this venture as well.

Meanwhile, with the assurance of August Rentschler looking after things at Waldorf Astoria, Emil began to relax. He made a point of going out in the evenings to attend concerts, operas and plays with his family and business associates. He still attended the various anthroposophical group meetings but avoided late night sessions. He also continued to attend tobacco meetings, where he served as an authoritative, calm and cool mediator when others fought. Whenever possible, he brought Walter and Berta on his trips to Dornach and Zürich.

Walter loved being with his father and learned quickly. He also paid serious attention to the enjoyment of life, packing as much fun as he could into his days. The car was Walter's ticket to freedom and gave him a great advantage over his peers—he wasn't at all averse to showing off in it and, although it worried his father, he let it be.

Help for Futurum

On November 14th, Emil was urgently called to Basel for a crisis meeting of Futurum. Arriving at his hotel, he found a delegation of the Executive Committee waiting for him. They handed him Futurum's balance sheet as of October, along with the following official letter:

Dear Mr. Molt: The Executive of Futurum AG Dornach requests that you take over management of Futurum in those areas and with those initiatives which are in its domain. We ask you especially to put the office and finances in order. We also ask you to take whatever steps necessary for the day-to-day running of the business. If you are willing to comply with this request, we ask that you sign your name to this letter. – Dr. Rudolf Steiner, Ernst Gimmi

Emil was stunned. He asked for an hour's adjournment and disappeared into his room. Had there been any hair left on his head, he would have torn it out. He called for a pot of coffee, momentarily regretting that it was not Schnapps. *Is there no one in all Switzerland*, he thought, *able to deal with this? Do I have to worry about The Coming Day and my factory and the under-financed school, and the Goetheanum and now Futurum too? I can advise them, but how do they expect me to take over Futurum without moving here?* He was in full revolt. Then he called Berta. "How can I do this?" he said. "The Board might want me, but the managers won't like my interference."

"Look," she replied, "Dr. Steiner needs it. The main thing is to find a solution. You can't be expected to run Futurum in the long term. Why don't you write them a response with your conditions; then perhaps it can be managed. I will help you do it." So he drafted a letter, read it to Berta for her comments, and brought it back to the others when the hour was up.

Declaration:
To the Chairman of the Executive of Futurum AG, Basel

The current condition of Futurum seems to be untenable. The various enterprises, with a few exceptions, are in a very unfavorable state. The finances of the organization must be considered as desperate. The October balance sheet is incomplete and not transparent. To achieve improvement will require an energetic, goal-oriented management. New persons cannot be found because of the urgency. I have been asked to attempt improvement. I will attempt this gigantic task, but state definitely that I cannot be held responsible for past actions of the managers, nor for the current balance sheet. Whatever I can do, I will, but I give no guarantee for success. I ask for unreserved trust and support from the managers and directors. – Emil Molt

The directors accepted Emil's terms, and from then on, Emil spent a great deal of time finding and training managers, making the rounds of the various companies, and poring over the books. Too often he was beset by feelings of helplessness and worry about the future—two deadly emotions for an entrepreneur whose effectiveness is measured by optimism and action.

Bank crash

On December 1st, 1921, the dollar dropped from 290 to 190 Marks in two days. There were terrible losses on the American stock market, and the day became known as "Black Thursday." Several days later, Emil had to rush to Berlin to get some direction from the government. Then he was back in Stuttgart for a day, looking in on Rentschler and his secretary, Wagner, reporting on financial measures decided in Berlin and approving purchases.

Rising early on the 15th, Emil went to the Annual General Meeting of The Coming Day, had lunch with Steiner and others, then sat with the Executive Council to review finances. In this meeting, he endured a great deal of criticism for his tobacco purchases and hotel and meal expenses. After supper, the meeting continued until 2:30 in the morning, during which time a decision was made to discontinue Emil's beloved *Waldorf News* as a cost-saving measure. Leinhas found its artwork inartistic and not in "Dornach style" and questioned the magazine's effectiveness. Marx agreed with him, and although Emil could have argued, he did not want to fight his colleagues. He found the meeting to be an ordeal, painfully aware of the extent to which he had given away his power. He feared that his boss, Leinhas, would use him to justify his own outlays because, instead of pulling in and belt-tightening, The Coming Day continued spending. After the meeting, unable to sleep, Emil paced the wintry streets until four in the morning.

The next day, Friday the 16th, Emil was pale after his sleepless night, but he bathed and dressed his best. With Berta he went to the festive cornerstone celebration for the new Waldorf School building. There, he signed the document containing Steiner's dedication, which was then cemented into concrete. He was heartened by Steiner's speech which mentioned him.

Steiner's cornerstone verse for the school:

May spirit-strength in love reign here;
May spirit-light in goodness active be;
Born from a certainty of heart,
And steadfastness of soul,
So that we may bring to young human beings
Bodily strength for work,
Soul inwardness,
Spirit clarity.
May this place be consecrated to this task;
May young minds and hearts find here
Servants of light, endowed with strength,
Who will guard and cherish them.
Those who lay this stone as a sign
Will think in their hearts of the spirit
That is to reign in this place,
So that its foundation may be firm.
Upon it will live and work
Wisdom bestowing freedom,
Strengthening spirit-power,
All-revealing spirit-life.
This we wish to affirm
In the name of Christ
With pure intent
And good will.

Worries for Futurum

Before the end of the year, Emil and Steiner met the Futurum directors for a financial review and evaluation. Steiner looked at the expenses and said that much of the money had been frivolously wasted. Emil said that under no circumstances should the Goetheanum be endangered by loss-producing businesses. "Why not keep the successful businesses and sell the rest?" he suggested. "You certainly won't come away with a huge profit, but you'll stop the losses." Privately he thought, *What a pity the Goetheanum Trust did not remain in Stuttgart where it functioned well.*

"I don't want to give up yet," Arnold Ith, one of the young directors, said. "With more capital, we might still be able to rescue all the existing ventures."

"I think we can find enough investors in Switzerland to get us through," someone else added, mentioning several names. Emil, reluctant and doubtful, had to leave then; he was summoned to an emergency survival meeting of German tobacco companies—they were stretched to the limit due to inflation. He promised to return for an intensive review of Futurum and ways to save it.

10,000-Mark note

Inflation out of control

In 1922 inflation worsened in Germany—foreign investors were snapping up German companies and speculation flourished. This created the very conditions Emil had feared when he attempted to set up the Stuttgart Credit Union in 1918. After borrowing heavily to pay off the national debt with a devalued Mark, the German government found itself in an increasing deficit situation. It started to spin out of control in the summer of 1922, causing galloping inflation. Prices increased by 700%, and over the next 15 months hyperinflation took over. Printing presses were kept going day and night, churning out almost worthless paper money. People sold furniture, clothing, jewelry and works of art just to have enough money to buy food.

Emil spent most of January 1922 in Switzerland with Futurum. It was precious time away from Waldorf Astoria, which needed him too, but despite the stress, some things were going well for Futurum. Emil was able to co-opt Edgar Dürler to help with outreach and marketing. Dr. Schmiedel's laboratory, adjoining Dr. Ita Wegman's clinic, was successfully producing a broad range of innovative remedies: Cardiodoron for the heart, Biodoron, a headache remedy, and Infludoron for the flu. Emil wanted to introduce these new medicines to the 2000 physicians practicing in Switzerland, and even entered into discussions with several people about possible sales to England and America. Berta cheered her husband on with encouraging messages from home. She avoided mentioning the financial stress at the Waldorf Astoria factory, with money flowing out to support The Coming Day. In the latter part of that month, Steiner left Switzerland for Stuttgart and to hold lectures in northern Germany. Shortly thereafter, Emil also returned to Stuttgart, believing that progress had been made with Futurum.

Need to sell Waldorf Astoria to keep The Coming Day afloat

On January 28th, the night before Emil was to leave for Dresden on tobacco business, Leinhas came by with a memorandum which he should have sent to Emil the week before. While Emil was in Switzerland, The Coming Day Board had met with Steiner to report a deficit and to discuss the difficulty of securing further financing. In that meeting, the group had decided that the only solution was to sell Waldorf Astoria. "Does Marx know?" Emil asked. "Not yet," replied Leinhas. "What will happen to my people if the company is sold?" was Emil's next question. "We will ensure that they are taken care of," Leinhas replied.

Emil showed Berta the memorandum. She was shocked but philosophical as usual. "You have been hard-pressed trying to do everything," she said. "The sooner you can gracefully let go, the better. Besides," she said, "they've done some very good things with the money."

Emil did not want to give up so easily. He wondered: *If Waldorf Astoria is sold, what will happen to the income for the school? Perhaps there is an alternative solution,* and he promised himself not to be hasty. "I will try to arrange a meeting with Dr. Steiner to discuss the issue," he said to Berta. "And although it is short notice, I will invite some of our friends from up north to attend. I promise to abide by any decisions they make." Berta thought it a very good idea to be in a neutral place, removed from Stuttgart, for an objective view.

A hopeful meeting in the north

Emil made some phone calls to arrange a meeting. Two days later, on January 30th, he met Steiner in Dresden and they traveled to Breslau. Count Carl von Keyserlingk and Rector Bartsch, the fiery proponent of Upper Silesia, met them at the station and took them to the Bellevue Hotel, where they arranged for a conference room and a meal. Ambassador von Moltke and the Countess Petusi von Moltke joined them, and Marie Steiner arrived shortly afterward.

It was a cordial gathering and, more than that, an unusual one. In conformity with that age, anthroposophical boards and committees were almost exclusively made up of men, although women numbered more than half the Society's membership. This particular meeting included two worldly, strong and practical women. There was no competition or posturing, just tactful willingness to find positive solutions. The group considered every aspect of The Coming Day: the people running it, its various companies, the political climate and the finances. Projects were placed in order of importance.

By the end of the day, Emil realized that, for the sake of The Coming Day, his company would have to be sold. He insisted, however, that the sale include tuition guarantees for the Waldorf Astoria children and pension security for his employees. "Of course," said the others. "We must find suitable buyers who will honor this."

Emil mentioned that a friend had recently recommended a reputable banker in Berlin, and said he would make contact with him. The group then enjoyed an early supper together, discussing agriculture and the farms of The Coming Day. Count Keyserlingk and his wife, Johanna, had a large farming estate near Breslau, and they were extremely interested in Steiner's ideas on soil improvement and animal husbandry. They wanted him to come and give an agricultural conference at their place.[22] In the evening, Steiner and Emil returned to Dresden.

The banker Dr. Nollstadt

The following day Emil took an early train to Berlin and introduced himself to Dr. Gustav Nollstadt, Director at the Darmstädter Bank, a well-established bank that dealt with a number of tobacco firms. An urbane gentleman with a keen eye for business and a lively expression, Nollstadt knew Waldorf Astoria as a respected, successful company which, he noted, had recently been mentioned less frequently in the news. He was intrigued to learn of Emil's social reforms in the company and of its patronage of a school. Emil described the difficulty of the large Waldorf company joining The Coming Day; he had hoped its addition would lend stability and opportunity to the venture, but it had proved to be a burden.

Emil's business card

Nollstadt immediately spotted a conflict of interest and the necessity of pulling Waldorf Astoria back out. He said he could envisage Waldorf Astoria joining a consortium composed of banks and tobacco interests, and he offered to talk with some contacts to see what they might come up with. He thought a transfer to such a consortium could be completed by May.

---

22 See Steiner's Agriculture Course, given on the Keyserlingk estate of Koberwitz in 1924.

Emil reports back

On February 3rd Emil returned to Dresden to pick up the Steiners and take them back to Stuttgart where, at the next Coming Day Board meeting, he described the visit with Nollstadt. "He would like to come to Stuttgart to view the factory and talk to the Board," Emil told his colleagues. Leinhas did not seem happy that Emil had taken this initiative and remarked that in the future Emil should consult him before taking any steps. "Very well," said Emil. But I hope you don't mind my following up on the consortium idea by talking to Georg Warburg, another potential investor." Leinhas was skeptical but the others encouraged Emil to go ahead.

He continues to seek connections

A week later, Emil met with Warburg in St. Moritz. Warburg was a member of a wealthy banking family that had helped make Hamburg into a shipping center. Emil presented Warburg with the idea of a consortium and gave him some background on Steiner, Waldorf Astoria, the school and The Coming Day. Warburg was an engaged listener and seemed intrigued. They parted cordially, Emil sure they would be able to work together. He promised to introduce him to Steiner.

Next he swung round to Bern to visit Dr. Wilhelm Muehlon, author of *The Vandal of Europe* and the friend who had recommended both Nollstadt and Warburg to him. Muehlon liked the idea of a consortium for Waldorf Astoria and provided some insight into Warburg, saying that he had ties to Prince Max of Baden and was financing a committee for refuting the German war guilt propaganda.

"Warburg probably has closer links to anthroposophy than anyone is aware of, and certainly is the man for such a consortium," Muehlon told Emil. Then he mentioned the defunct *Waldorf News*, saying what an interesting journal it had been, better than any other anthroposophical publication. He named friends in leading positions who had subscribed to it. They were sorry it was gone. *It wasn't the daily newspaper Steiner wanted,* Emil thought, *but it could have served as his "organ for communication."*

Back to Futurum

On February 20th, Emil's last day in Switzerland, he met with Steiner and the Futurum Board. Significant new investors had not been found. Steiner mentioned that Dr. Ita Wegman wanted to pull her clinic and Schmiedel's laboratory out of Futurum to avoid putting their work at risk. Emil looked at Steiner and saw fatigue and distress in his face. *What have I done?* thought Emil. *All along I assumed I was doing what Steiner wanted. I relied on him and he relied on me, but he is not the businessman, I am.* Emil took a deep breath.

"Let us end this meeting now," he said. "I will take a few days to contemplate our next course of action and will come back with suggestions." Later, in bed, after recording the sequence of the day in his diary, he pondered the ease of working with people such as Nollstadt, Muehlon and Warburg, compared with the difficulties of something as uncharted as Futurum and The Coming Day.

Emil assessing with Walter

The next day he traveled back to Stuttgart after breakfast with Steiner. He was happy to be home and desperately craved some rest, but instead he asked Walter to join him in his office so they could work on the Futurum problem. Walter was very attentive. They spent the rest of the afternoon writing extensive notes on the potential of each company, and ended by drafting a practical set of suggestions. In the evening, the three Molts and Felix went to a eurythmy performance at the school, Walter's cousin Lisa performing.

In the morning Emil went to The Coming Day Board meeting with Leinhas presiding. The group was surprised and happy to see modest overall gains for the publishing company, del Monte's factory, Unger's factory, and the medicine production in Schwäbisch Gmünd. Waldorf Astoria sales were up too. On the other hand, the financial needs for the coming year were estimated at 20,000,000 Marks—far beyond what the combined enterprises could produce. Unger said, "We must sell Waldorf Astoria as quickly as possible."

Emil's Futurum suggestion

Berta had not been to Dornach for a while, so Emil offered to bring her along on his next visit. The weather was glorious, and Dr. Roeschl, a young language teacher, came with them. Arriving in the early afternoon, they knocked on Steiner's door and brought him a birthday letter from Marie Steiner, who was in Stuttgart with her eurythmy troupe. Steiner greeted them and escorted them to his studio to show them the progress of his sculpture. Then Berta took Dr. Roeschl on a tour of the Goetheanum and its surroundings while Emil and Steiner met with the Futurum Board. In this meeting, Emil presented the memorandum he had worked on with Walter in the hopes that it would serve as a kind of birthday present for Steiner.

"While the simplest thing is liquidation, I believe there is another possibility. We can turn Futurum into a shareholding company with just one manager and one employee, keeping only the successful enterprises and making them self-administering. A manager needs a degree of freedom and autonomy. We now have capable managers in the various enterprises, but they lack freedom to act. I believe it is because their companies' income belongs to Futurum, and most of the decision-making too. They are not able to use the money they generate to build their businesses because it is needed for cultural initiatives. I would like to propose a new form—Futurum as shareholder in the ventures, with the dividends supporting cultural initiatives. As long as the ventures are successful, their managing directors have the authority to run them. This plan will also give the clinic and the laboratory their independence. The Board can remain as it is." He emphasized that he was in no way criticizing past problems but would help with this change if they wanted him to.

With this plan, he thought he had fulfilled his obligation, as Berta had advised, to set Futurum on the road to health. Steiner looked relieved, but some of the others seemed to consider the plan a danger to Futurum's governance and income stream.

Negotiating the consortium

On February 28th, Berta and Emil returned to Stuttgart with Steiner, staying overnight at their favorite inn in Freiburg. At home Emil grabbed the replacement overnight bag always at the ready with pressed shirts and ties, cufflinks and handkerchiefs. After a brief visit to his office, he and Steiner boarded a train headed north. Emil had booked adjoining sleeping suites and after a short chat they retired. In the morning they parted ways, Emil continuing to talks with Nollstadt in Berlin and Steiner going to Leipzig. Over the next two days, Emil met with various people interested in the consortium—Nollstadt, Privy Councilor Frisch of the Dresdner Bank, and representatives of tobacco companies. All were ready to participate in a consortium.

"How interesting," Emil told Berta on the phone, "Four years ago in Stuttgart, I tried to get a business consortium going, and now it's finally being realized. Waldorf School funds and pensions will be guaranteed and the *Waldorf News* reinstated." Then Emil rang Leinhas and August Rentschler, asking them to join the negotiations. They both arrived on March 3rd.

On Saturday, March 4th, Emil, Rentschler, and Leinhas met with Nollstadt who said, "Your organization is exemplary, but the Waldorf company needs a larger setting." He laid out his plan for the consortium, to include his own bank, Warburg, the Dresdner Bank, and selected tobacco companies. "It is a new model," he said, "but it's sure to succeed. A great deal of advertising is key, especially for the sake of the Waldorf School." He suggested an advertising campaign in the main Frankfurt financial paper. "This project is ahead of its time," he said, envisaging a 15% dividend instead of 12%, and sales to Russia and the border lands. He saw no problem with The Coming Day still being involved.

Leinhas spoke for the first time: "Let me be clear," he said. "If a bank consortium joins, The Coming Day will pull out because that would be diametrically opposed to its principles. Either one is pure or one is not. The consortium might provide Molt with shares," he continued, "but The Coming Day would not take it lightly that Molt chose opportunity over principle. Still," he added, "I am willing to negotiate." Emil was embarrassed and thought, *He thinks I'm just doing this for my own personal gain.* Nollstadt seemed taken aback, but the meeting continued and ended on a positive note, with August Rentschler going back to Stuttgart in an upbeat mood.

Emil, thinking about what Leinhas had said in the meeting, wanted to give him a better impression of the people they were dealing with. "Come to Hamburg with me," he said to Leinhas. "Herr Warburg is there this weekend. You will enjoy him. We can also meet with Marx and the Abrahams." Leinhas went along, but he remained dour to the point that Emil, looking back at the meeting they had just had, realized how engaged and forceful he had been and how little space he had left Leinhas.

Trying to appease Leinhas

Genuinely sorry and blaming himself for insensitivity (he was desperately trying to see the best in Leinhas), he decided to make an effort to meet him on a personal level. He booked them into the *Vier Jahreszeiten* (Four Seasons), one of the best and most comfortable hotels in Hamburg. *"Can we really afford this?"* was written on Leinhas's brow. *"Yes. It's my treat,"* nodded Emil. He recommended they leave all business aside and enjoy Hamburg on a Sunday, inviting Leinhas to lunch and to the theater.

Although the two men had a good day together, Emil might have realized that he could never win Leinhas over like that. In reviewing the day he tried to place himself into this complex person's shoes. He promised himself to step back and let Leinhas direct things more in the future. Then he thought about Marx's son Hans—how much Hans had wanted to join Waldorf Astoria and how Leinhas opposed it when the firm was transferred to The Coming Day. Emil thought that now, in this new situation, it would be easy to bring Hans in. That prompted thoughts about his partner, Marx, who had always wanted his son to take over Waldorf Astoria.

Suddenly, Emil was worried. *I am faced with an unfamiliar consortium,* he thought. *Can I suggest Marx as a Board member? Will he side with me or with them on crucial issues? I do need an ally.* He realized he would be entering a high-stakes situation that could end up completely out of his hands. With that worry, he fell into a restless sleep.

On Monday, March 6th, Emil introduced Leinhas to Warburg at M.M.Warburg & Co. and met with his 19-year-old son, Siegmund (who would one day go on to found a major investment bank in London). Together the group discussed Waldorf Astoria shares and the possibility of expansion into America. Warburg and his son were about to return to St. Moritz, but said a representative of the firm, Dr. Ernst Spiegelberg, would continue the negotiations. The meeting took longer than expected, so without seeing Marx and the Abrahams, Emil and Leinhas traveled back to Berlin, from where Emil sent Marx a telegram: *Am in Hamburg on Monday. Please telegraph if you are there. Greetings Molt.* He knew Marx had heard about the negotiations and was eager to connect. That night he and Leinhas had dinner together and all seemed well.

On March 11th Emil attended a major meeting of the tobacco industry. Stressful times were turning colleagues into competitors. One accused the other of undercutting, another of anarchy. Emil, looking to the outcome of his own negotiations and faced with the continuing tobacco treadmill, realized that his ideal of bringing his unique Waldorf Astoria into an anthroposophical setting was almost over. He suddenly lost his courage.

The final Darmstädter Bank meeting with Emil, Leinhas, Nollstadt and Spiegelberg took place that afternoon. All details, including the purchase price, were settled. Emil, as an employee of the consortium, would continue managing Waldorf Astoria. It remained for the contract to be written up and sent to The Coming Day for signing. They shook hands on the deal and parted.

Leinhas left for Hamburg to arrange a meeting with Marx, but Emil stayed behind because Steiner was giving a lecture in town. He went to the lecture, remaining in his seat afterward while the animated crowd dispersed. Then he rushed out, looking for Steiner, looking also for words of comfort, but Steiner was already gone.

Sorrow

Emil returned to his hotel room, a wave of sorrow washing over him. Many years before, after his successful negotiation with the Abrahams and Marx, he couldn't wait to ring Berta. Now he sat at his desk and didn't know what to say. *The direction of our life has suffered a setback,* he thought. *Berta can still work within her ideals at the school, but where will it lead me?* Eventually he took hotel stationery and a pen and wrote, not to Berta, but to Steiner, delivering it to the lecture hall early the following morning.

March 11th
Most respected Doctor:

I would have wanted to say good-bye to you this evening since I travel tomorrow to Hamburg and Stuttgart; unfortunately you had already gone. I must now take my leave in writing, while venturing to express a few words concerning the thoughts and feelings which move me on this day in which I see my fondest hopes, and with them a fair portion of myself, carried to the grave.

One year ago I returned from Hamburg to The Coming Day with the bill of sale for Waldorf Astoria. One year later it has to be sold again, and I am forced to serve the powers I have fought till now. A sad destiny—after the hopeful spring of 1919. Then and now! As matters stand I even had to propose the sale to the banks myself to unburden The Coming Day. In the present state of its finances, it would not have survived. And apart from me there is now no one able to direct Waldorf Astoria. So I have to return to the path of capitalism—if The Coming Day is to be preserved from harm.

Certainly, on the whole, "circumstances" are to blame—but I am nonetheless not quite able to get over the self-reproach that I failed in the task set me and which you honored me with. Had I faithfully and energetically followed everything you recommended in June

1920, I would perhaps not have failed so badly. On the other hand,
I also felt that one was much left in the lurch with efforts at
fundraising, even by the management of The Coming Day, especially
earlier on, and I have the feeling that all the many "digs" from
friends weren't especially helpful.

It seems paradoxical that the Waldorf News has a better
prospect of being continued under "capitalism" than under our
anthroposophical management…

And so I now go, heavy of heart, into a new period, with the sincere
and heartfelt plea to you, most respected Doctor, to hold your
protecting hand over me and not to let the "thread" connecting me to
the Society break. How much remains for me in the way of work for
the Threefold Social Order, The Coming Day, Futurum—perhaps
even the Waldorf School? I will be taking on a quite new, extensive
round of duties for these banks.

Please, do not lose sight of me altogether! I shall try to help with
Futurum; then I must proceed to my new tasks in the service of high
finance. In heartfelt and sincere esteem.
Your most humble, Emil Molt

Hans Marx

Emil took a noon train to Hamburg to see Marx, expecting to find
him waiting at the station as usual. Instead Leinhas met him, telling him
to prepare himself for a shock—Marx had gone to Frankfurt because his
son, Hans, had committed suicide. Hans Marx had fallen in love with
a Christian girl and she with him. He had proposed to her but she had
to reject him—her father forbade the union because Hans was Jewish.

On March 14th, Leinhas and Emil left Hamburg together. Leinhas
got off the train in his hometown of Mannheim, saying he wanted to visit
a banker he knew at the Süddeutsche Diskonto Bank. Emil continued
on to Stuttgart and went straight home, exhausted and burdened.

On March 15th, Steiner arrived in Stuttgart from Berlin in the early
morning and Emil invited him in for coffee. While they were sitting

together in the breakfast room, Leinhas appeared, telling Emil that the Mannheim banker would like to see a Waldorf balance sheet. He urged Emil to come along to meet him. Emil, still exhausted and recovering from the shock of Hans's death, did not want to go away again and reminded Leinhas that they both had a 10 o'clock appointment with the Commerzbank in Stuttgart. But Leinhas insisted that they go to Mannheim that afternoon—he particularly wanted to do this before The Coming Day Board meeting the following day. Berta was not happy about this.

The Discount Bank

Emil took Rentschler, Walter and Lisa with him to Mannheim where he, Rentschler and Leinhas met with Director Weil and the gentlemen of the Süddeutsche Diskonto Bank—a small, subprime local lender. Emil described Waldorf Astoria and the negotiations in the North, and gave them the company balance sheet. He understood that they were interested in the consortium and had significant funds at their disposal.

At The Coming Day Board meeting the next day, Dr. Steiner was surprised to hear Leinhas say that, in spite of the Board directive of February 25th, Emil had again taken it upon himself to negotiate the sale of the company on his own—until he, Leinhas, had finally been called in. He emphasized that The Coming Day didn't have the means to hold on to Waldorf Astoria and that the company would have to be sold quickly and at the most favorable price to avoid a reduction of programs. Emil did not respond to this since he had indeed acted unilaterally. Leinhas also said he had taken up contact with a bank in Mannheim which had inquired about an option on Waldorf Astoria shares.

Can Futurum survive?

On March 17th, Marie Steiner arrived in Stuttgart from a eurythmy tour. Emil picked her up and took her to his house to meet her husband. In the afternoon Wagner drove them both to Dornach. Emil spent the day in the factory preparing for his departure to Dornach, where he hoped to conclude the Futurum matter. He begged Berta to come with him, and they were just about to leave when he heard that Director Weil and two other gentlemen from the Süddeutsche Diskonto Bank were on their way to inspect the factory. Naturally, he delayed his departure to give them a tour, inviting them to lunch with Berta and Leinhas. After lunch, he excused himself, leaving the gentlemen with Leinhas while Berta and he traveled to Dornach.

The Molts spent the next morning with Steiner and his wife. Then Steiner and Emil went to a Futurum Board meeting at the Friedwart. Instead of resolution, they were met with the assumption that within three months Futurum would cease to exist.

"Does anyone have the means for continuing?" Steiner asked. One manager thought Futurum could survive if Switzerland didn't collapse economically and if a new Board could be created. Nobody took up this suggestion. The group's pervasive negativity and its failure to act on his recommendations gave Emil indigestion. Later that day Arnold Ith, the youngest member of the management team, tendered his resignation from the Futurum Board:

To the President of the Board of Directors of Futurum –

The writer regrets to tender his resignation as director of Futurum. I pointed out that we couldn't realize our goal of associative working among the companies bought in the first year. This was supposed to be our primary remit. In social life there are situations that prevent people from working together because of incompatible differences. Swiss law recognizes such cases. The present situation makes it impossible for me to be part of the management group of Futurum...One would have to find a different group of directors, capable of liquidating the old Futurum AG and starting a new one in the spirit of association. If the present group is convinced that a new Board can solve this task, I see it as my duty to make room for such... Ith

He warmly recommended asking Edgar Dürler to head Futurum, believing he would be the most able to lead and to communicate with all concerned.

A possible way for Futurum

Emil, exhausted, woke the next day much later than usual. He spent the morning writing, and in the early afternoon he was told there were gentlemen waiting in the foyer. He went down to find the two Futurum publishers, Dürler and Storrer, looking uneasy but determined. Storrer told Emil that they had talked things over and had formed an action committee willing to take on the responsibility for Futurum. Emil was courteous, saying he thought their initiative was very fine. Storrer elaborated a little, saying they intended to follow some of Emil's suggestions. They seemed to understand that Emil would not be part of this, and he was relieved that a natural conclusion had come about, believing destiny had resolved things with Futurum so he could concentrate fully on the Waldorf Astoria transfer. "It's actually a miracle," he said to Berta later, "just at the moment when Waldorf Astoria is being sold. I only hope they know what they're doing." His mind already turned toward Germany, he wrote:

> To the Futurum Board:
> Since my task has been superseded by the formation of the new responsible body, I ask you cordially to relieve me of my post as delegate to Futurum. I would have stayed for your next meeting, but must go to Hamburg in connection with my own firm…

Steiner was on his way back from a lecture on the morning of March 22nd. The Molts met him at the train station in Basel and drove him to Dornach. Emil described what had taken place with Storrer and Dürler. Steiner was surprised at the sudden decision and sorry that Emil was not staying for the meeting but said that, in view of the pending negotiation in Germany, Emil and Berta should go back to Stuttgart.

Sold!

The next day, March 23rd, Leinhas arranged another meeting with the discount bank in Mannheim to discuss, as Emil still thought, joining the consortium. When they arrived at the bank, Leinhas asked Emil to wait while he went into the boardroom to speak with the assembled bank gentlemen. After a time, Leinhas brought Emil in and introduced him around. Director Weil said he looked forward to meeting Warburg and collaborating with Nollstadt, who had been his financial advisor at one time. Weil was aware that Leinhas had not mentioned the discount bank to Nollstadt and the others, and said it would have been fair of him to do so. Altogether, Emil had the curious impression that Weil was being conciliatory. Then Leinhas again asked Emil to wait outside. An hour passed, during which, Emil learned later, Leinhas had signed a sales contract with the Mannheim bank. He later claimed to have shown the contract to Emil, who he alleged had not found the time to read it. Nollstadt had told Emil that the consortium transaction could be in place by May, a seemingly optimistic and speedy undertaking. Within ten days of bringing Emil to the discount bank, Leinhas signed away Waldorf Astoria in the name of The Coming Day. He then coolly traveled back to Stuttgart with Emil.

Later, meeting with Rentschler in Emil's office, Leinhas admitted that he had sold the company and Emil with it. He had no sense whatsoever that the consortium should have been included or given a chance. He admitted that Emil had requested approval by The Coming Day Board before any action or decision was taken but claimed that had not been possible.

How to explain

Emil felt completely humiliated. What could he say to Warburg and Nollstadt? *I was not awake enough,* he thought sadly. *For people like Warburg it was not just a business deal, but a strong human-personal interest. Now his faith in anthroposophy will be shattered.*

On March 24th, 1922, Emil traveled to Hamburg to see Marx for the first time since Hans's death. On the way, he stopped in Frankfurt to meet with Warburg's man, Spiegelberg, who he assumed had heard about the new situation. But Spiegelberg only knew from Nollstadt that Leinhas had sent a message saying the transaction was in question. Spiegelberg was shocked to hear that the company had been sold. He said that, in a business sense and in a human sense, he couldn't understand Leinhas. Emil told Spiegelberg that, as a member of The Coming Day Board, he couldn't comment, but that he was upset by the turn of events to the point of resigning. Spiegelberg encouraged him not to do that and not to underestimate his own capabilities.

Message from Emil to Leinhas in Mannheim:

Spoke with Spiegelberg. He is professionally and humanly upset and feels dealings to be an insult to the house of Warburg. Please implore Weil to do everything possible to include Warburg and Nollstadt. Greetings, Molt

Mourning Hans

The next day, March 25th, Emil went on to Hamburg to apprise his partners of the new development. Marx met Emil at the train station in Hamburg with great warmth, and Emil gave him a hug that brought tears to Marx's eyes. They went to a quiet place and reminisced, recalling the beginnings of the extraordinary road they had traveled together. They mourned Hans and mourned the path Waldorf Astoria had taken, feeling closer to each other and more compatible than ever before. They visited Hans's grave and then visited Stern and the Abrahams, who, although disconcerted by the sale of Waldorf Astoria, hoped that all would be well. Emil felt decidedly under the weather, so they adjourned to Marx's house where Mrs. Marx provided them with comfort and a nourishing soup.

Inner collapse

On March 28th Emil took the train back to Stuttgart. Although now feeling really unwell, he put on his best face for a State dinner with the German President, dignitaries, and ambassadors. The newspapers were full of the news that The Coming Day had sold Waldorf Astoria, and he was bombarded with questions at the event. At the end of the night he crept into bed feeling weak and ill. When Dr. Noll examined him the following afternoon, he diagnosed an enlarged spleen.

Warburg wrote Emil. He had already arranged sales in America for over a million dollars and was outraged that "such a little bank" could have won out over a major consortium. On March 30th, Warburg's son, Siegmund, arrived in Stuttgart with Nollstadt for a personal discussion. "I am so deeply sorry for the way things have gone," Emil said to Nollstadt. "Especially since you put so much effort into the merger. I hope we still have a future together."

"I can only do business with you in the future if I am assured that you were not part of the Diskonto Bank decision," Nollstadt replied.

"Please allow me to remain silent," Emil said. "I cannot discuss anything that would be harmful to The Coming Day or the personalities involved."

That evening he sat at home, staring at an abyss, shocked at the turn his life had taken in a few short months, not knowing the way forward. He wrote in his diary, illustrating it with a drawing:

Emil's sketch

> I perceive a pressure from the abdomen pressing against my head; the brain is pressed and I cannot think until the pressure subsides. Question: Can this pressure be arrested in the rhythmic sphere to prevent it from rising up? Lhs [Leinhas] has unusually..." (The rest is shorthand.)

Mending friendships

On April 3rd Emil visited Emil Georgii, finding him in good health, and still handsome and debonair. "We have not really talked since I left Georgii und Harr," Emil said to him. "I never had the courage to call on you because of the way our friendship ended."

"As time went on," replied Georgii cordially, "I saw how right you were and how far we could have gone together had I not been sidetracked. I never did get to perfect my machine, and other tobacco companies soon overtook me. Of course, I was young and impulsive and had to learn the hard way. But now," he continued, "you're the one suffering—all of Stuttgart is talking about it. Did your business sense desert you because of your association with the theosophists?"

"Yes, I guess you might say so," said Emil. "But it's anthroposophy, and it is part of my life. If there are consequences, I will bear them."

"Well," Georgii smiled, "that school of yours is certainly astonishing."

"I'd love to show it to you," Emil replied. "And I'd love to invite you both to our house for dinner. You've not seen Berta in such a long time and we have so much to catch up on."

The Georgii circle is closed and the wound is healed, Emil thought gratefully next day while sitting in the train to Mannheim. There he pleaded, unsuccessfully, with Weil at the Diskonto Bank to include Darmstädter Bank and other members of the Consortium in its plans.

On April 5th George Warburg came to visit him and, wonderful to relate, the link with him was not broken. Together they traveled overnight to Hamburg. Emil spent several hours with Marx, then went to see Spiegelberg again, who told him that Max Warburg (the senior partner) was very put out and considering a lawsuit. "I traveled with Georg Warburg last night and hope that he will put things right," said Emil. Spiegelberg mentioned how much he would have enjoyed working with Emil to get to know his philosophical background better. Emil was grateful to know that the personal connection was unbroken. However, when he reported to the combined Board of Asten and Abraham, he was sharply reprimanded about the course of events and how it would impact them. The meeting ended on a dissonant note. They parted on cordial terms but Emil traveled back to Stuttgart exhausted.

And yet…

When, on Saturday, April 7th, a telegram arrived notifying Emil that Dürler and another Futurum manager wanted his advice and were on their way to see him, Emil did not feel up to it and begged Wagner to make an excuse. Wagner told them, rather clumsily, that Emil was in a meeting. When they asked when he would be available, Wagner said he didn't know and that they should ring in the evening when he would have an answer. They left, frustrated, and went to The Coming Day offices, where they found a willing ear in Leinhas. They told him they had been turned away and he shook his head, saying they were better off not working with Emil. He looked at the proposal Emil had written up for them and called it rather simplistic. "I'm sure there are other solutions," he said. "And I suppose I shall have to take this on as well."

"Truly," said Berta to Emil, "You are not yourself. This is the second time you have aborted a meeting with Futurum." Emil would, in time, regret this omission more than any other because of the burden it placed on Steiner.

Berta's strength

Berta, who had often been frail and now suffering the intensities around her, began to assert herself. Whereas before she had kept her fiery nature hidden, she now led her husband. He was downcast and in crisis; she was upright and determined. "This is probably your life's biggest lesson," she said. "Leinhas, Steiner, Dürler—what are they teaching you? You have become vulnerable and now you are open. You have always followed your own ways, now you must listen to others. It is Easter week and Friday is your birthday. You have already gone through your Good Friday. Let us go to the mountains to see whether we can truly find our Easter Sunday and the further path you are to follow." She booked a hotel in Berchtesgaden, and they traveled with Wagner driving them. High up in the glorious Bavarian mountains, they found a view that made their hearts soar. The air was clear and warm. *My birthday. Hopefully there will be a change for the better*, Emil wrote in his diary on April 14th.

Early that morning, he and Walter went out walking and suddenly Emil looked at his sixteen-year-old son and thought, *Where have I been, that I have not really looked at my dearest boy? Why have I only noticed his weaknesses, his difficulties in school, his spending? Who is he, what are his thoughts? What are his ideals?* With a pang, he realized how often he and Berta had left Walter in the care of Maria and others while they traveled with Rudolf Steiner to Holland and Switzerland. In the fresh, sweet air of Berchtesgaden he asked Walter many questions and listened carefully to his son's answers. Walter had thought about going to England to learn English—an idea he hadn't had the courage to discuss with his father. Now Emil understood and, thinking back, realized how, at Walter's age, he had been out of school and challenged as an apprentice. They came back from their walk to a lovely breakfast on the terrace with Berta. This was Emil's Easter experience: meeting his son.

The Molts returned to Stuttgart a week later feeling refreshed and happier than they had been in a long time. Slowly, Emil got back on his feet. Slowly he took up his duties although he still needed compresses on his spleen almost every day. He walked with Berta and went to the theater with Walter. He visited a number of old friends, invited the Georgiis to dinner, and attended a school Board meeting.

And yet again...

On April 27th, before the next Coming Day Board meeting, Berta cautioned Emil not to get drawn into an argument with Leinhas—it would only harm Emil and the already fragile Coming Day. Emil went; Steiner was present. As usual there were problems, but there was good news as well. The sawmill had improved and the laboratory had successfully introduced the hay fever remedy (Gencydo). The migraine remedy (Biodoron) had been introduced to the market. But before the meeting was over, Leinhas, holding a sheaf of correspondence with Dr. Spiegelberger, once again justified his actions with the Waldorf Astoria sale while seeming to accuse Emil of dishonesty. For a while, Emil refused to comment, but eventually he became upset and got up to leave. Steiner gently told him he must stay and not take things so personally. After all, he had responsibilities as founder of The Coming Day. Emil then asked Leinhas for the correspondence with Spiegelberger.

Later that evening, at the anthroposophical representatives' meeting (a meeting Emil dreaded more than any other), Steiner seemed dejected, saying he felt betrayed by everything that had happened and that nothing had changed. People were still talking about bringing new ideas into business when in fact they were employing the same old economic practices.

Emil came home distraught. "I've practically been called a liar," he told Berta. "When have I ever told them a lie?" She asked him what had happened and he replied that he had simply refused to engage in an argument with Leinhas. He said he believed Leinhas's accusations stemmed from the day the Diskonto delegation came to Stuttgart. "Do you remember, we took them to lunch and then left for Switzerland while they went on to meet?"

"Yes," she said. "You did not negotiate with them. But you have damaged yourself. You have long had trouble with Benkendoerfer and Leinhas, but out of loyalty to Steiner you don't confront them."

"If, after all the time we've worked together, they don't believe me, it's a shame," he said. "Perhaps your true relationship with them will flourish in the future. Try to look at yourself objectively. Haven't we learned that we choose our so-called adversaries as medicine for ourselves, and if we succeed in working with them, something new can be gained?" Emil took paper and pen and wrote the following observations about his current state of mind:

When my thinking is lazy, it likes to postpone. This causes a lack of will. The lack of will becomes a lack of goal. I need independence without pressure from outside. I must not take on more than I can manage, but when I do take on a task, I must complete it. I will work more consciously...

The following day Emil read through Leinhas's correspondence with Dr. Spiegelberg. He was horrified by the content. Leinhas justified himself with many words, while casting Emil in a very poor light. Leinhas wrote of the pleasant relations he was able to establish with Spiegelberg. Spiegelberg wrote back, "As I've already told Mr. Molt, it is not the disappointment over the lost business, because in this transaction we did not do it for mere gain but rather because the perspective it offered seemed interesting, and because we felt trust in you and in Mr. Molt..." He expressed surprise that Emil had not been honest with him. The letters between the two men continued until Spiegelberg seemed to tire of Leinhas's long missives and stopped responding.

Emil showed the correspondence to Berta, who read it with compressed lips—she was unable to forgive Leinhas the betrayal she saw in these letters. Emil, on the other hand, reflected deeply on what had happened, trying to recognize that Leinhas would have seen the quick financial advantage to The Coming Day of the discount bank. He saw himself, how he waited outside the discount bank's meeting room during the negotiations, and he thought that perhaps Leinhas may have believed that they had, in fact, discussed everything together. *I had my blind spots, but Leinhas had his as well*, thought Emil. *He is not fundamentally dishonest, but he certainly interprets life in his own way.* Then and there, Emil decided to remain silent and never again defend himself to Steiner and the anthroposophical group.

Now Emil did something he would regret forever. He shut down temporarily, losing confidence in the whole complex of people and institutions. He even doubted Steiner's ability as a leader. He couldn't face the school, dreading chance confrontations or even glances. He spent long hours at the factory but stopped going to meetings and to Dornach. He was tired all the time. "How could I have been so led astray?" he wrote later in a terribly shaky handwriting. "We tried to make a leader of Steiner in the outward sense: the 'Führer' Germans craved, whom we could follow blindly. Instead he simply led by example."

Attack in Munich

In May, Steiner was nearly lynched in Munich. By now that city was the center of the National Socialist movement with General Ludendorf as one of its spokespersons and Hitler pulling strings in the background. A local anthroposophist heard that an attack on Steiner was planned and took him to police headquarters to ask for extra protection. A group of young friends of the Society pledged to stand guard in the hall. In the middle of Steiner's lecture the lights suddenly went out. Steiner continued speaking seriously and calmly until the lights came back on. Surprisingly, the students hired to attack Steiner remained glued to their seats. When he finished his lecture, the students made a dash for the podium but were blocked by Steiner's friends while the police stood by. Steiner left the theater through a side door and took an earlier train away, never to return to Munich. He canceled the rest of his public speaking engagements in Germany. He came to Stuttgart where he gave a private lecture for his shocked friends, after which they discussed ways of coping with the threats to all of them. During this meeting they decided to change the name of their publication *Threefold Commonwealth* because they felt the word "Threefold" was too controversial. The new name they decided on was *Anthroposophy*, a change Emil found heartbreaking.

Staying home

Emil spent more time with Walter, who was learning office procedure at Waldorf Astoria and had joined the fire brigade. After work they would dig the garden, plant bushes and flowers, and go to the observatory on the hill to look at Mars and Jupiter. They also visited art exhibits and helped Wagner plan his wedding. Walter still had time for friends and he developed a carefree social life.

Around that time a seventeen-year-old Swiss boy named Rudolf Grosse moved to Stuttgart from Zürich on his own initiative to attend the Waldorf School. In order to help pay for his tuition, he worked in the Waldorf Astoria factory during vacations, where Emil noticed him and was impressed with his performance. When Emil discovered that Grosse was short of money, he invited him to live with the Molts free of charge, hoping he would be a companion to Walter and Felix. The three young men got on well together and soon became close friends.

The teachers at the school had no idea what had happened to Emil, only hearing vague rumors. But when Steiner reopened the school in September, Berta insisted on Emil's attending. He was at first terrified at the prospect of being asked to speak on that opening day and then mortified when he was not asked to speak. This exacerbated his feeling of loneliness, and before long, he fell physically ill as well. Then, at least, he had a daily visitor in Dr. Noll, who came to care for him and helped him pull himself back together. As he recovered, Emil began to look back on the events and on his own actions and saw the things that he might have done differently. "Leinhas is Leinhas, and the others are who they are," he said to Berta. "I am the one who has to change."

Later in September, at Berta's suggestion, they ventured to Dornach for the first time since the previous spring. Emil heard Steiner lecture and met with him afterward. Steiner in his kindly way advised Emil to heal his relationships, be truthful, open, and clear in himself, and to rely on Berta. He warned of causing ruptures, saying, "Even though they can be repaired, some dross always remains."

"Do you think I am capable of all of this?" Emil asked him. Steiner just smiled.

Emil, glad to have breathed the Dornach air and spent time in the beautiful Goetheanum, told Berta he would try to win his colleagues back.

In October, Steiner came to Stuttgart again to lecture. He had pondered the issues presented by the young anthroposophists in 1920.

Aware that they still wanted separation from the German Society, despite the best efforts of the three chairmen, he responded with a set of social lectures.[23]

Waldorf Astoria sold again

On November 13th, Emil was at breakfast with his former partner, Mueller, who was visiting from Hamburg. The daily newspaper arrived. "Here," said Emil, passing it to him. "You can read about local Stuttgart gossip while I fetch more tea." Mueller leafed through the paper and gasped. He showed Emil the news that Waldorf Astoria had been sold to speculators by the discount bank. They immediately ordered the car round and drove to Mannheim to face down Weil. He confirmed that the tobacco importer Kiazim Emin had bought the majority of the shares. Weil claimed his bank couldn't discuss the negotiation in advance, otherwise a hostile firm would have forced a sale. He said that his bank still had an interest in the business and that Emil would be kept on as a traveling representative. "What about the agreement to support the school and the workers?" was Emil's first question. "That stays in place," promised Weil.

> In 1922, with inflation and speculation rampant, cigarette companies such as Waldorf Astoria were forced to import tobacco at foreign rates and then sell their cigarettes at a greatly weakened Mark. Many couldn't survive this situation and were bought out by foreign investors. Thus it happened that, very soon after the sale to the discount bank, the majority of Waldorf shares came into the hands of a Greek tobacco supplier: Kiazim Emin. His firm was looking to invest in cigarette companies as a means of ensuring a market for his tobacco. The transfer of ownership took place during the latter part of 1922. – Otto Wagner, Emil's secretary

---

23 *The Younger Generation, Educational and Spiritual Impulses for Life in the Twentieth Century.*

Christmas decision

Berta, on hearing the news, wondered where it would end and thought her husband should get out. "Waldorf Astoria is no longer the same," she said. "Tobacco is no longer the same, and you need to do something you can put your heart into." Emil said it would be his greatest wish, but he worried that the workers' contracts and the school payments would be dropped if he left. "If the school fails, it will destroy us both and Steiner too," he said. Berta sighed anxiously, convinced that her husband was now caught up in something that no longer was part of him, and she longed for him to be free.

"Come," said Emil, "Let's go to Vienna, go to an opera, visit friends." They did all that for a few weeks, but Berta's anxiety didn't lift. Toward Christmas Walter fell ill and had to stay in bed. The strain in the house was palpable. Christmas Eve arrived and, although they did not feel much like celebrating, Berta and Emil trimmed the tree, lit the candles and read the Nativity passages in the Saint Luke Gospel. One lone visitor, del Monte, came and offered them his friendship and his sympathy.

Then, wanting spiritual comfort, they decided to pack up and go to Dornach for the end of Steiner's Christmas lectures. Walter felt improved, but stayed at home. The weather was harsh and the drive hazardous, but they arrived safely on the evening of December 30th. The next day, they walked from their hotel in Arlesheim to the Goetheanum, breathing deeply of the bracing air. They paid a visit to Steiner, who sat chatting with Joseph van Leer, a businessman from Holland. Van Leer admired Dr. Noll's line of products and, having recently returned from America, he wished to promote them there.

"America is the land of opportunity," he said with a noticeable twang. "And they'll sell like hot cakes." The man's energy rubbed off on Emil, who imagined what an adventure it would be to represent anthroposophical products in the land he'd always wanted to visit.

Walking over to the Goetheanum afterward, Berta and Emil met up with their niece, Lisa. She was happy doing her eurythmy training in Dornach. She introduced them to her teacher and invited them to an afternoon performance in the large hall. They stayed together until it was time for Steiner's evening lecture.[24] At ten o'clock, after the lecture and after wishing everyone a happy New Year, the Molts started back toward Arlesheim through the woods. They did not get far before they heard sirens and saw an awful orange glow behind them in the sky. Retracing their steps, they were confronted by an inferno—the beautiful Goetheanum with its molded carvings and paintings was in flames. To the Molts, it looked as though raging demons out of the underworld had been let loose with hissing and cracking and tongues of colored fire devouring and melting the stained glass windows.

Flaming nightmare

If 1922 was a year of suffering for Emil, nothing he experienced came close to the horror and pain of seeing Steiner watch that incredible monument to peace and learning destroyed by fire, with no one able to save it.

Emil joined Lisa and others who were risking their lives trying to rescue books and whatever else they could. He hurt his arm on a burning beam, then sat on a cold stone, physically frozen and frozen in spirit, with every ounce of strength drained away. He looked for reasons why destiny could be so cruel. He thought about the millions in currency of all nations—from a child's saved allowance to a wealthy widow's bequest—that had flowed through the Goetheanum Trust under his supervision and how he had followed every detail of the thoughtful construction and artistic finishing.

Emil suspected it was arson; the culprit could have been sent by any number of enemies. *But who? Whom had the anthroposophists attacked? Was the idea of a spiritual world so dreadful that someone would try to burn it away? Where were the guards whose job it was to watch? Why did we not notice anything?...*" These questions plagued him as he sat among the

---

24 *The Spiritual Communion of Mankind*, Dornach, New Year's Eve, December 1922–1923.

251

The ruins of the Goetheanum

wreckage. Berta finally found him and gently pulled him off his cold stone. "You will catch your death sitting there," she said. "Come home to bed. Tomorrow we will help." He went home reluctantly but he couldn't get warm again. The shock was too great. The only consolation was that Steiner's statue, *The Representative of Humanity*, survived. It was still in the studio, awaiting the final touches. The fire was started behind the stage in hollow partitions between the walls. It had burned quietly during Steiner's lecture and then took hold after everyone was out. The arsonist was never found. In later years, Emil would write in his diary of this event:

> *On Michaelmas 1913 the building's foundation stone was laid. Seven years later, Michaelmas 1920, the Goetheanum was festively opened. Just two and one quarter years later, on New Year's Eve 1922, it was destroyed. Is it right to say that Steiner lost a part of himself in that dreadful fire and that his grief surely was the deeper cause of his later illness?*

> *Besides the good events there were sad ones. They caused us to feel solidarity with each other. On the night of New Year's Eve 1922, we were all shocked to hear of the Goetheanum burning. We felt*

so sorry for Dr. Molt. Of course many people also thought of Dr. Steiner. We hardly had the courage to begin work in the New Year.
                                                        – Friedel Reik

For days after the fire, with all other problems forgotten, everybody worked together clearing, cleaning, comforting each other. Steiner insisted that conference plans not be changed or postponed. He gave courageous lectures and was firm and eloquent. The traditional Oberufer Three Kings play was performed in one of the studios. Walter and Wagner arrived from Stuttgart to lend a hand. The Goetheanum Trust met in the Glass House, the studio where the stained glass windows had been made, to discuss immediate rebuilding—in concrete this time. They asked Rudolf Steiner to oversee the initiative.

Words cannot hurt

Berta left on January 3rd with Wagner to prepare for school. Walter and Emil stayed on for the rest of the week, Walter working with a young group of volunteers and Emil, his arm still bandaged, helping out where he could. *I am thinking clearly again,* he wrote to Berta, *without the emotional baggage that weighed me down.* The pain of his injury gave him a sense of perspective, so that, when attending a planning meeting with Uehli, Unger and Leinhas, he was calm in the face of some of the old criticisms.

Such words, he thought, *are just expressions of grief and feelings of bitter inadequacy.* He was convinced that the projects the anthroposophists had worked on over the years were not in vain and had been done because they were necessary. Of course there were repercussions, and if Steiner reprimanded them for not understanding or not getting the work done, it was certainly because he was frustrated himself at not being able to realize his vision. *What worries he must have endured as events initiated through him took their uncertain course.*

On his last morning in Dornach, Emil went to see Leinhas to share some of his thoughts and sensed a new connection beginning between them. Then he went to the afternoon eurythmy performance and evening lecture and left the next morning for Stuttgart. Berta met him at the station and took him straight to their garden. There, a large project was underway—the Molts were finally building their own house.

Over the next weeks, Emil traveled again; there was much to do for the business. Meanwhile Walter took his cousins, Dora and Lisa, and various girlfriends for wild spins in his car. Once, with Dora and Emil, he chased a train Emil had wanted to board and caught up with it at the top of a steep hill. Dora was full of admiration for her dashing cousin. She described him in her diary: *His hands are slim yet strong and dexterous. He plays piano well and has a wonderful sense of style. He is very discerning, able to judge people well and give practical answers. He has a very quick wit.*

At the beginning of February 1923, Emil's health broke down again. He spent two weeks at home in bed. He was feverish, with a urinary tract infection which was probably an aftereffect of the night on the cold stone in Dornach. Berta asked for a leave of absence from teaching to nurse him, and Dr. Noll prescribed anthroposophical medications and strict bed rest. Each day Wagner brought work from the office.

Meeting with delegates

On February 25th, 1923, anthroposophical delegates from all over Germany gathered in Stuttgart to discuss with Steiner the disputes between "old" and "young" members of the Society. The older group were people who had grown up before the war in an atmosphere of order and tradition. They had an enormous veneration for Steiner's words and resisted change. They couldn't understand the younger people, who grew up during the war. The latter wanted new experiences—some even calling anthroposophy "spiritual sport." The older ones saw them as frivolous but were seen by their juniors as unbearably heavy. Emil was out of bed by this time, but his doctor told him to stay away from the meetings. Berta disagreed and encouraged him to go with her, saying

Steiner would be there and that, with friends on both sides of the divide, he might be able to help.

Hoping to mend his own relationship with the Society, Emil went. After a presentation by Dr. Unger, Emil was invited to speak. He began by begging pardon for having been too sensitive in the past, saying nothing in his life was more important to him than anthroposophy and that he would work for it to his dying day—together, he hoped, with all of them. He was warmly applauded. "Now perhaps I can begin again," he said under his breath to Berta.

Steiner withdrawing from posts in Stuttgart

In spite of the best intentions, it was clear that neither Uehli nor Unger or Leinhas could hold the German Society together, and that became another source of distress for Steiner. One might have thought he would have imposed his will on them, but he did not. Rather, at the close of the meeting, he shocked everyone by announcing that he would withdraw from his posts in the German Society, the Waldorf School Association and even The Coming Day—to concentrate on his spiritual research and his teaching work. Back at home Emil made notes in his diary:

> Requirements for anthroposophical life: Strength for life is gained through experience. Memory is deeper than speech and binds people to each other, not through thoughts but through shared experience. Community is the key element. We might receive ever such wonderful ideas from the spiritual world but we won't understand anthroposophy until we understand the soul of the other person. There should be no divorce (two Societies—old and young) but rather union through differentiation—two groups of the one Society. Practice inner tolerance. Accept in equanimity even the most contradictory utterance as being a justified remark. Souls should not be expected to have to change themselves. The adversary knows what is needed to practice spiritual research, and he tries to prevent it by making us focus on controversy instead of having the time and peace needed for work.

His two new favorite mottoes were one from Steiner: *"Live in the love of the deed. Let live in the understanding of the other's deed. This is the motto of the free human being,"* and from Goethe: *"To understand the world, look into your own soul. To understand yourself, look into the world."*

Two days later, February 27th, 1923, Steiner was still in Stuttgart and it was his birthday. Emil and Berta went to see him and pledged their support. It was a poignant meeting for them, knowing he would henceforth be a rare guest in their city.

Emil's fever returned and he had to go back to bed instead of attending the teachers' conference with Steiner. Over the next several weeks, he worked a bit and rested, with hot compresses to his abdomen. Berta read to him and he dictated letters to her for their niece, Dora, who was studying in England. By now Dora had become the helpful and loving daughter they never had.

Securing support for the school

Leading up to Easter, Emil got a letter from Marx, urging him to take it easy and look after himself. Then he did get out of bed for an hour to entertain Philipp Reemtsma, a rising star in the tobacco industry, who wanted to tour the Waldorf School and the factory.

Later that spring, Emil mustered the strength to negotiate his contract with his new boss, Kiazim Emin. The current owner of the Waldorf Astoria factory flattered Emil, saying he admired his knowledge. He asserted that they would do great things together. He made that sound very tempting, but followed it with an intense and tricky negotiation, renewing Emil's contract for six years. Under this new agreement, Emil would serve as the Waldorf Astoria's general manager, overseeing finance, marketing and personnel, but not purchasing or technical matters. In return, Kiazim promised to uphold the Waldorf Astoria tradition of quality and to support the school.

That contribution was crucial. The Waldorf School had grown from 250 to 700 children, not counting the new kindergarten. Hundreds of parents were on the waiting list. As a private school it struggled financially, surviving on the donations of the cigarette factory and friends both at home and abroad. The Molts continued contributing out of their personal funds and helped finding "Waldorf godparents," people with no child in the school, yet willing to underwrite the tuition for a pupil.

The kindergarten

Berchtesgaden Hitler rowdies

In August, the family ventured forth for a holiday near Berchtesgaden where they had been the year before. By now, due to the devaluation of the Mark, their stay cost two million Marks each, but Emil probably paid in Swiss francs. On one very hot and murky day, they went to town and found it much altered. The rowdy and boisterous "Hitler people," as Emil called them, had arrived at the local dance hall. Walter and Felix were both fascinated and repulsed by their visceral self-confidence. Some of it rubbed off on Walter. He smirked at remarks made at the table, defied his father and was curt with a hotel guest. Emil decided that Walter would soon have to be cut loose, but Berta, good mother that she was, spoke softly to her son and brought him round. That crowd certainly infected the atmosphere in the place and the weather mimicked the mood, changing from beautiful to rain and thunder. They traveled back by way of Munich and Nuremberg, where a meeting that Emil was supposed to attend had to be canceled because of a massive National Socialist rally.

Playing brinkmanship

On September 19th, Emil met with Kiazim, who proposed selling Waldorf cigarettes in Italy and France, conjuring an image of Italy swimming in British pounds and France on the brink of extreme wealth. He was sure Waldorf cigarettes would fly off the shelves in both countries, and Emil could sell them in exchange for stable currency. Startup money, he promised, would be no problem—Emil could have whatever he needed. Emil calculated and came back to Kiazim next morning, saying he would need 20,000 francs to finance the new sales.

"Impossible," said Kiazim, thinking to play Emil, but he found himself matched in Levantine bargaining craft.

"How unfortunate," answered Emil. "I didn't know you were so short of cash."

"It was just a joke," Kiazim protested. "Everything is flexible, and we're just starting to negotiate." Then he mentioned that he could destroy Waldorf Astoria if he wanted to, since he now owned the competing company Turmac.

"Perhaps two businesses are one too many for you," Emil replied, beginning to enjoy himself. "But that is not my problem."

In time, Emil realized that the only reason Kiazim bought German companies was to use them as outlets for his own low-end tobacco. Once Emil knew this, he understood that his own insistence on quality was a potential thorn in Kiazim's side. For the moment, though, Kiazim needed him, and so Emil found himself more enmeshed in the business than ever.

Inspiration in a fragile Vienna

On September 27th, Steiner was to give the first lecture of a Michaelmas series in Vienna. Emil made the long trip because he found Steiner an even more powerful and poignant speaker since the fire. On his way from the train station to the lecture hall in Vienna's center, Emil's taxi was stopped. Hitler's "swastika people" were marching in the road and they looked intimidating.

"I wouldn't want to cross that crowd," the taxi driver said. Later, in the peaceful hall, Steiner talked about courage and about the spiritual powers waiting for human activity. "Failure should never prevent us from having an indestructible trust in the power of the spiritual world," he said.

The following morning Emil sat in the front row during the subsequent lecture about ancient Druid priests—their education relative to the cosmos, and their celebrations of solstice and equinox. Steiner described the cromlechs as receivers of the changing light over the course of seasons and what part this played in Druid ceremonies. A beautiful eurythmy performance followed.

Later that day Emil visited his former Patras boss, Albert Hamburger, and his wife. The company Hamburger & Co had been taken from them by Greece during the war. Since then they had settled in Vienna and joined the Anthroposophical Society. They lived a quiet life, content and glad to be home. *How courageous they are,* thought Emil, *to start life all over in a country that is becoming increasingly anti-Semitic.*

Together, Emil and the Hamburgers went to Steiner's late evening lecture. Perhaps because of the ungodly marching of Hitler's followers outside, Steiner talked about prayer and said, "If someone learns to fold his hands in devotion in childhood, he will be able to bless people in old age. Devotion in childhood and goodness in age allow the possibility of bringing peace into a room full of fighting, restless adults." Again he spoke of developing an active inner life rather than losing oneself in the external world and said that educating the heart to be a barometer of the cosmos is how to prepare for a true Michaelmas.

Later that night, Emil sat at the desk in his hotel room contemplating the events of the day. He had a profound experience which he recorded:

When someone lectures as Steiner does, truth is living in it. In my imagination I literally saw the Druid ceremonies as he spoke and was able to follow his research. I know it to be true. Tonight I make note of this inner experience while fully conscious. It is like a new life beginning and forces being awakened. I am standing before major decisions but in one respect I am different to the person I was before: I am clear and have the will to walk the path of destiny further with courage because I know it is the only way forward. I am sure I will be beset by darkness again—dragons will approach me. It is in my nature to counter these with emotion. But I shall

never again lose my trust in the spiritual world, nor trust in Steiner,
nor trust in my own spiritual self. I write this in case doubts arise;
it is a marker, as proof of the truth of these experiences. I pledge
faithfulness to Steiner and love for my wife as deterrents to these
adversarial powers.

The tobacco trust idea revisited

He went on to think about how to safeguard the tobacco industry in the continuing instability. He decided to try once again, if his business colleagues were willing, to create a cooperative structure in the form of a tobacco bank. He envisaged it underwritten by a financial institution and owned by the participants with their own currency, based on their combined tobacco holdings. Emil called Kiazim, who was immediately in favor of the idea.

On September 29th, his final day in Vienna, Emil visited his friend, General Consul Fanta, who was the director of the Bank of Vienna. Fanta saw merit in the tobacco bank idea but said Austrian banks were afraid of doing business with Germany.

"They didn't want to be seen as traitors to their country," he said. "It needs further discussion." They went to lunch, and by the end of it, Emil had Fanta's commitment. Happy with the morning's efforts, Emil joined his anthroposophical friends for the grand finale of Steiner's lectures.

Afterward, Emil decided to travel back on the Orient Express with Steiner. The Koliskos, Unger and Joseph van Leer were also among the passengers. The animated group chatted and discussed the impressions

Waldorf Credit Note, in billions
in the value of 1/4 dollar (Gold Mark –
fr 1.25)
"This note can be redeemed in most cigar
stores until December 31st, 1924, and is
guaranteed by the STK AG. Stuttgart
Nov. 1923"

of the past days. At one point, the conductor recognized Steiner from photographs and told the group proudly that he had a son in the local Waldorf school.

Berta met Emil in Munich. She traveled there to make sure his health was holding up. He assured her he was fine, and took her along with Kiazim's man Herbst to obtain approval for the tobacco bank idea from State Commissioner Gustav von Kahr.

After signing off on the bank plan, von Kahr felt compelled to demonstrate his allegiance to Hitler: "Hitler is a good person who wants a strong Germany," he told them. "The thing about the Jews is not meant badly. Nobody is thinking of being a Jew murderer, but their power has to be broken. Didn't Hitler manage to bring many communists and socialists under his wing with the German idea?…One only wants to cleanse Berlin of bad elements…The main hatred is against France. We have to arm, maybe sacrifice ten million people to free Germany. We have to forcibly throw the French out of the Ruhr, which will cause some devastation, but France will accommodate, then there will probably be a French revolution. England is behind us as an ally; it is only waiting for a strong Germany and will send us arms and munitions. Italy is behind us too. We have enough money for war…"

Emil backed out of there; he didn't even want to touch the signed approval, leaving Herbst to complete the negotiations.

A renewed relationship with the school

Back in Stuttgart, Emil turned his attention to the school, helping with its administration and correspondence in his spare time. This was his recreation, working with the teachers whom he liked and admired. He organized a meeting of business friends to find ways to cover the school's financial shortfall. At this meeting, the group was able to find 200 new godparents (each supporting one child), 200 business donors, and a number of individual gift givers—more than enough to keep the school in good financial health for a time.

In mid-October, Steiner arrived in Stuttgart to conduct another teachers' conference, and he invited Emil back to the faculty meetings. *I can hardly believe this,* thought Emil in response. *It is an honor and a reprieve.*

Establishing the tobacco union

On October 30th, the South German Tobacco Union was established with a nominal capital of ten million paper Marks. The Board included some of Germany's most powerful industrialists, who understood the benefit of this union not just to manufacturers, but to wholesalers, retailers, and ultimately the consumers. They issued scrip (stable credit notes). The practice was not unusual at the time. There was even "boot" currency, i.e., the value of a boot!

Emil went to the Finance Ministry in Berlin for permission to borrow gold for 500 million Marks backed by the tobacco bank. The official at the Ministry told him to just go ahead; there no longer seemed to be any authority. So they did; they created their own system in Stuttgart.

Hitler makes his move

On November 8th, while Emil was still in Berlin, Hitler and his leaders felt the time was ripe to make their move. Their base, Bavaria, was a hotbed of various groups opposed to the republican government. They demanded action. Hitler knew he had to move or risk losing the leadership of his party.

With Goering, Ludendorff and Himmler, he marched on the central beer hall in Munich where a large number of politicians and businessmen were convening. His intent was to kidnap the politicians and force them to accept him as their leader. Luckily his move failed and he was thrown in jail for five years.

Emil was glad to read about that outcome and hoped it would the end of Hitler's movement. His state of health was like a barometer of outer circumstances as he felt himself again.

Shortly after this the government stabilized the currency with the Rentenmark, and everything seemed normal for a while.

December 1924 diary entry

The Christmas Conference

…At the turning point of time
The Spirit-Light of the World
Entered the stream of Earthly Being.
Darkness of Night had held its sway
Day-radiant Light poured in the souls of men;
Light that gave warmth to simple shepherds' hearts,
Light that enlightened the wise heads of kings.
O Light Divine, O Sun of Christ!
Warm Thou our hearts,
Enlighten Thou our heads,
That good may become
What from our hearts we would found
And from our heads direct
With single purpose.

> – Rudolf Steiner, from the *Foundation Stone* mantram,
> given at the Christmas Conference 1924–1925 in Dornach

Emil traveled to Dornach to attend the Christmas conference. He went alone because Berta and Walter were both not feeling well. Lisa organized quarters for him. She told him about the many impressive guests coming from abroad, taking special note of Henry B. Monges, a suave American who had complimented her on her eurythmy performance. Seeing Monges at lunch, she introduced him to Emil, who liked his easygoing American style.[25]

During the conference, Steiner completely restructured the Anthroposophical Society. He appointed a Board made up of Marie Steiner (as custodian of the books, eurythmy and speech), the physician Dr. Ita Wegman, Dr. Elisabeth Vreede, Guenther Wachsmuth, and the Swiss poet Albert Steffen. Contrary to his former decision to remain independent of organizations and to devote himself to teaching and writing, Steiner took on the chairmanship of the Board—a decision he spent much time deliberating, but which he ultimately felt was essential. He emphasized the importance of the new Society as a world society. He said the times demanded complete transparency—books and lectures were all to be made available to the public. "It is to be a society of like-minded people, and not a society of statutes," he said.

Emil left the conference early in order to help Berta move into their new house. He found her feeling improved and eager to hear his report. They sat on the sun porch of their old apartment for the last time, looking over the city lights in a darkening sky, and discussed the conference. "It's all new," he said, telling Berta about the esoteric school forming in Dornach and that he had penned a request to Steiner:

> *Esteemed Dr: Please accept me in your school for spiritual science, in whatever class you think I am ready for. At this point I want to reiterate my promise to work for our sacred enterprise with my best forces. Heartfelt thanks for the rich spiritual treasures you have given us. In deepest devotion, E. Molt*

---

25 Emil could not have imagined that one day the shy Lisa would marry this man and move to America, settling up the hill from from his son Walter's family and the Threefold Farm. And that she would start a eurythmy school and bring her mother Paula and her widowed sister, Dora, with her son, Christoph, over from postwar Germany.

The Molt house and plaque

Berta's application letter soon followed Emil's:

Stuttgart February 11th, 1924. Esteemed Dr, may I request participation in the esoteric school in Dornach. As a teacher in the Waldorf School I would like to participate in everything related to education. With greetings and thanks, Berta Molt

Both Berta and Emil were accepted, and became members of what was called "The High School of Spiritual Science."

On January 4th, 1924, the Molts moved into their lovely new home, designed by Emil's friend Weippert. The house was on a quiet street, with a large garden behind it. It contained rooms for at least three students, a suite of rooms for meetings and study work, a large room each for Emil and Berta, and a library for over a thousand books Emil had acquired— including a Tauler bible and an ancient Merian. The centerpiece in Emil's study was a fountain of Saint Francis that a sculptor friend had made for him.

In the wake of his health issues, Emil found he no longer had the stamina to follow Steiner on his many intense lecture tours. But Steiner still occasionally came to Stuttgart, and meetings with him were very intimate in the protection of the Molts' new house. On March 27th, Steiner came to a faculty meeting at the Stuttgart school, where he talked with concern about the new children coming into the world. He said they would mature too soon and that regular schooling, which "stuffed brains with prosaic facts," would be especially hard on them. "It is shocking to see how old children are," he said. "We should give them back their childhood. Youth can be silly—the mantle of cleverness doesn't sit well on their shoulders."

Emil's health remained unstable. He continued to apply compresses to his stomach, which gave him an excuse to withdraw for a while each day, using the time to read Steiner's basic text, *The Philosophy of Freedom*, a study he would continue to the end of his life.

Four Waldorf students graduate

Four of Walter's friends—Rudolf Grosse, Karl Nunhoefer, Ulrich Schickler and Adalbert von Keyserlingk[26] were among the first graduates of the Waldorf School. They all knew Steiner well, and read his books with enthusiasm. They worried about the likelihood of harder times ahead and how to meet them, especially wanting a dynamic Waldorf-style college to prepare them for life in the best way. They called themselves the "Pentagram," and they included Walter in their group even though he was two years behind them in school. They often met at the Molts' house, glad to have Emil sit in as their mentor. After many discussions they penned a resolution and presented it to Steiner:

---

26 Rudolf Grosse went to Arlesheim to work with a special-needs boy, later rejoining the Waldorf School as a teacher. Karl Nunhoefer studied medicine and went on to a successful career as an anthroposophical family doctor in London. Adalbert von Keyserlingk walked in his family's footsteps, promoting biodynamic agriculture, and Ulrich Schickler became a scientist.

*At Easter 1924, the first Waldorf class will graduate. These days
a final exam is required for college. The Abitur (German leaving
certificate) is arduous and contrary to Waldorf principles because
this one-time test will decide the whole future of a developing soul.
We have to pass it to get into college. From everything we hear,
the sciences are no longer taught in a living way, comprehensive of
the whole human being. They are abstract and designed to serve
economic interests. We want a university that allows talents and
qualities slumbering in the human being to fully blossom and not
just be a place for learning a trade. We want a free college that
finds its task in fostering the anthroposophical understanding of the
world so that the abilities we have gained in the Waldorf School can
develop and become fruitful wherever they are needed.*

Steiner was pleased by the letter and read it aloud to the next group
he talked to, even though he was aware that such a wish could not be
fulfilled quickly.

Walter goes to England and a happy school

After his friends left the Waldorf School, Walter couldn't see himself
going back to finish his schooling without them. Emil agreed to let him
have one more year away from school on the condition that Walter go
to England to perfect himself in the language and learn British business
practices. Through Emil's connections, Walter was given a post at a firm
in England's North, and he learned the language quickly.

Meanwhile, despite the general malaise in the country, the mood in
the Waldorf School was positive—happy children were protected and
animated by the dedication and creativity of their teachers. The teachers,
in turn, were animated by the bright and eager young faces before
them—despite working hard for little pay. Many of the parents were still
workers at Waldorf Astoria, and while the factory no longer subsidized
educational activities for workers, its association with the school
provided the workers with more than enough cultural participation.

Berta and Olga Leinhas continued teaching handwork and bookbinding together, and Emil even set up a bookbinding workshop for them in the basement of the Molt house where they could practice. That year, under Berta's and Olga's tutelage, the children at the school were able to bind a copy of the four Mystery Dramas in leather, which they planned to give to Steiner as a birthday present. Berta and Olga grew closer through their work together, and Berta was a great comfort to Olga, whose husband had strayed from their marriage.

In early May, Steiner asked Emil to chair a meeting with parents and friends of the Stuttgart Waldorf School Association and to give an introduction and a financial report. As in former times, Emil initially felt trepidation, but then Steiner's presence gave him confidence and he suddenly broke through his anxiety. The meeting became warm and upbeat, full of lively contributions. For Emil, this meeting finally laid to rest the emotional residue of his earlier inhibitions. And yet, this 48-year-old businessman, used to conversing on equal terms with heads of state, knew he would always have to be extra vigilant to keep an objective middle ground between fearful doubt and over-assertiveness.

Basic guidelines for the Tobacco Trust

On May 10th, the Tobacco Trust Board members met to discuss inflation. "Let us leave old ways behind," Emil counseled. "Let us overcome animosities and apathy and combine purchases and advertising. Otherwise how will our businesses survive?" The members agreed and the meeting ended cordially. Emil had again achieved the remarkable social feat of bringing disparate businessmen together in an atmosphere of cooperation. He also managed to obtain an agreement from the Minister for Finance and Industry to let the Trust self-regulate rather than operate under State control.

"You see," Emil said later to Berta, "I must continue working for a while." Berta didn't agree; she saw him exhausting himself and running after a dream. Yet it was an important time for Emil. He was rehearsing, as it were, by trial and error and against all odds, for a future era when, according to Steiner, business life would be defined by selflessness. Emil was committed to bringing his tobacco colleagues with him into this future.

The demise of The Coming Day

At the next Board meeting of The Coming Day, Leinhas admitted that he could see no alternative to liquidation, although some members felt it might still be saved. Steiner suggested a supervisory board to implement a quick reform following the sale of everything non-essential. He told them, "Buying and selling should not be done by one person; it should be shared." *That is a truth hard come by*, Emil thought.

Accordingly, the supervisory board initiated the sale or liquidation of major holdings, paying back whomever they could while preserving the ventures that were involved in cultural activities. Del Monte took his factory out of the Trust. Miraculously, the Goetheanum project survived the failing Futurum in Switzerland, as did Ita Wegman's clinic. Edgar Dürler took over the medical laboratory in Arlesheim. He consolidated it with the laboratory in Schwäbisch Gmünd under the name "Weleda," making it into a company spanning two countries. Under Dürler's chairmanship Weleda took on the burden of paying back the accumulated debts, repaying shareholders over decades. This was an enormous source of relief for Emil, whose admiration for Dürler and Weleda grew.

An anniversary

Emil now turned his attention to a very special occasion. Shortly, he and Berta would celebrate their 25th wedding anniversary and he wanted to honor it with a carefully planned festival. First he ordered two rings from a goldsmith in Dornach, a master at fashioning jewelry with anthroposophical motifs. Steiner himself designed them.

On July 14th, 1924, the anniversary was celebrated in the flower-filled chapel of the Waldorf School. Walter, standing next to his parents, had come from England. Berta, in white, always slim, looked like a young girl, and Emil felt happy and devotional. Steiner sat with his wife, watching the ceremony with kindly attention. Afterward there was a reception at the Molt house. School-children brought flowers and sang. Dora and her brother, Siegfried, helped Walter and Felix serve guests. Emil gave a short speech recalling the past 25 years. It was a memorable day.

Walter, Dora and Felix Goll

Steiner's illness

On September 20th, 1924, while lecturing to theologians in Dornach, Rudolf Steiner said, "Before the etheric Christ can be understood in the right way, humanity will have to deal with confronting the Beast which will rise up in 1933." Nine days later, his strength was exhausted. News arrived in Stuttgart that he was seriously ill.

Berta and Emil followed reports of his illness. Together with their friends, they cared for the anthroposophical work without troubling him. They missed him terribly.

On New Year's Eve, the Molts traveled to Dornach to visit Steiner in his studio, where he lay in his bed at the foot of his statue, *The Representative of Humanity*. Dr. Noll assured the Molts that Steiner was slowly improving, but needed seclusion and rest and was too ill to receive visitors. Noll described Steiner's daily activities and how well Ita Wegman was caring for him while others looked after her clinic.

"She and Steiner are writing a book on medicine together," Noll said. "It will be a great work when it's done." Berta asked Noll to give Steiner the drawings and handcrafts she'd brought from the children in her class—they had also written to him of their love and devotion. Noll told Berta and Emil not to worry, that the love they brought was the best medicine, and that he would gladly pass it along to his patient.

Then Berta and Emil visited Marie Steiner, finding her dauntless as ever, willing to continue her travels and eurythmy work because her husband had asked her to. She would, she said, be his representative in the world during his illness, and the Molts promised their help and support. They went on to the Sonnenhof (an annex of Ita Wegman's clinic), where their young friend, Rudolf Grosse, lay recuperating. He had been called to Dornach by Steiner to look after a special-needs child but had fallen seriously ill on the way. He arrived only to learn that Steiner himself was ill. Berta and Emil brought him news of his friends in Stuttgart and wished him well for his work in the year ahead. They admired the healing atmosphere in the clinic—the caring staff, the colors on the walls, the fine linens and, permeating it, the Weleda fragrances. "You're in quite a hotel here," said Emil to Grosse.

Three Kings, three words and three things

That afternoon the Molts attended a performance of the medieval Oberufer Three Kings Play and in the evening a reading by Marie Steiner. Afterward, back in their lodgings, the Molts wrote to Walter in England. When they reviewed their day, Emil found himself remembering conversations he'd had with his revered teacher. "The question most people ask me when confronted with the term 'anthroposophy' is: 'Can you describe it in three words?'" He once asked Steiner, "What would you say?" "Doing your duty, selflessness, and contentment with destiny," Steiner had answered. "And what," Emil had asked, "are the three things that most harm a person?" "Untruthfulness, vanity, and ambition," Steiner answered.

Safeguarding support for the school

In early 1925, cigarette sales throughout Germany were stagnant and banks were not lending. Kiazim forced Emil to implement drastic cost-saving measures—older workers were sent into early retirement and others were simply dismissed. Then, as a result of Emil's extreme

271

sales efforts, orders began to flow in, and the company suddenly found itself short-staffed. Emil was constantly dealing with complaints and complications from the workforce, all of which were made more difficult by the volatile Kiazim. The fact that he was needed was the sole reason Emil stayed on, and he made sure his boss knew he would resign if pushed too far. In an effort to disengage further from the company, he sold his remaining shares to Kiazim.

Despite being constantly busy, when principals of the company came to Stuttgart, Emil made sure to show them the school, let them speak to teachers and observe the children. He would then bring them to his home for dinner with Berta. Emil's warmth and enthusiasm were so infectious that these business associates felt comfortable with him, and many became admirers of the school and company.

Berta's agitation

On February 26th, anxious about Steiner, the Molts drove to Dornach, this time with Olga Leinhas and the Waldorf teacher, Helene Rommel. They had hoped to be able to visit with Steiner this time, but were told that his state of health was still too unsettled. They attended a birthday celebration in Steiner's honor, although his friends celebrated in his absence. The party began with a rather somber address by Steffen, followed by a poignant rendering by Lili Kolisko of one of Steiner's verses, "Springing from Powers of the Sun."[27] As a birthday gift, the Molts had brought Steiner the copy of the Mystery Dramas that the children at the Waldorf School had bound in leather.

In Dornach Berta was agitated and fearful. She felt so poorly that they cut short their stay and drove back to Stuttgart. She went to bed with stomach cramps, and Emil canceled all of his appointments because he didn't feel too well himself. Dr. Kolisko came to see Berta, and she was comforted, speaking to him admiringly of his gifted wife, Lili, and her presentation in Dornach.

---

27 The last address by Rudolf Steiner, Dornach, Michaelmas Eve, 1924, GA 238.

The Simons' recommendation

Shortly after this, Ambassador Simons and his wife visited the Molts. They had just been to Italy and praised Sicily in particular, saying they'd been to many beautiful spots in Italy, but never any as interesting as the country's foot and the island it was kicking. But Emil had a strange dread of the place because he had read about the evil magician, Klingsor, and his castle Kalot Enbolot in Sicily. "We saw nothing evil there," laughed Simons. "No darkness at all."

On March 3rd, with the Simons' recommendations still fresh in his mind, Emil tidied his office and went home. "We're leaving," he said to Berta. "Where to?" she asked. "I don't really care," he answered. "Easter will bring a new beginning wherever we go." Berta was still weak, so he packed for them both, eager to be on their way. He helped her to the train and settled her in a first class carriage. Then, feeling ill himself, he agreed to stop for a few days at a spa in Zürich. This time their favorite Swiss town was depressing, the weather was cold and unfriendly, and instead of enjoying Zürich, they sat in their room. "Why don't we go to Dornach for Easter?" Berta said. "We will go on our way back when we're stronger, since our last visit there made us ill," Emil said.

The next day they looked out the window at the snow and decided to move on. At the train station, Emil went to the counter to buy tickets, but when he looked through his wallet, he realized that in his hurry he'd forgotten to take enough money for the trip. He rang his man Bruckhausen at the Zürich Waldorf factory who, rushing to the station with minutes to spare, brought him some cash.

Into the South

The Molts traveled to Genoa and booked themselves into the Miramar Hotel before taking a short evening stroll through the bustling town. The weather now was lovely and clear, but they were told there had been a fire on their steamer, and it wouldn't be available for several days. Emil didn't mind the wait, and Berta went clothes shopping since the things Emil had packed were completely inappropriate for Italy and its climate.

273

His yellow woolly suit, loden coat, and oldest hat were only outdone by her gardening hat, English tweed coat, and heavy boots. "What a fright we look," said Berta. She was an astute shopper and Italian fashion had a great allure for her. She came back from her excursion looking chic and wonderfully improved.

Finally, on March 10th, they were able to board the steamer and enjoyed their trip past Elba and Corsica. They arrived in Naples in the morning and booked a day room with a view of the sea at the Hotel Continental. They went out to visit San Elmo, sighting Mount Vesuvius and the islands of Ischia and Capri from afar. In the afternoon, after a walk to Castel Nuovo, they booked a sleeping compartment on an overnight train.

They admired the changing landscape out their window and settled into their bunks when the light faded. The next morning, they crossed to Sicily by boat and checked into the tourist resort of Taormina. Their suite overlooked the town and the expanse of sea beyond. As they explored, the Molts saw sure-footed donkeys and goats climbing among the rocks and the high villages that had been built to avoid the swamp fever of the plains. They admired the local people, finding them beautiful and graceful, with a noble bearing. They thought of Pyrrhus and Garibaldi, who both had landed here.

A strange wildness

But the weather turned, and over the next few days all they could see from their balcony was rain turning to sleet as the temperature dropped. Mount Etna was blanketed in snow, and they were trapped indoors waiting for better weather. When it didn't arrive, they ventured up to the lava beds in the Alcantara Valley, below the volcano that had erupted recently. There they watched hot air hissing and steaming over an area of approximately 30 square kilometers, and saw that the road had been completely blocked by hardened lava and sulfur salts. Fissures up to 20 meters deep lined the verge of the road. While the Molts watched, the snow began to fall again, mingling with the hot air to create a beautiful scene in black and white. One brief break in the clouds revealed to them a long mountain range, barren and vast, that quickly disappeared again. Now Berta was glad of her warm tweed coat and heavy boots—her thin little Italian outfits were of no use to her at all.

The Molts spent the next few days in the hotel taking shelter from the relentless weather, which even the locals marveled at. The grand finale on March 20th was a dreadful storm with rain, thunder and lightning more severe than local residents remembered having seen ever before. Nature had gone mad, and the Molts asked each other what had unleashed these forces. They had had enough and wanted to get away from that strange place, but no boats were venturing out on the wild seas, and they were trapped.

Uneasiness

On the 22nd, they moved to Palermo to be closer to whatever ferry might be leaving. They went out briefly for some sightseeing, but without enthusiasm, as they were weary and demoralized. Finally, five days later, they boarded a steamer and endured a stormy, sleepless passage to Naples, arriving there on the morning of the 28th. The weather was still cold and rainy, so they went straight on to Rome, passing through yet another thunderstorm on the way. They stopped at the Hotel Eden and ate in their room, feeling uneasy and wondering what fate was trying to tell them with this onslaught of violent weather. Deciding to spend one more day in Rome, they went to the Villa Borghese and, on impulse, visited the Catacombs, the "city of the dead."

On Monday the 30th, they left for Milan in bad weather, arriving at the Hotel Pellera late that night. A telegram from Emil's business associate in Rome awaited them:

Just received news from Stuttgart: Doctor Steiner passed away this morning 10 am. Walter informs that he is in Basel. Waldorf car brought Frau Doctor to Dornach. Greetings, Wagner.

Their revered teacher and beloved friend, Rudolf Steiner, had died and they had not been at his side.

Grief

The Molts took the first train to Basel, the weather now serene and clear. Walter met them at the station and together they went to Dornach to the studio where Steiner lay, surrounded by flowers.

Walter, introspective and highly sensitive to his surroundings, was overwhelmed. He was anxious for his parents and didn't have the heart to go back to England. Emil observed him and thought, *He will need much love.* In an effort to deal with his own shock, Emil looked for something to do, checking with the kitchens about providing food for the people streaming in, and assisting in whatever practical thing needed attending. Berta went to their room in the house of Mrs. Frey and sat by the window, quiet and immensely sorrowful as she remembered Steiner.

The Stuttgart school closed and sent its teachers to Dornach to participate in a memorial gathering organized by Albert Steffen. After the funeral service, the Molts attended the cremation. Then they returned to Stuttgart to attend another memorial, with eurythmy, held for parents and children at the school.

Despite Steiner's long illness, his death came as a surprise to many. Even his wife, Marie, who had been in Stuttgart with her eurythmy group, had been shocked to hear of Steiner's deteriorating condition on Sunday. With the Molts away and the Waldorf Astoria factory closed for the weekend, she hadn't been able to access the car that was usually at her disposal. She tried phoning Leinhas, but he was out and didn't see her message when he returned. At six the next morning she rang him again, desperate to get back to Dornach. Leinhas got in touch with the Waldorf Astoria chauffeur and drove with Marie to Dornach, but even so, they arrived two hours after Steiner's death.

Emil was sick for most of the following month and always tired. He was not sure whether his ailments were physical or psychological. He couldn't bear going in to his office and instead worked at home with August Rentschler. Dr. Kolisko prescribed him an iron remedy to balance what he characterized as "too much sulfur." He told Emil not to give in to his lethargy but to get up at six in the morning as always and to continue with his work at Waldorf Astoria. "You will only improve," he said, "if you are among people." Emil followed this advice, and even prepared a Steiner retrospective at his home, to which he invited the office staff.

On April 26th he ventured out to vote for the next German president and was disgusted when old General Hindenburg won by a small margin. *How can he take this country forward?* he thought. The radical right was beginning to assert itself over the powerful socialist left.

A threat to the school

The results of the German election immediately threatened the Waldorf School. For six years the school had been allowed to develop in freedom. Then an old federal law was invoked, stipulating that an experimental independent school could only operate for a maximum of seven years before being closed by the government. The Waldorf teachers received notification that from 1926 onward, a new first grade class would be discontinued and additional grades would be closed each year thereafter. Emil suspected the Waldorf School was being singled out, and he met with Mr. Niefer of the school board with his attorney, Dr. Lenkner, citing other independent schools in operation far longer than seven years. Emil learned that this law had never before been enforced, and Niefer advised him to wait while working toward State accreditation. "The school has enough friends who will stand by it if necessary," said Lenkner.

Meanwhile, Emil watched helplessly from the sidelines as The Coming Day plunged into final liquidation. Leinhas, the current director, claimed the world had failed to understand The Coming Day, and therefore the organization could not expand enough to realize its original idea. But Emil felt that it had actually expanded too fast, and that his associates were not able to keep step with the rapidly changing world. After The Coming Day's collapse, the Waldorf School was the sole remaining Threefold organization. Leinhas changed The Coming

Day company name to "Uhlandshöhe Corporation" and continued as the financial administrator of the school.

Walter goes to Rome

When things settled down after Steiner's death, Walter wanted to leave home again. Emil got him a post in Rome at a friend's bank and gave him some pocket money while imposing certain conditions:

- ~ Answer letters
- ~ Keep his parents informed about his health
- ~ Report on his work
- ~ Describe his cultural-artistic activities
- ~ Report on letters, etc., from others
- ~ Remember birthdays and inquire about people at home
- ~ Send economic reports
- ~ Send political reports
- ~ Inform his parents about books and articles he read
- ~ Let Emil know about meetings he attended.

For a while, Walter did write to his parents from Rome, but eventually his letters stopped coming and Emil wrote to Walter in search of news. Finally, in early August, Walter rang and asked his parents for money. He claimed his letters had stopped because he had been unwell. After this phone call, and against Berta's advice, Emil hopped on the next train to Rome. Walter was not too thrilled to see his father, but assured him he was indeed now fine. At the bank, Walter's manager told Emil how sorry he felt for Walter, so often sick and having to mind his bed. Emil noticed that Walter was more dreamy. He found it quite charming and invited Walter to his hotel for several meals to help build up his strength. On the last day of Emil's visit, he insisted on seeing Walter's quarters, probably imagining that Walter hadn't taken him there because his rooms were too shabby. "All right then, come along," Walter said. He took Emil to the top floor of an apartment complex, opened the door, and introduced him to Alma, the beautiful young Roman actress who had been taking good care of Walter.

When Emil came back home to Berta, she was genuinely angry with him. "Why can't you mind your own business?" she asked. "You are impossible. You have no trust in your son and, in fact, no trust in me. I had to let my maid go, although she was well within my budget, because you kept talking about our finances. And yet you spend money on useless trips and expect me to make do."

"I'm not tolerant enough," he pleaded with her. "I see that now."

"Walter is coming back for his summer break," said Berta, giving in. "We will take the young ones for a break." They went to Riva with Walter and he invited his friend Rudolf Grosse. Rowing out on the lake in the evening under the moon, father and son had a long talk. Emil apologized for his behavior in coming to check on Walter, and he promised to learn to understand Walter better. Walter told him about his life in Rome and about his girlfriend. Then he said he wanted to return to school to prepare for final exams, having realized that he needed a certificate to get on in his career. They rowed to shore in the best frame of mind.

Still working hard

From August through December 1925, Emil achieved incredible sales at Waldorf Astoria. Much of this was due to reorganization and a new advertising campaign. "Go for luxury, choose quality in tobacco," Emil insisted to his boss. "And don't spend too much on packaging—we are a cigarette factory, not a packaging company."

He still traveled a great deal, since most tobacco meetings took place outside Stuttgart. During these trips he read Steiner lectures, chatted with fellow passengers, and made use of his portable anthroposophical medicine kit. He tried to compensate for the tedium of travel by enjoying expensive meals in fancy hotels with friends and by visiting museums and theaters. But when he got back home, he was often met with disapproval from Berta. She told him he had put their own future on hold and too many pounds on himself—he was getting rather portly. "I am doing too much," he admitted. "But then, you are too. Why do you stay at school meetings until one in the morning?"

Reemtsma

Around this time, Kiazim entered into an alliance with the Reemtsma Company through their representative, the American businessman, Gutschow. Reemtsma, headed by two brothers with a large interest in New York, was already a leader in German industry. They wanted American tobacco to surpass the Orient in terms of quality and fame. Kiazim told Emil about plans for consolidating Waldorf Astoria, Reemtsma, Manoli, Zuban and Karnistri into one central firm with combined bookkeeping, manufacturing and storage facilities. This new conglomerate would be centered in Stuttgart, thanks to Waldorf Astoria's spectacular increase in sales and public respect.

Toward the end of the year, it became apparent that Kiazim had overspent and sent the company into debt. A number of investors were after him—one of them, while traveling on the train with Emil, pulled a pistol out of his pocket and told Emil he was so furious he had almost shot Kiazim. "Are you mad?" asked Emil. "Take that thing home and lock it away."

Kiazim, under stress, became abusive and claimed Emil was losing the company money. But Emil called Kiazim's bluff, saying he would be quite willing to resign and make room for a different director. "Nothing has changed," Kiazim said, "and there is absolutely no need to bring someone new in."

Emil told Berta that he was doing it for the school and that, without him, Kiazim would have gone broke long ago. Berta felt it unbearable that Emil had to keep working. She said her heart was giving her trouble. "You need rest," said Emil. "Take a leave of absence from the school."

"Winter has always been the worst time for me," she said gratefully. "Since we can still afford it, I will go and leave you to it." Emil booked her into the clinic in St. Moritz, and she made all the arrangements for the household. Then, with her friend Alwine, Berta spent three long months recovering in St. Moritz.

The attempt at an international Waldorf School Association

In 1926 Dr. Willem Zeylmans van Emmichoven in Holland, along with Emil and some teachers at the Stuttgart Waldorf School, initiated the international Waldorf School Association project. The group envisioned this new association as a network and means of collaboration, financing, and support for Waldorf parents, friends and teachers around the world. The Association was to assist startup schools and serve as their public proponent. The startup group discussed having the Anthroposophical Society appoint a board for this new venture, thus linking the Association with the Goetheanum. Dr. Zeylmans believed Holland to be well-suited as a base for this new Association, but the plan immediately ran aground when objections arose from some teachers in Stuttgart and from the administration in Dornach. Emil and Berta found themselves in the middle of the dispute, with friends on both sides of the issue. Leinhas traveled between Dornach and Stuttgart trying to mediate but couldn't resolve the conflict. He reported that Marie Steiner and Steffen would remain opposed to the Waldorf Association plan until everyone acknowledged Dornach's supervision.

Kolisko suggested having the spiritual center in Dornach, the educational administration in Stuttgart, and the practical, initiative center in The Hague. But even this proposal wasn't accepted and the project was abandoned. To alleviate stress and strengthen its relationship to Dornach, the German Waldorf School Association asked Steffen to become its new chair. He accepted, although he rarely came to meetings, leaving the vice chair, Emil, to preside.

In 1927 Fritz Lange released the movie *Metropolis*, a vision of the future set in the year 2000. The theme of his movie was anger, apathy and lack of trust in government—all real undercurrents in Germany during this time. Hated by their neighbors, reviled and caricatured in the international press, many Germans were not recovering from their poverty.

At a tobacco trust meeting in Berlin, Philipp Reemtsma became more dominant and Emil admired him for his success. However he

Emil holding on

experienced the same malaise among his partners that he saw gripping the country: The members could not gauge the future. Interest in the organization had diminished, and non-member competition had become fiercer. Clearly, the glow of togetherness had waned. They talked of temporary price cuts to survive against the competition. Emil pleaded against reneging on their own policies, but they scolded him for not going along with the times.

In March, Kiazim sold half his Waldorf shares to the Banque Belge in Paris and sold the Swiss Waldorf Astoria outright. He had to sell because he had incurred too many debts. Emil went to Zürich to supervise the transition and found it hard to say goodbye to his employees, some of whom, like Sophia Kaiser, he'd worked with for years. Wanting solace, he ate at the Baur au Lac, remembering lunches there during his honeymoon when he'd struggled to be nonchalant while marveling at the high "service charge." He rang Berta to tell her about his lunch and the sale. "I don't care who buys the shares anymore," he said. "It's a game that's out of my hands. I still have my contract, and whom I work with on a day-to-day basis is more important to me than who owns the company."

"This is cause for celebration," Berta said. "Come to St. Moritz, just for the weekend! The weather is perfect and I'd love to see you. Shall I meet you in Chur?" He agreed, happy as a boy going to meet his sweetheart. Arriving in Chur, he found Berta waiting for him, looking beautiful and assured in ski pants and a leather jacket.

"I feel so well," she said as they drove off. The long road through the woods and the stretch over the pass to St. Moritz brought back fond memories. The Chantarella hotel, unaffected by downturns and upheavals, stood as solid as a castle above its frozen lake and the crystalline mountains framing it. Emil put on a pair of skates, delighted that he still managed to cut a good figure after ten years, and Berta skated even better than she had before.

At the end of the weekend, Berta accompanied Emil back to Chur. They stayed the night in the same hotel they'd found on their honeymoon. Strolling through town, they enjoyed every detail, watching shops close their shutters and restaurants open their doors for dinner. At the train station they parted reluctantly, Berta heading back to St. Moritz while Emil went on to Zürich and business life. But their separation would not be for long, as they planned to meet in Venice in time to celebrate his birthday.

The following week he met with Mrs. Olin Wannamaker, a wealthy American whose daughter attended the Stuttgart Waldorf School. She wanted advice on how to involve herself in an anthroposophical activity in the States. Emil, who still had dreams about America, took her on a tour of the various anthroposophical initiatives in Stuttgart. The experience filled the lady with such eagerness that she and her husband soon started the first American Waldorf school in New York City.

Birthday

Soon Emil was on the road again. After a short stop in Munich, he traveled to Trieste in northeastern Italy, now the most important tobacco gateway to the East. On April 14th, his business done, he met Berta in Riva on the Lake Garda, at Signora Zantini's cozy hotel. They ordered lunch and he got a surprise birthday cake for dessert. Afterward, they strolled along the lake, and the beautiful weather was like an additional birthday present. Berta, fit and ready for the next part of the celebration, had booked a trip to Venice. But Emil needed rest, so they spent an extra quiet day in Riva. By Saturday, Emil declared himself ready for the excursion, and over the next two days they did a grand tour of Venice—beginning with a gondola ride to the Rialto. They admired San Marco inside and out, sat in a café listening to music and throwing crumbs to the pigeons, and visited museums and churches. They took a boat down the Canale Grande to the Lido and watched glass-blowing in Murano, and in the evening they lingered in a bistro and caught a moonlit gondola back to the hotel.

In Germany in those days, the school year still ended in the springtime and the new school year started after the Easter break. At the end of the year, the school always presented the work of the pupils in a final assembly, which Berta and Emil attended. Afterward, Emil wrote:

Burdened by business cares, I attended the school end-of-term assembly. Class teachers stepped to the podium one after the other, describing the past year and talking about plans for the coming one. Their pupils were attentive and applauded enthusiastically after each speech. I had the impression of teachers and students as one integral whole. An invisible web of belonging filled the room, and in this atmosphere my clouds of worry dissipated and a sunny wave of joy broke through in an elemental way. I returned to my work renewed.

We live in an unhappy time. Economic uncertainty and a terrible pessimism pervades. Everyone experiences this on a daily basis and it weakens our courage and our will. Our former remedies for overcoming problems are ineffective now. We are going through a dark period of materialism. The longing for inner life fills our hearts, but it keeps getting harder to find it in our outer life.

This is why I experience the school as so important and it is not the first time I've experienced it. Every assembly, every demonstration, whether eurythmy, gymnastics or music, brings a transformation of mood. The shadows recede, the light breaks through.

What is the element that creates this miracle, this real and not imagined medicine for the illness of our times? My observation teaches me: It is the power of love which conquers the powers of darkness. It arises out of the hearts of Waldorf teachers and penetrates the children's souls. Admiration for the teacher opens their hearts and allows them to receive their teaching. Not with dry intellect alone but with the heart, organ of life, do the children take up their lessons. It makes them happy, it makes them delight in their school. – Emil Molt, Easter 1927
Personal impressions of the Waldorf School

284

Both the Swiss and the German Waldorf Astoria sold again

That year the Dresdner Bank bought Waldorf Astoria for a 500 million Mark guarantee. Emil visited Kiazim and found him devastated and in debt, his dreams shattered. Kiazim said the sale of the Swiss Waldorf Astoria had not been enough to bail him out, and Emil felt sorry for this adventurous businessman. *If not in this life, we'll definitely meet again the next time round,* he thought. Colleagues and adversaries in the tobacco industry found Emil interesting for this reason. He acted according to his understanding of the laws of karma, believing that once a relationship is formed with another person, threads are woven that have an effect on future lives.

When Emil heard that Kiazim still had a large amount of tobacco lying in the warehouse, he was able to persuade two shareholder friends of his to buy it from Kiazim.

That summer the American businessman Gutschow, whom Emil had first met during his time at the United Cigarette Works, turned up again at a tobacco gathering in Dresden. The nervous sales representative of previous years now wore a comfortable mien and invited Emil to lunch. He said his business had almost failed in Germany before he was able to connect with Reemtsma and persuade him to amalgamate with Gutschow's American sponsors.

"It's been easy ever since," he said. When Emil said he'd be in Hamburg and would like to visit the Reemtsma factory, Gutschow was delighted. He arranged for Philipp Reemtsma to take Emil and Marx around the plant, and Emil found it fascinating, modern and efficient. He admired the large mixing funnels, the ventilation that sucked tobacco dust away, as well as the efficient packaging methods. The Reemtsma brothers, Philipp and Hermann, were dynamic young businessmen, clearly on the rise, and they chatted with Emil about connections abroad and business associations in German industry until late that night.

After this visit, Emil was hardly back in Stuttgart before aggravation began again. His tobacco master, Sterghi, was in hospital after crashing the company car, and a warehouse inventory revealed large amounts of unregistered and now useless tobacco. On top of all that, the finances were in a critical state. By now, Emil realized he felt unwell whenever he was in Germany.

I am bereft, he now thought. *I have lost my fair and precious country, or rather it has lost me because I don't understand it anymore. I long to travel abroad because I feel helpless to change the dark cloud hanging over Germany.* Through sheer force of will Emil had kept Waldorf Astoria together, but the company had sustained too many shocks, and with Emil's weakened health keeping him out of the office, the company's sales took a downturn.

Walter and Dora graduate

In March, Walter and Dora took their final exams. The written tests went on for four days followed by oral exams. Then everyone held their breath in anticipation, waiting for the results. The family took walks, played music and read to pass the time.

Both Dora and Walter passed their exams, and Walter decided he wanted to go to university in Berlin. Emil took him to an

Walter Molt graduation

interview, but for one reason or another, the university did not accept Walter. When Emil found out, he was outraged. "Who do they think they are?" he said. "There are plenty of other universities." He wanted to get in the car and take Walter to visit more schools.

"The deadline is past for the next semester and I've decided my next step," Walter told him. "I have business experience. Perhaps I can find something in the medical field."

This exchange left Emil thinking of the trip to the Orient he'd promised Walter. Where would they go and what could he show them? For once Berta was supportive of his travel plans—she felt sorry for his loss of spirit and would go anywhere with him to find it again. Besides, she was curious to see the lands he had praised so much.

Revisit the East

So on March 23rd, the family took a train to Munich, then Agra, and from there a sleeping train through Serbia to Saloniki. They traveled first to tobacco markets, Emil always doing a little business as they went. After his final business transaction, Emil took on the role of tour guide, taking Walter and Berta to see the sights and showing them landscapes dotted with wandering shepherds. They were met with wonderful, warm hospitality, and, surprisingly, modern German appliances.

The Enfiezioglou family hosted them in the beautiful coastal town of Cavalla, and Berta took an immediate liking to the matriarch, who spoke some German. Leaving the women together to explore the town for a day or two, Emil and Walter took a side trip further east along the coast to Drama, where the swamps had been drained and converted into fine tobacco fields. Finally, Emil brought his family to Athens, showing them the Acropolis and Piraeus. On April 7th, in rainy weather, they boarded the ship *Cleopatra* to Brindisi and then took the train back home.

Berta's mother joins them

On April 14th, 1928, Emil's 52nd birthday, his sister-in-law, Paula and her husband brought Berta's mother to visit for a birthday celebration. Mother Heldmaier ended up staying with the Molts, as she needed care and had become too frail to live alone.

This new houseguest didn't prevent Emil from taking Berta and Walter along to Paris on his next business trip. "After all," he said to Walter, "had you been accepted to the university in Berlin, you could not have come. I go to Paris frequently, but you and Berta have never seen this fairest of all cities. While I'm busy at Banque Belge, you can enjoy yourselves." Berta and her son took Emil up on this offer and savored the romance of the boulevard cafés, the museums and the parks—they even went to Chartres. Berta found this trip particularly enjoyable and invigorating.

Mürren

In July, Emil chose the Swiss Alpine resort of Mürren as a summer retreat. Emil and Berta went to Mürren by way of Dornach because Emil wanted to bring Steffen up to date on the school. Steffen seemed burdened and asked whether he shouldn't step down as Association chair. Emil thought it would be a shame to lose this important link with Dornach. "Besides," he told Steffen, "coming from Switzerland, you have a more objective view. We are going to Mürren—come and spend a few days with us. We'll have more time to talk."

Steffen agreed to join them later on, and the Molts traveled over the Bruenig Pass to their hotel—a resort with a sanatorium perched on an enormous cliff with views to the Swiss mountain peaks. Emil was prescribed a rigorous schedule of treatments and sent to bed. His entertainment was reading about Frederick II, the king who had reigned in Sicily, while Berta and Walter hiked through mountain meadows and to the Rhone glacier.

Mother and son

Walter was glad to be escorting his mother, but he felt a bit trapped, thinking about how often he had tried to start a life of his own and found himself returning home in response to a feeling that his parents—particularly his father—needed him. His name, which Steiner had chosen for the Molts, means "caretaker," and indeed he had become his parents' caretaker. Despite his inner turmoil, Walter kept his thoughts to himself so as to avoid spoiling his mother's holiday. But he too fell ill with a fever shortly thereafter, and Berta found herself tending to her two men.

While still in Mürren, Emil received a letter requesting his presence at an awards ceremony at the university in Tübingen. This was the town where, nine years earlier, Emil had lectured to the student body about the Threefold Social Order. Now he was surprised and moved to discover that the university wished to present him with an honorary doctorate:

> *The Eberhard-Karls-University at Tübingen grants Councilor*
> *of Commerce Emil Molt, General Director of the Waldorf-Astoria*
> *Cigarette Factory in Stuttgart, in recognition of his achievements*
> *for peace among workers and community, the honor of a doctorate*
> *of Political Sciences.*
> *Signed by the Chancellor of the University, Tübingen, June 16th, 1928*

Emil accepted the honor and became "Dr. Molt." Walter congratulated him but was secretly sad in light of his own thwarted academic hopes. Walter was also very aware of his cousin Dora's activities, as she was pursuing her own studies in London with Emil's financial help. The family returned to Stuttgart with Walter searching for his own next step.

Doctoral award

Inauguration

At Michaelmas, September 29th, 1928, the Molts traveled to Dornach for the inauguration of the new Goetheanum. It had been built in record time with the insurance money from the fire and was an enormous achievement—a powerful building made of concrete, with stained glass windows and a huge hall. Steiner's mystery drama, *Portal of Initiation*, opened the festivities, while teachers and physicians, poets and philosophers spoke from the large stage.

The Molts were deeply impressed by this new headquarters of the worldwide Anthroposophical Society, and Emil was relieved to find that, in this celebratory atmosphere, his old rift with Carl Unger was quite healed.

The new Goetheanum

The European Union idea

In Stuttgart after the Goetheanum celebration, Emil attended a conference of people promoting a united European Union, initiated by Count Richard Coudenhove-Kalergi, an Austrian aristocrat and political activist. Some of the principles of this new idea were interesting to Emil—the union supported the abolition of national borders and the facilitation of international business. But Emil had concerns that this new union might create giant conglomerates, stifling politics and culture.

Emil's attention was diverted from the European Union idea when a large amount of Waldorf shares changed hands. The Reemtsma conglomerate had bought out the other shareholders, thereby becoming majority owner in a move that worried August Rentschler. Rentschler's worries proved well-founded when, just before Christmas, Emil and the other managers were notified that Reemstma was closing down Waldorf Astoria in the coming months. Emil was told that the workers would be let go. No amount of meetings and arguments on his part made the slightest difference, and Christmas was a gloomy and sorrowful event.

Waldorf Astoria closed down

On March 7th Emil received personal notice that his contract was to run until the end of the year. Exactly seven years after The Coming Day had sold the company to the discount bank, the liquidation of Waldorf Astoria had begun.

April 6th, 1929

The Management of the Waldorf Astoria Cigarette Factory to its people:

We are obliged to give you notice of the following: The main shareholder of Waldorf Astoria, citing the difficult situation of the tobacco industry, took advantage of the opportunity to sell a large part of his shares to the Reemtsma company. The latter does not wish to continue production in Stuttgart; the plant will therefore be closed.…We will do what we can to delay the closing and will keep you informed, asking you meanwhile to please continue to do all you can in the interest of the company.

With best regards, E. Molt

In economic life, thought Emil, as he prepared to say goodbye to Waldorf Astoria, *the fate of thousands is decided by one person buying and selling shares.* Emil accompanied the Mayor of Stuttgart to a meeting in Hamburg with Philipp Reemtsma, and together they were able to get Reemtsma to promise continued support for the school over a period of ten years. Additionally, Reemtsma promised to keep working with Waldorf's suppliers as far as feasible, to give laid-off employees severance, and to pay the city a significant amount to alleviate the financial difficulties of the firm's older workers.

From 1925 on Herr Molt began to be absent more and more for health reasons. This alone can explain such an end as that in 1929. It came like a cataclysm of nature and we were thunderstruck. A factory doing so well—bought out by the competition: Reemtsma! Much later, I came to think that a sacrifice had to be made for

all the beauty and goodness surely awakened in many hearts—
a sacrifice for the Waldorf School, which then still had to prove its
success. Yet the greatest sacrifice was made by Herr Molt and his
family... – Waldorf Astoria employee, Friedel Reik

Reviewing their lives

April 14th, Emil's birthday, was a strikingly beautiful day that year. It fell on a Sunday, and in the early morning as the bells rang in town, Berta and Emil walked in the budding woods together and hoped that the day's beauty was a good omen. They were both 53 years old, but their life together had been so intense that the time seemed much longer. It had been five years since Steiner's death, ten years since the school opened, fifteen years since the war began, twenty years since Emil's first trip to the East with Marx, and twenty-five years since the Molts had found anthroposophy. After their walk, their heads filled with thoughts of the past and future, they went to the Sunday children's service and, later that evening, celebrated with a small group of friends and family.

Marx and the Molts in Berlin

On April 22nd, Emil and Berta went to Berlin for further negotiations—Waldorf Astoria had a thousand threads that had to be carefully cut. Marx met Emil in Berlin and stood by him during the negotiations, despite managing the burden of his own financial loss and Germany's mounting animosity toward his religion. The Molts and Marx went to the opera in the Charlottenburg Theatre that night, and it seemed a gesture from the artistic hand of fate that the program was Mozart's *Magic Flute*—the same opera that had marked the Waldorf School's opening.

The next day Emil met with Marx, Rentschler and Privy Councilor Fischer to plan the company's closing. They agreed that liquidation was to be accepted gracefully but without compromise. In the evening, after sorting everything out, they decided to go to a comedy show to put things in perspective. The title was, appropriately: "When will we see each other again?"

> *From 1920 on I worked in the payroll office, and we sometimes stayed longer, with those cleaning up. On one of the last days I visited Herr Meyer in the machine room. His job was to supervise the running of the large machines, which were now going to be destroyed. I found him sitting on a crate, with dirty hands and face, crying. He was suffering pangs of the heart. "I myself have to smash what I've tended for years. Sometimes I spent hours under these machines when something needed fixing. Oh, I just can't, I can't go on!" I could do nothing but sit down beside him and cry as well—it was wretched. Herr Meyer later got a position as supervisor in a cigarette factory in Holland. As a farewell he brought me chocolates, saying, "Nothing consoled me as much as you did, when you sat down beside me on that crate."*

> *Once I saw Herr Molt again at a school assembly, and later still I wrote him. One day I happened upon an old tobacco-woman who told me that several of them still got together every week to pray for Herr Molt. Hearing this, Miss Allmendinger said to me, "Write him that. He'll be pleased. He always asks after you when I visit." When I did this, he sent me a few lines. – Friedel Reik*

Earlier in his life, Emil would have fumed and raged against the liquidation, but now he proceeded calmly, swimming through the devastation as best he could. Years earlier he had felt forsaken by his friends, with only Berta standing by him. But now he had warm support from Palmer, Kolisko, Rentschler, Mayor Lautenschlager and Marx. Marie Steiner also sent Emil her heartfelt condolences at the loss of Waldorf Astoria.

A final invitation

On Friday, May 24th, Waldorf Astoria's formal closing gathering took place in the large hall of the Wulle beer factory. Emil addressed his workers.

My dear Waldorf people!

It was the heartfelt wish of Mr. Rentschler and myself that we meet once more in the closed circle of the "Waldorf work community." It is deeply satisfying that we can be together.

Strange to say, our very first Waldorf gathering was in this very hall about twenty years ago. Looking through the hall at so many dear coworkers, we deeply feel the calamity that has broken over us, and we cannot quite take in that we are really to part from what has united us for so long. I believe it will take many weeks until we fully realize what it means to no longer come into our—I would like to say beloved—Waldorf, greeting each other and exchanging a word or two.

According to modern views, a company consists merely of workers and a certain quota of production. We had a completely different background, people who were connected: their destinies, their joys and their sorrows. It created a spirit that bound us together and only now, when we are to be dispersed, will we see what it means to have been such a community within an economic venture...

When the war came, production took off. Waldorf workers were in the field of battle, some from the first day to the last. We had luck; many of those people came back to us and for that we are still grateful. Then came the year 1922. Before that, during the time of the revolution, we tried to initiate change. When the old social order broke apart, we were looking for new forms...If we did not succeed it was not only because our own forces were not enough, but also that the world resisted...I believe if our efforts had succeeded we would not be standing in the face of the present calamity. I must say that, unless business people change their thinking and find new forms, we will not see an end to difficulties.

Waldorf Astoria will not be forgotten because the Waldorf School remains...We who are grown up and already old at 40 know that change will only come from a maturing younger generation; they can bring new ideas if they are allowed to develop toward a future that is different to the one we experienced. We were young in a past when ideals still existed, and with peace and a certain security we were able to pursue our dreams. Now we have behind us a lost war and inflation brought about by the impoverishment of the whole of Germany. I will say, the more we pull back, making do with less...the less chance we will have to keep our cultural gifts...

If we admit to ourselves that our whole nation is in a state of extreme straits, we will understand that the more we reduce and close enterprises, the more the population will become impoverished....

One last request: On going out into the world, you are truly cast abroad as once the nation Israel was after the destruction of Jerusalem. But please be assured, we had a work community that was built on human inclination. Carry this spirit of Waldorf with you to your new places of work and show how exemplary this spirit is. Then good will come about out of what seems so hard now, in the knowledge that we are merely seeds in a new social order, in a new way of thinking and feeling. Then you will be aware, even if we are physically apart, that we still have an inner connection. Be assured: Herr Rentschler and I will never forget a single one of you. The image of each one, the face, the gestures, the way of working, often the fingers, this we will carry into the future and we don't yet know what it will bring.

And now I will hopefully have the opportunity of talking with each one of you before this evening is ended, and I want to wish you good luck from my innermost heart, in spite of the sorrow of today. In this vein I say: Be well and happy in your future. – Emil Molt

On October 17th, 1929, the daily paper, *Stuttgarter Neues Tagblatt Nr 484*, featured an article by Emil:

The [Waldorf] school was formed in revolutionary times to help heal society. Why is it so hard to bring about such a future? Have things improved since then? We need only look at our public life for the answer. The political domain is filled with party-egotism. Goals that could bring Germany respect do not prevail. What Rudolf Steiner said in 1919 is still valid now: "Party opinions are wandering around us like judgment mummies, rejected by reality." The best among us are kept at a distance and can't become active in political life, and the young cannot find any relationship to circumstances. In the economic domain, egotism is rife as never before. Americanization under the motto "rationalization" has moved in, which fosters the battle of all against all. The more foreign capital is pumped into the empty blood vessels of our economic body, the more we forget our main national task which is to manage business in such a way that it creates social fairness and a basis for our cultural offerings. How far we are removed from that is shown by the common phrase in large corporations: "Eat or be eaten." Waldorf Astoria has been sacrificed to this principle and the Waldorf School has become endangered, deprived of its protective sheath.

Our cultural life is in decline instead of serving growth. All we have to do is read our newspapers. It can only improve when the spirit living in the Waldorf School flows into all parts of our social life. If it can fructify our cultural life as well as bringing to birth true rights and true service, then the social question will go toward its solution. To form this future in the right way is the noblest task of today's youth. Our time is short, we cannot wait. An awakening out of the daze which has caught hold of all of us will show that the reprieve our Western people are still enjoying will be over.

Stock market crashes again

On October 24th, 1929, the stock market in new York crashed. Many American companies called in their overseas loans and European banks failed subsequently. In Germany, the economic downturn had begun in the middle of 1928—first in agriculture, which suffered from overproduction, then extending to industry with concomitant unemployment—and now the economy plummeted. The Goetheanum suffered as well, with former large donors no longer able to contribute, although many small donations still flowed in. For the second time in that decade, the German people lost their savings and their confidence, and again protests arose. "Bring back the old ways!" called the monarchists. "Down with capitalism!" shouted the communists. But the National Socialist voice proved most persuasive, calling for Germans be proud and fight back.

The country longed for strong leadership, and, to the distress of most German anthroposophists, many people were taken in by Hitler's words. "For this at least I am thankful," Berta said to Emil, "that you are no longer responsible for the company and that all contracts with Reemtsma were made before the crash. This present stroke of fate you could not have survived."

"Berta," said Emil, "Walter has moved out, you are often away, and I don't have the strength to work in our large garden. Let's put vegetables there again for teachers and others, as a kind of 'Liberty Garden' during this financial depression." Berta agreed and soon found a capable gardener. He came and often brought his little son Walter along. This garden, along with the school, gave the Molts strength through these difficult economic times.

The Waldorf Spirit

In 1930, while Berta was still teaching, Emil questioned whether his entrepreneurial days were finished. Although he was financially fairly secure, thanks to his pension and some savings, he knew that the days of large spending and donations were behind him. He also realized, with a pang of regret, that his moment for joining Weleda had passed: Dürler was managing the company's facility in Switzerland, and Leinhas was managing the Schwäbisch Gmünd branch. Van Leer headed the

Austrian Weleda and Madame Gracia Ricardo the tiny American branch. Meanwhile, Walter applied for a job at Emil's friend Walter Rau's soap factory and was accepted as an apprentice.

Emil then turned his attention to helping some of the newer Waldorf schools, advising them on building plans, teachers' salaries and fundraising. He spoke of Steiner's social ideas and suggested ways out of the depressive economy. As part of these efforts, both he and Berta visited school conferences in various communities. In Stuttgart, he advocated opening a second school to accommodate the many parents who were being turned away. Through this work, Emil began hearing more about Waldorf initiatives around the world. He even received a letter from a Dr. Mehta in India that described a new Waldorf school there where Waldorf toys and handwork were in use. Mehta called this new initiative an "educational revolution." Emil also met regularly with economists and business people, engaging them as potential school supporters.

A destiny contemplation

On a summer's day in 1930, Emil was invited to Dornach to give an account of the circumstances surrounding the demise of his firm. In essence, it was to be a lecture about destiny. In preparation Emil contemplated Saint Luke (12:12): "For the holy ghost will teach you in the same hour what ye are to say." He opened Steiner's *Anthroposophical Leading Thoughts* in search of more inspiration. There he found Meditation 90: "In dreamless sleep-consciousness man experiences, all unconsciously, his own being permeated with the results of past earthly lives. The inspired and intuitive consciousness penetrates to a clear vision of these results and sees the working of former earthly lives in the destined course—the karma—of the present time." These two passages gave him strength and inspiration, and he found himself feeling more prepared.

On his way to give the lecture, Emil paused at the studio where Rudolf Steiner had created his great sculpture and where, in the summer of 1920, he had asked Emil to assume responsibility of "Curator" for the Threefold movement. Emil then proceeded to give his lecture, and it was well received. Afterward he thought about the descriptive images he had used—how, after a burgeoning, blossoming life, a deathly quiet had entered Waldorf Astoria, and how it became like a cemetery within the space of six weeks. It suddenly reminded him of Klingsor's garden in the medieval romance *Parzival* by Wolfram of Eschenbach, a story all Waldorf high school students get to read. Klingsor's beautiful magic garden disappeared after Parzival redeemed the spear and took it to the Grail castle. In the same manner, Emil said to himself, the Waldorf spirit was brought to the Uhlandshöhe: to the school!

Edith

In 1932, while taking a mutual friend to the train station, Walter met Edith Emma Elisabeth Lichtenberg, the daughter of the popular Stuttgart physician Friedrich "Fritz" Lichtenberg. At twenty-two years

Edith

old, she was a fearless, modern flirt who wore her hair in short curls and her skirts short as well. Walter was taken by her style and asked if she'd like to have supper with him—he was going to meet his father at the Hotel Marquardt. She didn't hesitate to accept, intrigued by the prospect of meeting the famous Emil Molt, although she was not too impressed by Walter. Emil, sitting quietly at his usual table, was suddenly beset by a whirlwind of energy— Walter laughing with uncharacteristic merriment beside a freckled, redheaded young woman.

"We walked into the dining room and met an energetic, small man with a round, bald head and penetrating blue eyes, sitting alone at a corner table," Edith recalled. "He was obviously a powerful personality, with much warmth and humor. I immediately felt drawn to him."

Emil jovially began interrogating Edith, testing her mental capacity —a strategy that had, in the past, reduced some of Walter's girlfriends to tears. But Edith was different, boldly giving back as good as she got and making Emil laugh. By the end of the meal, he had invited her to a concert at their house, and she promised to come, eager to see this fascinating man again.

A concert in the Molt house

"Dr. Molt is expecting you," the maid said to Edith when she arrived at the Molts' house on the night of the concert. The maid led her past three elegant reception rooms and two grand pianos to Emil's study. Edith was astonished by the luxuriousness of the house. The study was a smaller room with a working fountain and a hand-carved desk. Three walls contained floor-to-ceiling shelves of books, some burnished with age, some with linen covers and gold lettering.

"Do you like my fountain?" Emil asked. "It is Saint Francis preaching to the fishes and was made specially for this room."

"I am very impressed by your fountain," she answered, "but I am even more astonished at your library." She saw an endlessly rich variety—classics, novels, history, religion, and a special shelf holding books by Rudolf Steiner.

"I have collected them over a lifetime, and I have read every single one," he answered.

He told her to find a seat near the entrance hall, from where she'd have a good view of both pianists. She did and was amused when Walter suddenly appeared, dragging a chair and setting it up to face her instead of the pianos. *Go ahead and stare*, she thought. *One day you'll marry me.* Surprised by her own thought, she immediately dismissed the idea— she loved her freedom and had no intention of getting married.

After the excellent concert, Walter was busy greeting people and offering them refreshments. Edith mingled with the crowd, wondering at the absence of the lady of the house. She heard Walter's mother was in poor health and in a clinic in the mountains. Before Edith left, Walter shook her hand and asked to see her again. She said yes.

The friendship between Walter and Edith grew, and she often came to the house. She rarely saw "Father Molt" after the concert, though, as he was always busy. So busy, in fact, that given the medical insight she'd gained from working in her father's office, Edith believed Emil's lifestyle could lead to collapse. She also noticed that this family was never alone. "There are always guests at their table," she reported back to her family, "even when both Molts are away. Some of them don't seem to deserve the hospitality and take this horn of plenty for granted. I know Walter suffers about this."

"Don't be too critical," answered her father. "Be helpful and enjoy it." Although she had heard of anthroposophy and as a child had played with children going to the Waldorf School, it was new territory for her and she became an acute observer and listener. Walter served as her interpreter, providing a measure of wry humor.

Edith's "bad influence"

"Who is this saucy person?" Berta asked when she finally met Edith, taken aback by the young woman's worldly manner.

"She is," answered Emil, "a serious and strong-willed girl who hides her light under a flippant exterior." Fragile, serious Berta worried that Edith was too much of a free spirit who might burn her sensitive son and then drop him. She tried to warn him, but he moved out of the house to a bachelor pad near Walter Rau's soap factory and, to Berta's dismay, often went away with Edith

Edith's "bad influence"

on weekend hiking or skiing trips. Berta still had Felix in the house, but suffered Walter's absences, regretting his preference for Edith over some gentle young eurythmist or another eligible anthroposophist.

Commitment to stay in Germany

"Should we consider leaving Germany and settling in Dornach?" Berta said to Emil. "It is our spiritual home. Maybe our work in Stuttgart is done. Switzerland is peaceful—just think, we'd be near the Goetheanum and Ita Wegman's clinic where we could get care."

"True, Switzerland is peaceful, safe and stable, but our home and our work is here," Emil told her. At the next parent-teacher conference, the teachers' presentations were courageous and insightful and they appeared as a united professional group. Emil listened and when he got home, he described the meeting to Berta. He recalled that in 1919 Dr. Steiner told the first parent meeting: "The spirit of the Waldorf School will slowly trickle through to the whole world and will be a force for a better and more dignified social existence."

"You see," Emil said to Berta, "that is why we are here, to support the school.

The Nazi takeover

On January 28th, 1933, Germany's president, General Hindenburg, advised by a coterie of conservative politicians, appointed Hitler to the post of Chancellor after the incumbent was forced to step down. Crowds of people in Berlin flooded the streets to boisterously applaud the appointment.

In a way, Hitler was a demonic counterpoint to everything Steiner stood for. He was born in the same country as Steiner and was well aware of his teachings, but like the magician Klingsor, he brought darkness instead of light, copying Steiner's teachings in an eerie way. While Steiner worked out of love and toward a future consciousness, Hitler invoked a regression to a mythical past based on hatred. His visions were distorted, fueled by drugs and, in his youth, magical practices. Steiner used words such as "folk spirit" and "destiny" which Hitler distorted into an evil and abiding caricature.

"Why could Hitler's rise not have been prevented?" the Molts asked themselves. "Isn't Hitler Austrian? How can he rule in Germany?"

Edith Lichtenberg wrote to her brother, Werner, in America:

Well, now Hitler, that monkey, has managed to become Chancellor. What a beastly sideshow, you can't imagine! First the Nazis blamed Hindenburg for the war and now they raise him to high heaven as the "brave Field Marshal." On the night of the inauguration, they gave their "Führer" a torch-lit parade. We heard a report of it on the radio. Such sh-t, I never heard the like.

The Molts, remembering the great war of fifteen years earlier, dreaded the beginning of a greater nightmare. Steiner's predictions in Stockholm in 1910 were fresh in their memories—he had spoken of windows into the spiritual world beginning to open for people in the 1930s and had warned that if those windows didn't open, confusion and the shadow of evil would follow.

Minding Steiner's message to be awake and aware—to guard beauty, truth and goodness—they confirmed their resolve to stay in Germany with their friends. "We must bring support to those with a Jewish background in particular," said Emil, despairing because he had never classified his Jewish and Muslim friends by race or religion.

Emil's illness reflects the country

Shortly after Hitler's appointment, Emil went to Zürich to give a lecture at the university. He was feeling tired and had pains in his bladder, and the morning after his lecture, he discovered a large amount of blood in his urine. Frightened, he went to a Swiss specialist. The diagnosis was unclear, but the doctor advised Emil to go home and rest. The doctor would run some tests and send the results on to Stuttgart. Arriving home, Emil went to bed with a fever. A few days later Dr. Palmer brought him the test results, which indicated that his kidneys were clear but there was a suspicion of stones or "sand" in the bladder.

"Don't worry," Palmer reassured Emil. "Such stones normally pass by themselves and if not, a surgical procedure will get rid of them." Emil remained in bed and was there the night of February 1st, when he heard Goebbels and Hitler on the radio.

Exactly fourteen years after Steiner's "Appeal to the German Nation," Hitler delivered a haunting parody of it, also titled "Appeal to the German Nation." Emil was horrified and sick for a month. Berta tended him, and Walter visited often with Edith, but Emil now found the young couple tedious, and he was unable to listen to their chatter.

On the evening of February 27th, the Parliament building in Berlin was set on fire. As if choreographed, Goering, followed by Hitler and Goebbels, immediately appeared on the scene. They announced that the fire was arson and was the beginning of a communist takeover. "Not a moment to lose. Soon they will strike in force," Hitler said, proclaiming that all communist leaders ought to be hanged that very night.

Freedoms gone

Early the next morning, a written and signed emergency decree was issued by the government "for the protection of people and state." This decree suspended freedom of speech and association, freedom of the press, privacy of mail, telegram and telephone communications—and authorized house searches and seizures. It paved the way for the arrests of opposing political candidates and rendered void many previous laws. Berta and Emil were shocked at the speed with which this took place, and the thorough planning behind it.

A couple of days later, Dr. Palmer took Emil to see a urologist at the Wilhelma Hospital. The specialist, an irascible man, examined Emil extensively and painfully, finding an infection and bladder stones. He recommended a surgical procedure and suggested a date. It took Emil days to recover from the examination, and Dr. Palmer visited him every day, clearly concerned. Berta worried about the surgery too. *Where is Dr. Steiner now?* she thought sadly.

Parliamentary elections were held on March 5th, and the Nazis took the majority, winning because 81 communist deputies had been arrested or had taken flight before the vote. In addition, a number of opposition politicians had likewise been imprisoned.

Emil spent a few sunny days in the garden and checked into the hospital on March 7th for his procedure. He underwent a lithotripsy five days later to remove the stones. Nowadays this procedure is done by laser, but back then it was a cruder surgical intervention and Emil stayed in hospital for ten more days before being sent home to recuperate.

On March 23rd the Reichstag (Parliament) passed the *Enabling Act for the Protection of People and State,* effectively voting itself out of existence and allowing Hitler's cabinet, and thus himself, to act with impunity. The German Communist Party was banned and all trade unions dissolved. On April 1st, the Nazis declared a general boycott of Jews.

What will our friends do now? thought Emil, concerned for his Hamburg associates in particular. He got sick again, suffering an infection, running a fever, and enduring serious pain. Berta took him to the specialist, who was in a hurry to go on vacation. He admitted that there might be some remaining stones, and both Berta and Emil insisted he take care of his patient before leaving. He operated again, this time with a general anesthetic, and removed seven or eight splinters. Whether his mind was already on a mountain resort, or he disliked the troublesome patient will remain a mystery, but his instrument went astray during the surgery and inflicted an internal wound that was never to heal.

Dr. Lichtenberg advises

For six weeks, Emil lay in the hospital after the procedure. Edith sent her father, Dr. Lichtenberg, to look in on him, and he was dismayed by the medical report. "You must see an expert," he told Emil. "I know the best man in the field. Dr. Kielleuthner has a practice in Munich and can surely help you. I will refer you, but go as soon as you possibly can."

"I will," said Emil, "but I have to improve first." Actually, he couldn't bear the thought of another examination and was not ready to see another specialist.

On April 14th, Good Friday, Emil celebrated his birthday in hospital with the nurses singing to him, after which he received a procession of visitors. His son sat by his bed for a long time, reading from a new book by the poet, Christian Morgenstern. That night, Emil dreamed of Rudolf Steiner. He was allowed to go home for a few hours on Easter Sunday. The trees were in bloom, the weather beautiful, and the cook prepared his favorite dish with vegetables from the garden. Visitors came, although he also spent time alone with Berta. His two physician friends, Palmer and Kolisko, found him in good form.

"Be patient," they said in regard to his recovery. On April 20th, an auxiliary physician discharged him, and he never saw his surgeon again. "May the gift of time be granted me, to make use of what I learned through this illness," he said. "Perhaps I can still make a difference, only not in the old way!"

Reflection

For a year Emil remained at home and often in bed. His illness put a ring around his world, limiting his movements to his house, his garden, and a few short strolls in the neighborhood. He had his Steiner books and biographies and the days took on a comforting rhythm, sheltered from the madness outside. No more rushing off to city after city—now he had time to think.

Berta hired a male nurse to look after Emil at night, and his niece, Dora, attended him during the day. Dora's brother, Siegfried, who later became a physician in Mannheim, helped with kitchen duty; Drs. Palmer and Kolisko came often to care for him, and a great number of people came to visit. Then, in September, Walter and Edith came by one day to announce their intention to get married. "When did this happen?" asked Berta.

"Oh," replied Edith, "it was nothing formal. Walter and some friends brought me home one night. He lingered in the courtyard after I went in. I saw him from my window, opened it and called out 'good night.' He walked away, then turned around and said in an off-hand kind of way, 'I don't suppose you'd want to marry me' and I said 'yes I would' and that was that. He got in his car and drove off."

Young lovers

In October, Walter and Edith celebrated their engagement in a glorious summit restaurant on the *Rotenberg* (Red Mountain) beyond the city. Emil was able to attend and told the story of his own romance with Berta. Now that Edith was to be a member of the family, Berta softened toward her, and Emil also got to know her better. She often stayed to read to him before his bedtime. Saying he had done enough serious reading in his life, she brought him light literature to brighten the hours. They laughed together and he called her his "sleep angel," and had a more peaceful night afterward.

Berta and Edith's mother, Friedel, got to know each other better. They enjoyed being together and exploring areas of the city they didn't know. They looked at potential apartments for Walter and Edith and things the young couple might need for their household. At the time, Walter was still working in Walter Rau's soap factory in Möhringen, a town set among cabbage fields on the outskirts of the city.

To everyone's delight, around that time Dora also found a partner in Max Emil Kimmich, whom she had met in college. They were both studying to be Waldorf teachers. She introduced him to the Molts one lunchtime, and they took Emil out for a short walk. Kimmich was a quiet, charming, soulful man, and the Molts felt that he and Dora were made for each other.

Max Emil Kimmich

Polling and Albert Steffen resigns

On November 12th Emil got up to vote. The election was rigged, but a consensus among historians is that it was also a successful referendum for the Nazi regime. Walter and Edith drove Emil downtown. Stuttgart was not as extreme as Berlin, but when he saw swastikas floating above the polling station and was required to fill out long forms with personal details, handed him by guards in uniform, he almost exploded. By the time he got home, he was pale and tottering, and suspicious that his ballot might not be secret at all and would be used inappropriately.

The teacher of the special class at the Waldorf School, Dr. Schubert, was waiting for him with a letter from Albert Steffen, who had announced that he wanted to resign as head of the Waldorf School Association Board. He would, however, still expect accountability. Emil, discouraged, said he'd send a reply.

Dear Albert Steffen:

In the name of the College of Teachers and Waldorf School Association, I beg you to give us your trust and reconsider your position as Chairman of the Board. My own illness doesn't permit me to come to you personally and this letter is a poor substitute. I know there are issues, but the teachers are in a tragic situation... You do have support. It just takes time and I beg you in the name of the Waldorf School to wait with patience for things to resolve themselves. We, who have made this our task, promise you that we will not rest until we achieve what is in the best interest of the larger whole. – Emil Molt

Advent 1933 and the "children"

In December the Molts celebrated the First Advent on Saturday instead of Sunday because Walter and Edith planned to go skiing the next day. Berta lighted the first of the four candles on the advent wreath, but Walter couldn't seem to tolerate the stillness of the house and the young couple soon left. Berta waited until the next morning, when she and Emil were alone, to read the Steiner Christmas lecture that she had originally planned for the night before. At noon, she invited him to her room (they each had a spacious upstairs room that served as a cozy retreat). Emil reclined in a lounge chair while she served up an elegant little lunch. Later, after his nap, she read to him from the life of Alexander the Great.

That evening Walter and Edith returned, glowing from their ski outing. They were excited about an apartment they had found which was bigger than the apartment Walter was currently living in. Edith hinted that she had also found a couch set she loved, but it was out of their price range.

Then Walter complained about his boss, Walter Rau, who he said wasn't interested in his sales and marketing suggestions and didn't give him enough space. Somewhat impatiently, Emil told Berta, "Call Lola Rau tomorrow and find out what's going on, woman to woman...Also," he added, "if Edith thinks she can make eyes at me and get whatever she wants, well, she's wrong. Anyway, we shouldn't be buying couches, we're not rich anymore."

The next day, Berta talked to Lola Rau, who sighed and said Walter was like a racehorse at the plow. He often arrived late and disappeared without telling anyone where he was going. "He feels that he should determine what he does and when, and he is often moody and unapproachable," she told Berta. "He does his job well, but I don't know if we can keep him—it's not good for the other employees." Berta promised to see what she could do. Emil was embarrassed by his son's behavior when he heard Berta's report. "His problem is that he never went through the discipline I did. All his jobs, whether in Italy, England or Germany, were bent to suit his lifestyle," Emil said. He summoned Walter, who arrived with Edith. "No more playboy," Emil said to Walter. "The Raus are giving you another chance. Don't embarrass me." To Edith, he said, "The gay twenties are over. Give him boundaries, otherwise what kind of life will you have once there's a family?" She looked startled, but clearly understood him.

Then Dora came with her fiancé, Max Emil. Berta served them tea and couldn't help thinking how easy Dora was compared to Edith. In the evening, Dora's parents, Gotthilf and Paula, came to supper, and after that Emil's secretary, Otto Wagner, rang with a long list of questions. Emil was still in a dark mood, and Berta realized she would have to cancel visitors and unplug the phone for a while—the days before Christmas shouldn't be stressful.

Christmas 1933

Three weeks later, Berta had a tree brought up to Emil's room and decorated it with candles, red paper roses and golden planetary symbols. The tree filled the room with its fragrance. "There," she said to Emil. "Almost like the mountain air we love." Then she accompanied Edith's parents over crunching and sparkling snow to the school to see the traditional Nativity play put on by the teachers. Fritz and Frieda Lichtenberg enjoyed the simple beauty of the play, and even the Nazi surveillance officer at the rear forgot himself and shouted with laughter when the shepherds in the field slipped and fell on the "ice."

Berta prepared a basket of presents for her friends and needy acquaintances. When Walter and Edith came around, they offered to deliver the presents, glad to go out again. Later, Emil got up and Berta bundled him into a comfortable chair in the living room downstairs, wondering what was keeping Walter and Edith. Eventually, they celebrated Christmas Eve with Dora, her fiancé, the Lichtenbergs, and Felix with his fiancée, Christa. Fritz Lichtenberg asked Emil whether he had consulted the physician he had recommended and looked concerned when Emil said he hadn't. Late at night, when Emil was in bed, Walter and Edith returned with the empty basket, drenched and shivering from their deliveries.

"Oh, my poor dears," said Berta, chagrined. "You should have left the rest for tomorrow." She served them a little midnight snack by the warm fire and gave them their present—a gift voucher for their couch set. She was rewarded with a grateful smile from Walter and a hug from Edith. Then they toasted the first minutes of Christmas Day with a hot toddy of elderberry juice.

The school threatened

Emil had little energy in January 1934, barely even putting notes in his diary. The sole entry is about a dream he had on January 14th, in which he saw Rudolf Steiner, who asked him very kindly, "Are you still depressed?" He woke up and felt comforted.

In February, Berta took Emil to a sanatorium near St. Moritz. Dr. Palmer accompanied them on the train, Emil lying down for most of the trip. The sanatorium was not the elegant one of their affluent earlier years, but the resident physician, Dr. Zambail, was glad to consult with Dr. Palmer who, in turn, was glad to know his patient was in good hands. Emil was given a raw food diet and sitzbaths, otherwise spending the days ensconced on a glassed-in terrace. Eight days later, Berta received a letter from a Waldorf School teacher:

Stuttgart, February 12th, 1934
Dear Mrs. Molt!

I am sending you my memorandum of the State's intention to close the school, not knowing whether Dr. Molt's health is strong enough to bear this news. I leave it up to you. Could you forward my enclosed memorandum to Mr. Steffen soon and say we are doing everything possible to stay calm. We have informed only a few parents…

Sending greetings and best wishes for Dr. Molt's health,
Your Paul Baumann.

Memorandum, February 9th, 1934

…At a meeting with Cultural Minister Christian Mergenthaler, he told me he intends to close the school as soon as possible. Taking effect immediately there will be no new admissions. He says it's not the method nor the inadequate treatment of certain subjects (both criticisms made during a recent inspection) but the underlying world view. "Rudolf Steiner and the Steinerians follow hazy, pacifistic, internationalist ideals," he claimed. My counter-arguments were brushed aside as personal conviction and not reality. In his opinion, the fact that all the teachers work out of anthroposophy makes it impossible for the school to align itself with the National Socialist State.

"Prepare yourself for a shock," Berta said to Emil. "You will want to see this."

"How can we deal with this additional stroke of fate?" asked Emil. "We must not let these difficulties weaken us! Tell them to plan every move carefully and keep us informed. Tell them to be strong. We will be back soon."

Shortly after this, they heard that at an emergency teachers' meeting on February 10th, Baumann had requested the attendance of a Nazi advisor who, he thought, was favorably inclined toward the school. Some teachers had reservations because this man was not trained in the Waldorf method, but they agreed because they wanted to be conciliatory. The advisor told them clearly that the school would have to be reformed to meet the conditions of the times and that they should appoint a Nazi party supervisor to facilitate this.

Several teachers suggested parents with a family member or friend in the Party who might be suitable. Others thought it might be wise for teachers to join the Nazi Party. "We can just go along while keeping our thoughts to ourselves," they said. Yet others wanted to create a circle of parents with links to the Party who could become "guarantors" for the school. The faculty member Ernst Lehrs said all of this was a direct attack on anthroposophy and Dr. Steiner. "The present parent body," he said, "is the only one responsible and everything else is compromise."

The attacks continue

The threats from the government didn't stop, and the Waldorf parents struggled to help the school. One parent knew someone with ties to Hitler and suggested reaching out; another suggested that teachers Ege and Boy drive to Munich to talk with Hitler's deputy, Rudolf Hess, who was known to be interested in biodynamics, the agricultural method initiated by Steiner.

Meanwhile, Baumann reported back to the parents and teachers at the school. He said that Cultural Minister Mergenthaler disapproved of Karl Schubert teaching the free religion class because of his Jewish background. Mergenthaler felt that the Nazis would not change their demands until they were assured that "non-Aryan" teachers were no longer involved in the school. A Nazi official who was friendly toward the school asked a parent why the school couldn't align itself with the times by temporarily suspending the Jewish teachers, Drs. Friedrich Hiebel and Alexander Strakosch. When he heard of these comments, Strakosch declared that he did not want to be a hindrance to the school and would step down. Dr. Ernst Lehrs, Karl Schubert and Dr. Hiebel all said they would do the same.

Dr. Strakosch

These four were among the most gifted and inspired teachers of the school, and their colleagues were distraught at this announcement. "All means at our disposal must be exhausted before we send anyone away," Baumann said, feeling that a solution shouldn't be decided unilaterally.

Karl Ege, another teacher at the school, reported that the Department of Education wanted to install its own director in the school. If that happened, Ege said, he wouldn't want anything more to do with the school. "From the time I was a child, I wanted to be German," the Austrian-born Strakosch told his colleagues. "Now I beg you to relieve me of my school duties. I beg it." Hiebel and Lehrs had the same request, and all three left the school and the country. "The decision these gentlemen made is a heavy sacrifice," Baumann said. But Strakosch went to Switzerland, Lehrs to England, and Hiebel to America, and all three contributed to the growth of the Waldorf movement there. Karl Schubert alone decided to stay in Germany, where, miraculously, the Ministry of Education allowed him to continue his classes for special-needs children throughout the course of the war.

Seeking the specialist

Emil, feeling better in Switzerland, was drinking tea in the St. Moritz hotel lounge when the radio announced a speech by Hitler's deputy, Rudolf Hess, in Munich. *Perhaps,* Emil thought as the speech began, *Hess will be reasonable.* But Emil's tea went bitter when he heard Hess say of Hitler, "Through our pledge we bind our life anew to one man through

Emil and Berta after doctor's visit

whom higher powers of destiny are at work." *Spiritual perversion*, Emil thought. *It's been a year since my operation and my condition is worse than ever. How helpless I feel.*

Indeed, Emil's condition had begun to frighten Berta. "The mountains have not helped you," she told him. She rang the physician that Edith's father had recommended and begged him for an emergency appointment. Then she packed their belongings and booked tickets for Munich.

"I am glad to get back to the school and am worried about what's happening there," he told Berta. Before they left, Emil received a letter from Leinhas confirming his fears that Nazi Party members were being co-opted into the collegium of the school and would surely try to take it over. Leinhas asked Emil to sign an affidavit, deputizing Leinhas to act as Chairman in Steffen's absence. Emil decided to talk this over with the collegium as soon as he returned.

On March 15th Dr. Lichtenberg's colleague examined Emil and shook his head. "You are too late," he said. "Your illness has progressed too far. Nine months ago I could have helped you." Berta and Emil were devastated by this news, as they traveled back to Stuttgart. Walter met them at the station and, despite being in the midst of his own wedding preparations, tried to comfort his despairing parents.

On March 24th Walter and Edith were married, and in spite of Emil's poor health, the day was marked with joy. After the ceremony, the Lichtenbergs hosted a lunch for the two families. After the celebration

Emil and Berta went home. The weather was warm and the garden full of flowers—more beautiful than ever—and Emil spent the rest of the day sunning himself on the balcony, loving the springtime after the cold of St. Moritz.

The courage of the teachers

Walter and Edith wedding

Waldorf teachers visited the Molts regularly to report on the school. Some teachers had shown extraordinary courage in the face of the Nazi onslaught. Leinhas described the ways in which the Party member parents who had been chosen as a friendly oversight board for the school were attempting to change the school's governance. He thought the anthroposophical industrialist, Mahle, who had a fast-growing business making pistons for the automotive industry, could be helpful with his influential contacts. Emil invited Mahle to his home. Together they discussed ways of keeping the school's principles intact, and at Emil's request, Mahle agreed to manage the school's oversight board. Emil was deeply relieved by this appointment.

In early May, Mahle called Emil to report that progress had been made with the parent group in the Association and that the teachers were feeling more confident. The following week, the Collegium sent a letter to members of the Waldorf School Association:

> We wish to inform you that Mr. Albert Steffen has resigned his
> role as Chairman, feeling it to be better that a German and not
> a foreigner occupy this post. We know that he remains deeply
> connected with the spirit of Waldorf and thank him for all
> his kindness and help. The Board meanwhile has looked for a
> replacement and has decided unanimously to propose the current
> Vice Chairman, Dr. Emil Molt, for this post, asking him as well to
> direct the activities of the Waldorf School Association.

The school chairman

Emil wrote back to the Collegium that same day:

Previously I rejected as impossible the idea that I could occupy a post once held by Dr. Steiner himself and since his death by Albert Steffen. I begged the latter to reconsider his resignation, at least for the duration of my illness. However, since the external situation of the school has become so very difficult, I place myself at your service, but only if I can remain in closest spiritual connection with the Goetheanum and its leadership.

The hard tasks of the present and future can be undertaken only if every member carries the school in his or her heart and if complete trust is given to people in managing positions. The Waldorf School must be kept alive. It was created by Dr. Steiner, not just for us but for everyone. Young people will go forth from it, healthy in body and soul, able to work toward a renewal of the State. If we can maintain the Waldorf School spirit, then in spite of all difficulties we can look to the future with joy and hope. Dr. E. Molt

Although the weather was hot and muggy on June 3rd, the Annual General Meeting of the Waldorf School Association was harmonious and positive. Emil was confirmed as Chairman during the meeting, which he felt was a gift from the spiritual world. "Even though he was not often present, he helped with advice," Emil said of Steffen to his colleagues. "Everyone knows how great his interest and love is for the school."

Excerpt from the Waldorf School's report (January 1st, 1933 to Easter 1934):

This time is among the most difficult the school has ever experienced. We miss our founder, Rudolf Steiner, whose concern from the beginning was how to carry this art of education forward and bring healing into social life, how to prevail against the hindering forces of a materialistic time. This year we are faced with a new and serious worry. The opponents of the work of Rudolf Steiner have managed to label the Waldorf School as harmful and conflicting with the new State and its goals. The authorities believe that anthroposophy makes it impossible for teachers to work constructively within the new German State.

The Württemberg Cultural Ministry has forbidden new students by closing the first grade and even declared that the entire school must be dismantled… Nine teachers will leave at the end of the year… The remaining teachers feel deeply connected with those who have left, some who have been with it since the beginning. They know how much they owe them and what they are losing…

When the state inspector, Bauser, came to the school in the spring, he found arithmetic, spelling and dictation lacking, but he admitted essays to be much better for content and liveliness than in state schools. He praised music and technology lessons and found oral presentations better than average, especially in the choice of words. He did not approve of foreign language studies, but said that, while reading skills were behind in the lower classes, the upper classes did very well. Gymnastics was good, but he recommended separating the boys from the girls. He found the Collegium faithful and hard-working, and in spite of all the "dogma," he saw serious striving, which he felt deserved praise and admiration. "*It is an interesting pedagogical experiment*," he wrote of the Waldorf School. Around this time, Mahle reported to Emil that 53 Waldorf parents had become Nazi Party members, participating in more than twenty patriotic clubs.

Brissago

Berta, acutely aware of Emil's declining strength and the impact each new crisis had on him, hoped to take him away from Germany for a while. Their budget was tight, as she was no longer working, but they had sold part of their back garden and therefore had some discretionary funds. St. Moritz felt like a bad memory to her, so she proposed the Motta in Brissago, a picturesque village on the west side of Lake Maggiore, several villages down from Ascona. The Motta was a modest guesthouse owned by two German anthroposophists, and Berta learned that they had rooms available at a price reasonable enough to allow her to bring her housekeeper.

In preparation for the trip, Walter took Emil to see his accountant, a reliable young woman named Miss Federer. She was responsible for Emil's official business correspondence, and she had become very dedicated to him. He, in turn, affectionately called her "Federlein" (little feather). Knowing that he was worried about the large amount of mail and dispatches he was prone to receiving, she offered to come along with the Molts to Brissago at no extra cost to take care of correspondence. Much to Emil's delight, she said she needed a holiday and loved the Italian part of Switzerland.

Hoping for healing in Switzerland

The Molts had just arrived at the Motta when they received a surprise message from Leinhas, who happened to be in Ascona and wanted to visit them. "Oh dear," said Berta, worried about putting strain on Emil. "Can we put the visit off for a few days?"

"Let him come," said Emil. "I'll be glad to see him."

Emil's first excursion that same afternoon was to a forgotten mill with a stream bubbling out of a spring. He watched lizards lounging on the warm rocks and washed his face with the cool spring water. The walk made him happy and he felt a bit better. Back on his veranda, he sat for a long time looking at the majestic lake and the mountains of Gambarogno beyond, with their forests of pine and chestnut trees. He spotted a tiny church on the outcropping of a hill, unaware that years later Walter and Edith would rebuild an old farmhouse in the village behind that church. Eventually they would retire there, often looking across the lake to Brissago, where Emil now sat. The day waned but Emil lingered on the veranda until the moon rose. Then he went inside, put on his jacket, and took a short walk with Berta through a vineyard above the village. "In the end," he said to her that evening, "Edith is right. We mustn't be too serious. Happiness cures all."

Next day Leinhas came with his new wife, Flossie. Berta set out tea and pastries under the fig trees in the garden. Leinhas gave such a uniformly pessimistic report of happenings in Stuttgart that Emil felt glad to be away from home. To change the mood, Berta invited the couple to stay for a reading of Steiner's Michaelmas Imagination,

Berta smiling at Emil

hoping to bring warmth and courage to the afternoon. It worked, lifting the group's thoughts beyond their troubles. "He is really drawn to you and wants so much to do the right thing," Berta said of Leinhas later.

Then the weather changed, bringing thunderstorms and long days of rain. Letters from Stuttgart bore conflicting messages—one sober, another full of optimistic statements. But all reported that a meeting with the State official had brought even more restrictions to the school. "I have to go back to Stuttgart," Emil said anxiously, but his anthroposophic physician in Ascona, Dr. Zehnder, told him he must stay.

"You have made progress," Zehnder told him, "but you mustn't risk traveling." "I think the school needs me," he answered.

"Make up your mind," Berta said. "There you will be sick again. Here you have a chance to be productive. Have your colleagues come and visit you. It's not so far away." Emil relented, and found that not having to face the journey back to Stuttgart was a relief for him. He had a long conversation with his landlord, Doman, who told him, "Regard this as a safe house. Let people come to you. You and all the rest are under surveillance in Stuttgart; here you are free to speak. They all need respite too."

Staying in touch with the school

Please send good thoughts, Mahle wrote to Emil on September 12th. *I will be meeting with the State schools official again.* Shortly afterward, Emil heard from Mahle again, who reported that the meeting with the State Schools official had not gone well. *Do you want me to come back?* Emil replied, sending a copy of Mahle's letter to the school. *Wait, perhaps we can handle this,* Baumann wrote back.

In early October, Emil received an extensive report from Mahle of a meeting with an education official who had insisted that an older, non-parent Nazi be added to the Association. The Collegium had been called upon to hire an "objective" Party teacher as well, and both appointments were to be accomplished by January 1935 at the latest. Furthermore, all lessons were to be based completely on natural scientific principles and not on "unproven fantasies." In response to this request, the Board of the Association agreed to add Mr. and Mrs. Link to the Collegium for Nazi oversight.

Visit to Dornach

In early December Emil's doctor advised him to go to Zürich to be checked out by a specialist. Emil agreed to this, but said he wanted to visit Dornach first. Before leaving, he took a bath, had his hair cut, and chose his travel gear.

The next day, he and Berta got on the train in Bellinzona where, by chance, they met their old friend, Hermann Hesse. The trip through the Gotthard tunnel and past Lucerne to Basel was relaxing, with a pleasant meal in the dining car. In Basel, Professor Tuch met them, bearing flowers from Steffen, and drove them to his beautiful house in Dornach where his wife had supper waiting.

On December 8th, Emil met with Mahle, Baumann and Steffen to discuss how to proceed with the school—how much compromise should they undergo to preserve it? Mahle thought they might still have political recourse, and Baumann thought the new Nazi representatives in the Association could be convinced of the school's ethos.

"Our constant task is fighting fear," Mahle and Baumann told Emil, glad of the chance to talk openly on the safe and neutral ground of Switzerland. They reported on relentless and increasing restrictions on ordinary citizens, who seemed unable to oppose anything. All State school-children were pressured to join Nazi youth groups, and people were often watched by their neighbors for evidence of disloyalty to their country. The Waldorf School children were supposed to start each day by saluting Hitler and singing patriotic songs, and there was a pervasive fear of the consequences of not complying with these guidelines.

Steffen's play

That night, after a productive but inconclusive discussion, they all went to the Goetheanum to see *The Fall of the Antichrist*, a play that Steffen had written in 1928. Seeing many familiar German faces gathered to watch this play, Emil recognized the importance of the Goetheanum and its location—just across the border from Germany—a neutral place to preserve anthroposophy.

The next day Emil met with Edgar Dürler, the Weleda director. Together they recalled the traumatic year of 1922. Emil told Dürler that he'd been haunted by regret over refusing to meet with him and his associate when they'd come to him for Futurum advice in Stuttgart. "I was so tired," Emil said, "and I thought it was more important to save Waldorf Astoria, when in fact the company was already gone."

"It wasn't," Dürler replied. "You didn't save the factory, but you saved the financing for the school—that was your task and your gift. Besides," he said, "I was able to take over from you with Futurum, and your written suggestions made it easier." Dürler talked about the challenge of holding those disparate member companies and their employees together until they were sold or closed. He felt fortunate that Steiner had supported him with the resolution of this ill-fated enterprise.

Emil was curious about the method behind the merger of the German and Swiss branches of Weleda, and Dürler was happy to explain. "The Basel office furniture company that Futurum owned," he told Emil, "had a registered trademark called 'Orga.' I knew that the large German firm Orga Berlin was interested in acquiring the Swiss trademark. I negotiated a good price and then drove to Stuttgart to present Steiner and Leinhas with a draft sales contract. Steiner then suggested that Futurum buy the German Weleda with the proceeds of the furniture company sale."

"I am astonished at your creative thinking," said Emil, "and I'm impressed with what you have done with Weleda. As a matter of fact, I'm a little jealous, because I had a secret desire to work for Weleda myself." They parted cordially, and Emil invited Dürler to the Ticino.

A Weleda product

Preparing for the clinic visit

For ten days, Emil lay in bed in Brissago recovering from his trip to Dornach. Then he prepared for his next journey. On December 19th the Molts traveled to Zürich, where they found comfortable rooms in the Glockenhof hotel. Emil checked in to Dr. Zbinden's clinic, where he was pushed and prodded and found to be somewhat improved. Grateful to put this trip behind them, they went back to Brissago for Christmas. Walter and Edith arrived shortly after them, and Leinhas and his wife once again surprised them with a visit for tea. Leinhas wanted to talk about the school, but it became clear to the Molts that he was interested in the donation Emil always gave around this time. Emil could hardly afford it anymore, but felt he couldn't say no, so he wrote a check with greetings to the school and wished Leinhas a happy Christmas.

Later that day the Stuttgart Waldorf teacher Karl Ege came by. He and Emil told each other jokes until suppertime—anthroposophical jokes, Stuttgart jokes and irreverent Nazi jokes. Walter and Edith joined in until they were all breathless with laughter.

On the last day of 1934 Walter drove the whole family to Locarno, and then across Lake Lugano to Montagnola to visit Hermann Hesse in his rustic hillside retreat. They ate with Hesse by the stone fireplace, simply enjoying each other's company, and then drove back in the early evening without any ill effect to Emil.

Molts in Ticino

Fading finances

Emil wrote to the teacher Max Wolffhügel in the new year, 1935:

My illness and the double household costs have swallowed a huge amount of money, I don't know when I'll be able to earn again; it depends on my regaining health and strength. Since I need my secretary here, we've had to send our housekeeper back to Stuttgart. We couldn't manage the extra expense. From April 1st we will have to take serious measures so I don't go broke too soon. It's time for Felix to get a job and his own accommodation, because we have to rent out our upstairs rooms. If you can help in this, we'd be grateful. I must be free of constant money worries; otherwise I'll not get well.

While Emil was worrying about his finances and Felix's employment, Hitler introduced general conscription and Walter received a call-up notice for military service. It put him in a terrible quandary—how could he join something he didn't believe in? Luckily, when presenting himself for registration, he found out that unmarried young men were taken first, while married men would be deferred for a short while. He noted that men with children were even lower on the active duty scale.

Threat of Walter drafted

Emil was unable to sleep for six days after hearing that Walter might soon become a Nazi soldier. On the seventh day, he was visited by a gentleman who wanted Emil to facilitate a position for his son-in-law at Weleda. Emil called Dürler, who was glad to come spend a few days in Ticino to meet with Emil's visitor. Afterward, Dürler told Emil that Weleda was paying off the entire remaining Futurum and The Coming Day debt—news that astonished Emil. They also talked about the quarterly publication, *Weleda News*, which Dürler had launched and that Emil found delightful. He saw it as an improved version of his former *Waldorf News*, and he told Dürler the story of the journal's popularity and its subsequent demise through The Coming Day.

They then stopped for tea with Emil's host, Doman, and Dr. Ita Wegman, who was also visiting from her clinic in Arlesheim. As the group chatted, Doman mentioned that he wanted to do something more worthwhile than hospitality with his guesthouse, and Dr. Wegman suggested he make it into a curative home for people with special needs. The friends casually discussed the idea, never guessing that Doman would in fact follow through on this suggestion and that Dr. Wegman would one day direct this initiative, called "La Motta."

Stages of illness

On January 25th, 1935, the Nazi Party members, Mr. and Mrs. Link, visited Emil and Berta. By including the Links in the Waldorf School Association, the school had been able to start an additional first grade, but the Links seemed clearly out of their depth when it came to the Waldorf ethos. Over the course of two days, they talked and talked with the Molts about how to fit the school into the Nazi educational system, but the discussion was inconclusive.

In early February a letter arrived from the teacher, Ernst Bindel: *Regarding the school: the joy over the approval for grade one is mixed with a bitter pill in that we suddenly are allowed only 40 pupils even though we already have 58 applications.*

In spite of the turmoil and heartache surrounding the school, Emil began sleeping through the nights again and had renewed energy for long dictations.

On March 1st, he woke feeling he had come through a catharsis. Sunshine followed that morning's gentle rain, and Emil walked and sipped tea in the garden with Berta. When the evening paper arrived, he read about an armed uprising in Greece led by Venizelos and recalled the uprising in Crete. Thinking about his time in Patras inspired him to begin dictating his memoirs, and Dora offered to be his scribe while she was visiting.

On April 6th, 1935, Emil wrote to Erich Schwebsch, one of his favorite teachers: *I know you are going to the Annual General Meeting in Dornach. Would it then be possible to sneak down here? This time of year there are probably cheap train tickets available...* Unable to go to the meeting himself, Emil longed for updates from the goings-on in Dornach.

A split in the Society

April 15th, the day after Emil's birthday, Erich Schwebsch arrived in Ticino with dire news. While Emil had been enjoying a quiet birthday celebration, the Anthroposophical Society suffered a major split. The conflict centered around a difference of views about the mission of the Society, now that Steiner was no longer there. This disagreement came to a head at the Annual General Meeting, when a decision was made to remove Dr. Ita Wegman and Dr. Elisabeth Vreede from the Board of Directors. Schwebsch told the Molts that hundreds of members had their memberships revoked. In addition, hundreds of members resigned. This news came as a terrible shock to Emil and Berta, as they had close ties to people on both sides of the issue. Emil was grateful that his illness had prevented him from attending the meeting.

Countering perception

In the beginning of May 1935, the Molts returned to Stuttgart. Emil was glad to be home, but found it difficult to adjust to life in Germany.

Nonetheless, he immediately threw himself into confrontation with Nazi Party member parents, who claimed to be faithful to Steiner's ideas but quarreled amongst themselves for control. Herr Link now regarded himself as the only official voice for the school, but another new member of the Board, a man named Schickler, also felt himself to be the authority.

"The children should be given fifes and drums and allowed to participate in parades," said Schickler to the Board. "They should be allowed to salute the flag. It is not good for them to go to the cinema and not raise their arm in salute to the Führer at the end of the film. The non-Aryan teachers should have been sent away immediately before State intervention became necessary. You are too bound up with Dornach and the hidden undercurrent of anthroposophy. Teachers shouldn't keep running to the authorities. They should leave it up to me." It was clear to Emil that Schickler was hoping to push him off the Board.

"It is known to the Nazis that many anthroposophists are critical of the regime," Mrs. Link said to Emil. "And therefore you will have to reckon with the Society being banned in Germany. However, the School must not be drawn into this." She said her intent was not to camouflage anthroposophy, but to save the education. One way, she thought, was to take on more teachers with Party membership, insofar as those persons were interested in the method. The teachers who were not Party-friendly should keep their opinions to themselves. Emil pointed out that the best teachers had already left the school, and asked if she wanted to eliminate the rest.

"Certainly not," she said, "but they are a hindrance. That was proven by their lack of attendance when the school inspector came and did an efficiency study." When Emil mentioned that Steiner had wanted notices of public educational conferences posted in town, the Links said Steiner wouldn't want that anymore. Both Links felt that their jobs as government liaisons were made especially difficult by the need to collaborate with anthroposophists.

"Your problem," Emil said to them, "is that you don't want to deal with me."

"Your generation has prepared the way for the younger ones," Mr. Link said. "You didn't quite succeed. You have a patriarchal relationship with the teachers, and that is no longer appropriate." Emil thanked the Links for sharing their thoughts, which he said he would discuss with the collegium.

The Nazis' attempt to eliminate Emil as Chairman of the Association with the help of the Links was not successful, so they tried another tack. "Perhaps," they said, "he is of Jewish heritage. He's certainly a sympathizer. Hasn't he been working with Jews all his life?" They demanded verification from him. Emil possessed the records of all his parents and grandparents save for his grandmother on his father's side. Angrily, he asked his secretary to make inquiries in his grandparents' hometown, and his grandmother's birth certificate was retrieved. As it turned out, Christine Henrike Molt had been a Protestant. The Jewish ploy having failed, the Gestapo performed house searches at the Molts' several times, even rummaging in the sick room looking for incriminating evidence. They disapproved of the anthroposophical and other esoteric books they found on Emil's shelves, but couldn't confiscate them because Emil and Berta were too well known and respected in the city. They even tapped the Molts' phone in the hopes of catching them in some unlawful act.

No relief

The summer of 1935 was unbearably hot and humid with frequent thunderstorms, and Emil found venturing out almost impossible. His teeth started to give him trouble, and his nights were restless. The heat and humidity subsided with the arrival of autumn, but Emil was sick and bedridden all the way through December. He bore it patiently, with only a few irritable intervals—brushing off Mahle once when he visited to tell Emil that "the 'orthodox' versus the 'liberal' school leadership must be decided soon." His full-of-life daughter-in-law, Edith, was the other victim of his irritability—she bothered him with her opinions. "Edith should keep her nose out of Walter's business questions and not think she has to contribute to every business conversation," Emil said once to Berta. "She shouldn't feel so sorry for her 'poor Walter.'"

"Come on," said Berta, "you know she's the only one who can make you laugh and besides, her father treated her like a partner."

Excerpt from Edith's memoirs

The invalid has not lost his sense of humor even though we are all under surveillance by the Nazis. They suspect Father Molt and the other anthroposophists of being enemies of the Third Reich. They are very suspicious of Waldorf education and believe that we are perhaps involved in surreptitious political agitation. Whenever Father Molt rings us, we hear a little click on the line and know that we are being listened to.

One day Walter and I went to a fair and came home with two ugly dolls Walter had won at the rifle range. We showed them to Father Molt. He was amused and gave them the names Hansel and Gretel. Soon afterward he rang me and we heard the click. During the conversation he asked me how the children were doing. Since we had no children at that time I knew he meant Hansel and Gretel. I told him they were very naughty and I'd gotten so mad at the little boy that I throttled him and he was now dead. Father Molt played along, recommending I bury the child in the trash can. Then he asked when I intended murdering Gretel. We discussed various ways of doing this until we heard a sharp intake of breath at the other end of the line. Then we knew that we had won and managed to shock our spy.

In November 1935 the Nazi regime banned the Anthroposophical Society in Germany.

Im ganzen Reich verboten!

Das Ende der „Anthroposophischen Gesellschaft"

Berlin, 16. Nov.

Die Geheime Staatspolizei hat, nachdem bereits die Auflösung der Anthroposophischen Gesellschaft in Baden gemeldet worden war, nunmehr diese Gesellschaft auf Grund der Verordnung zum Schutze von Volk und Staat vom 28. Februar 1933 für das gesamte Reichsgebiet aufgelöst und ihr jede Weiterbetätigung verboten,

Banning notice

One more attempt

> O Spirit of God,
> Fill my soul.
> My soul lend me strength
> Also for my heart.
> My heart seeks Thee
> With deepest longing,
> Longing for health,
> For health and power of courage,
> Courage streaming in my limbs,
> Streaming like a noble gift
> A noble gift from Thee, O Spirit of God
> O Spirit of God fill me.
>
>   – R. Steiner, *Meditation for a Severely Ill Person*
>   1924, GA 268

Routine

Early in 1936 Emil began feeling better again and his life settled into a quiet routine. Each morning he read Steiner's *The Philosophy of Freedom* and worked on the story of his life. Weather permitting, he would take a walk with Berta to the knoll above the school afterward. Occasionally, a former City Mayor named Hartmann joined him for a walk, and Emil loved testing his own views and ideas on Hartmann. In the late mornings he regularly joined the teachers in their meetings, and in the afternoons, after his nap, he often had tea with visitors. In the evenings a male nurse gave Emil a bath. Then Berta would bundle him to bed and read to him, often something historical or a biography. Occasionally they went to a school event, or to a concert or play.

Continuous surveillance

The continuing Nazi surveillance made members of the Waldorf School Association very insecure. Some called for courage—to stand against the dictates of the regime and continue public lectures and events. Others advocated caution and diplomacy with concessions if necessary.

Emil mentioned his concerns to Count Fritz von Bothmer, one of Emil's most important supporters and a personal friend. (Bothmer had joined the school years before and introduced a method of modern gymnastics for Waldorf children.) Bothmer suggested they chat with a government acquaintance of his, Ministerial Director Dill, about whether Waldorf teachers giving public lectures could jeopardize the school. Dill, he said, was kindly inclined toward the school. Accordingly, late one evening (to avoid spying eyes) Emil and Bothmer visited Dill. "I am responsible for the Waldorf School Association and need this question resolved. Otherwise we will have continuing conflict," Emil told Dill.

Fritz von Bothmer

"There is no final decision about this," Dr. Dill said. "It ought to be a harmless matter, but right now we don't want to risk a negative outcome for the school. These things are decided in Berlin. Did you know," he added, "when the order came down from Berlin to dissolve the Anthroposophical Society, the head of the political police in Stuttgart procrastinated because he didn't want to do it? Eventually he was severely reprimanded, and I had to cover for him. Your people in Switzerland don't understand the gravity of the situation here. Be happy your school is still open, and people are able to keep their Steiner writings in spite of the ban." To double-check his own advice, Dill phoned a colleague, who affirmed his cautionary stance: "Such lectures here or abroad could easily be classified as treason against the State," the colleague said.

Describing the dictatorship in Dornach

Bothmer and the Molts decided to go to Dornach to explain the situation to those in charge. At the Goetheanum they met with Marie Steiner and Albert Steffen, and although the meeting went well, the

Molts and Bothmer found it difficult to describe life under a dictatorship to people operating in a free country. Later they met with Günther Wachsmuth, the third member of the Goetheanum Council, who promised them his understanding and help. In the afternoon, Berta took Emil to Ita Wegman's clinic in Arlesheim for treatment, where he was warmed through and refreshed.

On his last day in Switzerland, Professor Suter examined Emil at his Basel clinic, and the prognosis was not good. Emil's illness had progressed and was causing greater damage to the kidneys. With this news hanging heavily over them, the Molts breakfasted with Bothmer at their hotel in Basel.

A visit to the museum

"Are you up for a short visit to the museum?" Bothmer asked Emil unexpectedly. "There's a wonderful Holbein and Böcklin exhibit, and they have wheelchairs available. I'll push you." Emil was delighted at the opportunity—it was an unexpected pleasure, and for a while the Molts absorbed themselves in art. Then they boarded the train for Stuttgart, where Walter met them at the station. Emil noticed how much more acute his perception had become since his health had declined. Every emotion was intensified for him—the beauty of the landscape he saw from the train window, the happiness he felt at seeing Walter, Edith and Felix. He was savoring these moments with the gratitude of a lifetime that was coming to a close.

Shortly after this, the chemist Otto Eckstein visited from Dornach to discuss the question of the canceled science lecture. He had been one of the coordinators of the science conference, and he felt Emil had overreacted by cautioning Waldorf teachers against lecturing abroad. "Actually," Eckstein said, "fifty Germans came to that conference, which seems to prove that the situation here in Germany is not as dire as you say."

"It doesn't take great courage," responded Emil, "to cross the border as an individual. You've no idea what's going on here. You've been away from Germany too long. The Gestapo have been placed in all government branches and their tentacles reach everywhere. We are under surveillance."

"I am so sorry," Eckstein said, "I had no idea."

Standing strong

On February 4th, 1936, Frau Link submitted to the Collegium her proposal to save the school. In it, she asked to be made school director and to replace Emil with Mahle as Association Chair. She insisted that Herr Toelke, a school parent and another Nazi liaison, backed this proposal. Emil told the Collegium he would meet with Toelke face to face to discuss the matter, since Toelke seemed to be the driving force behind the proposal. The meeting took place that evening, and Count Bothmer took notes:

> *Minutes of Meeting between Emil Molt, Chairman of the Board of the Association, and Leo Toelke, speaker of the National Socialist Waldorf parent group, an extended arm of the Württemberg Cultural Ministry under the leadership of Minister Drück. (abbreviated)*
>
> *Molt welcomes Toelke and thanks him for coming.*
>
> Toelke: Are you aware of the big picture?
>
> Molt: I believe I am.
>
> Toelke: I'm not concerned with the educational aspects, but the school cannot continue as a private school.
>
> Molt: We have been waiting for the decision from Berlin for a long time. It should be arriving shortly.
>
> Toelke: The law gives guidelines; the local authorities are free to decide. It is absolutely necessary to change the Waldorf School Association and the Board because it is impossible that so many former members of the Anthroposophical Society are connected with it.

Molt: What is your view, your intention?

Toelke: I want to see the school continue as an experimental State school with Dr. Steiner's pedagogy.

Molt. Why can't it exist as it has?

Toelke: The government expected more accommodation, more alignment with general methods. We, myself especially, are extremely grateful to you for everything you have done. Now however you have the opportunity to make us even more grateful by resigning your post.

Molt: I would like to say, in the words of Friedrich Schiller: "Lady, I don't desire that thanks." For me the decisive thing is my responsibility toward Dr. Steiner and the spiritual world. Of course I don't reckon with thanks. … I can only say that I will act as my conscience dictates. I want to be able to step before Rudolf Steiner in such a way that there are no failings on my part. The College of Teachers must play a decisive role too. Reorganizing the Association doesn't really change anything.

Toelke: The government has to see that the people around the school will now want what they have not wanted before. Then the decision in Berlin will be different. But if they don't see any accommodation on the part of the Waldorf School— Dr. Drück specifically told me this—"then we will just close the enterprise."

Molt: So, that is a definite intention? I have the feeling the school needs a respite for a while in order to work properly.

Toelke: You will have that if you allow those changes to take place. I can imagine an ideal that would do justice to Rudolf Steiner's pedagogy and at the same time to the State.

Molt: In what way have we not done justice to the State?

Toelke: There is much to criticize. If the government sees change: a restructured board, teachers and pupils that connect with the life of the State to form a real people's community (*Volksgemeinschaft*).

Molt: I thought the Waldorf School was an exemplary part of the community, even from its beginnings in 1919. Can I have been so wrong? What you are saying is a question for the teachers. The Association is concerned with the finances and, I think, hasn't done a bad job.

Toelke: In its present configuration the Board of the Association is perceived as an ideological club.

Molt: You can't say that. If the political police thought so, they would have banned the Association together with the Anthroposophical Society. One can't separate the method from anthroposophy!

Toelke: Do you believe that one has to be an anthroposophist in order to teach this method?

Molt: Do you believe one can practice this method without being an anthroposophist? You can't just copy the pedagogy. It can only be practiced properly if one is an anthroposophical teacher.

Toelke: The State isn't at all against anthroposophy....

Molt: But if the teachers are not willing? If they can't go that route?

Toelke: The teachers will go that route if they love the children. I would show the government what the method is, to make them interested in it, perhaps with some restrictions, for example without eurythmy, etc.

Molt: It would not be a sacrifice for me to resign; it is a sacrifice remaining in the Association.

Toelke: In the eyes of others it would be a great sacrifice if you resigned. Then the School could remain in existence.

Molt: What is your opinion, Count Bothmer?

Bothmer: We can't fall prey to the illusion that the Collegium will submit to any given board. It won't work with a Board which it doesn't find suited to represent the spiritual interests of the school.

Molt: By the way, does all of this arise with you personally, or have you discussed the matter with Mahle and Leinhas? Or with Dr. Schwebsch?

Toelke: I haven't seen Mahle for a long time, but I have been in touch with Leinhas. I have a circle of National Socialist parents behind me whom I have promised to do everything to preserve the school with its pedagogy as a State school.

Molt: Isn't that a contradiction: State school and Rudolf Steiner's pedagogy?

(Toelke answered that he would submit his written suggestions within a few days.)

The teachers' decision

On February 6th, Emil rose early and, for the first time in many months, prepared to join the faculty meeting. It was an important meeting, as it would decide the future of the school. As was their custom, the teachers first discussed a pedagogical theme together and then plunged into a discussion about the demands from Link and Toelke. Emil was pained to discover that one or two of the more fearful teachers were inclined to go along with these demands.

"Shouldn't we follow their recommendations?" they asked. "And is it not better to discontinue some subjects, such as art and eurythmy and main lessons?" They thought these moves would appease the supervisors and keep the school open. Emil thought that these individuals didn't understand the tactics of a dictatorship—the strategy of achieving goals while preserving appearances by cutting away at support. One teacher asked whether Frau Link should be Chairperson.

"Is this a pedagogical question?" Emil responded. "Would you be asking it in normal times or if she wasn't a Party member? If the only motivation for changing the chairperson is political or tactical, is that compatible with a truly free spiritual life? The Power behind the politics will allow no freedom of speech. If you think you want to restructure the Board, you must go ahead, but then in the full awareness that it will mean the beginning of the end of free spiritual life and of the conference as well. What would Rudolf Steiner have said to this demand?" Emil was both persuasive and determined, and he managed to turn the few dissenters into a committed part of the whole. By the end of the meeting, the teachers agreed that the school's ideals must prevail no matter what the outcome.

The Collegium reconfirmed Emil as Chairman of the Board, and he was thankful that his physical and mental strength were enough to have seen him through this crisis.

At home

After the meeting he went home, leaning heavily on Bothmer's arm. That evening he recounted the day's events to Walter and Edith, but it was Felix's birthday so they put shop-talk aside in order to celebrate, looking at slides of past holidays instead. The next day, Emil and Berta went into town for new eyeglasses and to sign a notarized statement affirming that Emil was not conspiring against the State. Toelke sent his written memorandum to the school the next day, but the teachers refused to meet his demands.

The following Sunday, Emil and Berta read a copy of the Sunday service in the privacy of their home, since the service had been banned. In the following days, they started reading *Reincarnation*, a book written by their friend, Wachsmuth. One night, Walter and Edith noticed the book lying on a side table and were intrigued. Emil suggested that they all read the book together whenever Walter and Edith came to visit, and the family enjoyed the shared interest. This activity aside, Emil was frustrated with Walter. He couldn't understand why Walter didn't want to become a partner in Rau's firm. *He is not connecting himself enough, not taking on responsibility,* Emil thought to himself, and he worried about this at night. Walter didn't have the heart to tell his father that he did not see a future for himself and Edith in Germany.

On February 14th, the school advisory group gathered at the Molts' house to put the issue of the Toelke and Link proposal to rest. Mrs. Link reiterated that the school should be run by Party members but said, "Even if my suggestions are not accepted, I will not leave." She believed she had been brought to the school by destiny and told the group that some teachers had been coming to her house to instruct her in basic anthroposophy. The advisory group was happy to hear this, but they rejected her proposal that the school be run by Party members.

Relapse

After a bad night on February 19th, Emil suddenly started shaking with chills and fever—a delayed reaction to the ongoing uncertainty at the school, he felt. He stayed in bed for several days, attended by his doctor. Meanwhile, it was carnival time again, and although Emil couldn't participate in the fun, Walter, Edith and Berta dressed up in costumes and went to a concert and ball at the school. They came home that night elated, the evening having been full of humor—a lively, happy occasion amidst the anxiety they had become accustomed to.

A week later Emil started eating again, savoring a light breakfast in the terrace room with Berta. Afterward, they went to the school where the teachers and students quietly celebrated Steiner's birthday with an assembly. Two nights later the Molts hosted a gathering at their home to commemorate Rudolf Steiner. Several teachers gave excellent presentations, and one read a section from Steiner's lecture to teachers, given September 7th, 1919, in which he described them as pioneers. Emil had attempted to prepare a presentation for the commemoration as well, but gave up when he felt uninspired and stuck on various ideas. He decided to remain quiet and to be open to whatever the spirit might inspire him with during the gathering. At the end of the lecture reading, the thought suddenly occurred to him to commemorate each of the teachers, so he got up and spoke in a wonderfully warm and animated way, without any self-consciousness. He was warmly applauded.

A meeting of banned study groups

March 1st was a sunny day with crocuses blooming in the garden. The Molts went to the Waldorf School to meet with representatives of the now banned anthroposophical study groups around the country. The teachers had prepared for the gathering with an exhibit of student work. At five o'clock, each class performed in a fine assembly. Much later, the adults sat together, sharing experiences. Someone described hearing of a Waldorf class outing to the country. They stopped off at a restaurant where Hitler youth were dancing. The Waldorf girls danced as well, but when the Hitler youth started singing their "Horst Wessel" theme song, one girl made fun of it. *"Das ist ja quatsch,"* she said. "That's just nonsense," and the class had to beat a hasty retreat.

Going to Berlin

The school still had not received a decision from Berlin regarding whether or not it would be allowed to stay open, so Emil and Berta went back to visit Ministerial Director, Dr. Dill. Emil told Dill that the suspense was nerve-wracking for the teachers and that he wanted to make one more attempt to work with his personal connections in Berlin on behalf of the school. Dill looked at him with sympathy and gave him recommendations for whom to see in Berlin. Then, with a superhuman effort and much planning, Berta and Emil boarded the night train. Count Bothmer and the teacher, Dr. Erich Schwebsch, accompanied them, and the whole party expected to return within two days.

The Molts arrived at the Anhalter Station on Saturday, March 7th, and booked themselves into Emil's favorite hotel, the Habsburger Hof. The following day they went to the Foreign Ministry to see their acquaintance, Foreign Minister Baron von Neurath—Emil making the visit in a wheelchair. Neurath was out of the office and Consul Walter Hinrichs told them that Neurath would be unavailable for a few days. Hinrichs himself was in a great hurry as Hitler was about to address the nation, but he told them to come back to see him on Monday. The Stuttgart party returned to their hotel in time to hear Hitler's grating voice announce over the hotel loudspeaker that German troops had entered the previously demilitarized Rhineland in contravention of the Treaty of Versailles and the Locarno Pact.

On Sunday, government offices were closed, so the four Stuttgarters visited with representatives of the Berlin and Altona Waldorf schools, who said that they expected their schools to be shut down soon because they had refused to compromise in accordance with the regime's demands.

On Monday, Bothmer went alone to meet with Consul Hinrichs at the Ministry, who recommended that Bothmer present his case to the Cultural Ministry. Bothmer accordingly made an appointment to do so the following morning. Despite miserable weather on Tuesday, Emil insisted on accompanying Bothmer to meet Director Fahlen of the Cultural Ministry. Berta first wheeled Emil to the barber for a shave and haircut, and then to a shop for some smart new shirts. In Fahlen's office all three waited in vain, talking to Fahlen's staff about the Waldorf School and their concerns. They were so sincere, and Emil looked so frail, that Fahlen's staff couldn't help feeling compassion and warmth toward them. Nonetheless, the Molts were told that Fahlen was not the one to help them, and that they should instead go to the Ministerial Director of Education, Helmut Bojunga, who would not be back in town until the following day.

On Wednesday morning they received a phone call saying Bojunga was not the right person to see either and that they would be referred to another department. They waited and waited by the phone in the hotel, realizing they had been deliberately deflected. Finally, in the evening, they were told they had an appointment for the following morning with Federal Councilor Thies in the Department of Education. This meant waiting yet another day.

On Thursday they took a taxi to the Education Ministry to meet with Thies, who was indeed available and granted them an entire hour of his time. The meeting went well, and they felt they were able to connect with Thies on a personal level. Feeling positive after their unexpectedly long week in Berlin, they went to back to the Foreign Ministry to visit Privy Councilor Böhner, a former Waldorf student, who promised to do his best to keep Waldorf schools untouched. Coincidentally, this was the very day that the Education Minister Rust ordered a ban on admissions to all Waldorf first grades in Germany, but the Molts did not learn of this until later.

After meeting with Böhner, the Stuttgarters felt they had done as much as they could and decided to return home. Despite the trip's headaches, deferments, and misdirection, this visit to Berlin and the conversations the Molts and Bothmer had with officials ended up buying the school another two years of operation.

A pledge and a celebration

To celebrate the good news that the school could stay open, the teachers threw a birthday party for both the school and Emil, inviting parents and friends of the Association.

March 1936

Dear Friends, the school will celebrate its 18th birthday in April. We owe its existence to the prescient initiative of the former director of the Waldorf Astoria Cigarette Factory, Councilor of Commerce, Dr. Emil Molt.

For all the years of its life, the Waldorf School has enjoyed the fatherly care of its founder. April 14th will be his birthday. The best gift we can give him on this special day is the joy of knowing that we will actively and faithfully stand united at the beginning of the new school year.

As long as the significance of Rudolf Steiner's art of education hasn't been generally recognized, it will always be necessary for us to be an advance guard with all of our strength and devotion.

After his trip to Berlin, Emil felt unwell again, but he continued to consult with the Waldorf teachers, who arranged meetings by word of mouth rather than by phone or mail, since their phones were tapped and their letters censored. On sunny days, Berta and Emil would go walking together, just as far as he was able. Sometimes they drove through town or to their favorite scenic places in the woods above Stuttgart. On one memorable day they watched the great Zeppelin L127 come floating by overhead. Early spring and warm weather had brought blossoms to the garden, and the Molts turned their attention to their family, spending as much time as possible with them.

Putting affairs in order

As Emil's health declined, his secretary, Federlein, helped him write his testament and sort his papers, and Berta prepared to take him back to Brissago, where Emil had felt best. He looked forward to what he hoped would be a short break away from Germany. Before leaving, the Molts attended the Waldorf School's closing assembly before Easter, where they were presented with flowers. The next day, Berta and Emil visited Hermann Mahle in his factory in Cannstatt to convey their gratitude for the risks he had taken on behalf of the school.

Emil met once more with each teacher at the school, wishing them courage, hope and faith. He said he would be only a phone call and a short journey away if they needed him. In the evening Dr. Schubert came. They loved this kindly man and admired him because, although Jewish, he had elected to stay in Stuttgart to look after his special-needs class. He was the gentlest of all the teachers, but his will was made of pure courage.

Early in the morning on April 1st, the family took Emil on his favorite woodland walk before breakfasting together. Then Walter loaded Berta and Emil's suitcases into the car and drove to the train station. Walter helped his father into the carriage and arranged the compartment with pillows and blankets, then said his goodbyes. As Berta and Emil watched the scenery go by outside their windows, they were surprised to find no snow on the north side of the mountains, while on the south side everything was covered in white. Even the blooming mimosas and camellias in Locarno were blanketed in a layer of snow. When they arrived in Brissago, the Molts were warmly welcomed by the new managers of the Motta, but found the place to be run down since their last visit. They settled in easily in spite of the conditions, and Emil began reading a historical series on the Stauffer dynasty. As usual they had visitors stop in periodically over the next few weeks.

On Good Friday the weather cleared and the sun came out, showing Brissago and the lake at their best. The Molts read an Easter lecture with Count Bothmer, who was visiting, and then Emil and Bothmer took a leisurely walk over to the next village, where they ran into Leinhas by chance. Emil greeted him in friendly fashion and invited him to join them at tea on his birthday. He had come to accept Leinhas and appreciate his wholehearted love of anthroposophy and his pain at the failure of the various ventures he had been involved with. Bothmer and Emil then stopped at the Café Mimosa before taking the bus to Monte Bré—Emil had regained his appetite slightly and was able to enjoy the outing. The next day, Bothmer, Berta and Emil took a boat trip to an island on the lake. The weather was cold, and at one point the others left Emil in the warmth of an enclosed restaurant patio where he napped while they explored. They returned to the Motta that evening feeling tired but happy, having absorbed the beauty of the scenery and the warmth of each other.

Emil's 60th birthday

April 14th was Emil's 60th birthday, and love-filled letters and telegrams poured in from all over Europe. The Molts had a special birthday lunch and, in the afternoon, a few more friends joined them for tea.

Soon, however, Emil's pain became unbearable and Dr. Zehnder advised him to go to the specialist in Bern as soon as possible. On May 16th Walter arrived. He and Berta helped Emil into an ambulance that took them to Bern. After settling his father in the hospital, Walter then went back to Germany. Soon he was back with Edith. They had special

Emil's last birthday

news to share with Emil, and they sat by his hospital bed, waiting for
him to wake up. When he opened his eyes, they told him that Edith was
pregnant and that he was to be a grandfather. From Edith's memoir:

> When he asks what his prognosis is, the doctor says quite honestly
> that his days are numbered, so his family decides to bring him home
> to Stuttgart.

> Because of Hitler's restrictions against taking money out of
> Germany, they have very little left, so Berta goes to the consulate to
> request a loan to pay for a private rail car. The Consul, Freiherr von
> Weizsäcker, says, "Even if it were my own mother, I couldn't help."
> He is afraid of Hitler. When the doctor, Professor Wildholz, hears
> this he is so outraged that he lends Berta the money out of hospital
> funds under his personal guarantee.

On June 5th Dora and Felix arrived to help take Emil home to
Stuttgart. Arnold Ith, the former Futurum Board member that Emil was
fond of, heard that Emil was being transported home and came to offer
his assistance. He was just in time to help a medic carry Emil to the
ambulance, which drove to the train station and then directly onto the
platform. There, Emil was moved to a bed in the train's special hospital
compartment. Arnold Ith had brought roses and he set them up in a

vase by the bedside. When the train arrived in Stuttgart, Edith, Dora, Miss Federer and six medics waited at the station.

News of Emil's arrival had spread throughout Stuttgart and it caused a sensation, Dora wrote in her memoir. *Masses of people were at the station, and we were glad when we had him home.*

Once safely back at home, Berta dedicated herself to caring for Emil. She was relieved at night by an orderly, Brother Klaiber, but did not sleep much, mostly staying by Emil's side and greeting his friends when they came. Edith still had the ability to make Emil laugh, and his face lit up whenever he saw her come into the room. She would often read to him with great pathos from a comical book about life in Berlin.

Gradually, though, Emil lost his ability to laugh and soon could only communicate in a whisper. Dora understood him better than anyone else and sat at his bedside taking notes of what he said. At one point, in what the family later saw as uncanny foreshadowing, Dora heard him say, "Walter—notices, Walter—Weleda." In one of his more conscious moments, Emil said, "It is so hard to have to lay down my work so soon."

On June 14th, Walter and Edith spent the day at Emil's bedside. Emil was surprised and joyful when he was told that it was Sunday. On Monday, June 15th, Emil's appetite suddenly came back and he enjoyed a meal. On this day Edith almost lost her child and had to be rushed home to her parents. She was bedridden for a week.

That evening Berta washed Emil and, wrapping him in a white towel, told him how much she loved him. The next day, June 16th, 1936, at noon, Emil died with Berta and Dora at his side. Dora wrote of the moment:

Almost imperceptibly and without complaint, Emil separated himself, following the call into the spiritual world. He lay, looking youthful and full of light, with a half smile on his face.

Emil on his deathbed

Emil's wake lasted for three days and three nights, and Berta was comforted by teachers, family and friends. Edith was still ill and in bed, but Walter was there to take care of matters as needed.

Early on June 19th, Waldorf teachers, former Waldorf Astoria workers, and many friends gathered for Emil's funeral. People came from all over. It was a major event in Stuttgart. The entire school, with all the Waldorf children, dressed in white, accompanied the flower-laden casket through the park-like avenue of the Prag cemetery in something of a royal procession. Berta, in black veils, was led by her son, Walter. The weather was warm and sunny, with bright clouds in the sky. Birds flew overhead. Over a thousand people attended. Since the crematorium chapel was too small to hold the crowds, the casket was placed on the steps in front of the entrance.

The girls' choir standing inside sang Mozart's *Ave Verum*. Count Bothmer was the first to speak. He described Emil's social deed as the founder of the Waldorf School and said that no one who participated in or even saw the funeral procession would ever forget it.

Emil Leinhas spoke of the endurance of Emil's faith through the most difficult trials and emphasized that he never held a grudge and always courageously stood by his convictions. Otto Eckstein of Weleda in Arlesheim brought greetings from Dornach. He said that Emil, having found his teacher, saw the spiritual world in every aspect of life and worked accordingly. Eckstein promised that he and his friends would continue to send their love to Emil in the spiritual world into which he had now entered. Berta's sister Paula said, *"We, his family, will keep faith with him, feeling connected with him in love, and we will model ourselves on him as example and guide until we meet again."* As the organ sounded, the coffin was taken into the chapel and given to the flames.

From Dornach, Albert Steffen wrote this short tribute:

Emil Molt was one of the most faithful helpers of the Goetheanum. It seems unbelievable that this strong yet delicate figure and open face with its light-filled, kind look, the friendly penetrating blue eyes…is no longer with us. His fine hands had a poignancy, revealing how much this healthy and, until recent times, youthful man had suffered. They had become thin, like deep and inwardly experienced destiny in the patient struggle for spiritual victory which, together with the transparency of his face, was shattering. That is how we saw him the last time he was in Dornach.

Emil Molt was a true German who remained faithful to his native land with his whole soul…he had the piety of a Swabian mystic while in spirit he was a citizen of the world. The study of German philosophers led him to universal truths. The cultural elite gathered in his home and were welcomed by his soulful wife. It was an echo of the great idealistic epoch of Goethe. Colleagues found it almost a wonder that he understood every detail of his business and had a more perceptive nose than any of them. But not just for tobacco, he had a fine artistic sense too, for example in packaging, and so he put German literature into his cigarette boxes.

Then came the School.

The State University honored him with a doctorate for his achievements in peace in the workplace and the work community. I was there when he received the letter in Mürren, where this friend had invited me, within view of the Eiger, Mönch and Jungfrau mountains. It seems typical of him; he looked for the highest in the life of the spirit, so also in the enjoyment of nature. His greatest pleasure was discovering a flower growing out of a glacier. It kept him youthful.

Then the tragedy of his life began. The factory was sacrificed to speculation and he lost it, he who had always done business on trust. The worry about the Waldorf School grew. His outer standing did not diminish; his inner worth grew. He is a living example of self-development and service to humanity.

And Emil's friend, Walter Rau:

"…As such, money meant nothing to Emil Molt. He enjoyed it, but it was just a means to an end. What end? At first it was to build his work, then ever more, to help the School. And here is where Emil Molt the businessman began to stand back behind Emil Molt the school patron. This may have been part of his basic inclination, not working with physical substances but rather working in the social domain. The more his inner nature worked itself out, the more the horizon was transformed. It was a kind of self-direction which went beyond business.

Often it is difficult to recognize such a development in a person, and he did receive criticism for not living just for his firm. But he broke old molds and left them behind. For some companions along his way, this must have been painful. How did he present himself as a businessman? He had an obvious gift for bringing people together. His way of looking a person in the eye and of speaking was pleasant. He understood how to put thoughts into words. Had he wished, he could have pulled people into his orbit, but he did not want this, at least not in later years. He did not want to curtail the freedom of others. Bringing people together was a need for him, even though that might place him in the background. He enjoyed creating such connections.

Epilogue

Walter goes to America

After Emil's funeral, Edgar Dürler asked Walter whether he would be willing to manage the Austrian branch of Weleda. Walter, recalling the moment when Emil had whispered "Walter—Weleda" on his deathbed, said he'd love to take the job but had no inclination to stay in a National Socialist country. In response, Dürler mentioned that the tiny Weleda in New York needed a director. Walter thanked him for the offer and said he would talk it over with his family and his boss.

Edith insisted that Walter accept this passport to freedom. Berta, sensing the inevitability of war, also told him to go, saying that he must protect his family. When he begged her to come along, she refused, saying she had to stay to support the school in Stuttgart and that her health would not permit such a trip. Walter Rau generously told Walter he was free to leave, provided he could train someone into his position. Then Walter called Dürler to accept the position under the condition that his departure be delayed until after the birth of his child. Over the next months, he took care of his mother and wrapped up his affairs.

In the first days of January 1937, when his daughter was ten days old, Walter crossed the Swiss border on the pretext of paying his father's financial debts. From there, he went to France and boarded a ship that took him to safety in America. He was now deemed a traitor to his country and for years worried that the Gestapo would follow him and bring him back to Germany as a prisoner. Edith spent the next three months trying to obtain a visa in vain—she was a traitor's wife and was probably denied by the authorities in the hopes that Walter would return for her. When Edith tried one last time, she dealt with a consular official who saw her name and asked: "Are you the daughter of Fritz Lichtenberg, the physician?" When she nodded he said, "He once saved my son's life. Here is your visa."

In America, for the duration of the war, Edith and Walter were classed as enemy aliens. However, he was able to pursue his work at Weleda and the family found a haven in the Threefold Farm in Spring Valley, New York. Walter's cousin, Lisa, was already living there with her husband, Henry Monges. It became a well-attended anthroposophical conference center after the war.

The Nazis close the school

Despite the strong defense of the school put up by Berta and others, and as a result of the teachers staying true to the Waldorf ideals and refusing to compromise, the doors of the school were closed on March 31, 1938. Berta attended the last school assembly. Class teachers addressed their children with words of hope and love. Walter's friend, Georg Hartman, the seventh grade teacher, told them the following:

Dear children of Class 7a:

You have been in the school for seven years. During the last year we learned about health and how a person's body renews itself completely every seven years. You will now be carrying a different body out of the school than the one you came with. But some things have not changed. Your name is the same because it is not formed of material substance, but is a mark of your spirit living in your body. Some of you even have names given by Rudolf Steiner. Look, dear children, we must have reverence for names. You will find people who want to revile the name of the Waldorf School, who would like the name of Emil Molt, our founder, to be forgotten. Don't forget him! There will be people who will try to tell you untruths about Rudolf Steiner. You will, however, prove yourselves worthy of these names. Be thankful for those seven years that you had the privilege of being in the school, founded by Rudolf Steiner and Emil Molt.

And this is my parting greeting to you, my dear children of Class 7a: Never allow your hearts to forget the three names: Waldorf School, Emil Molt and Rudolf Steiner.

School in 1938

Waldorf students 1938

Teachers at closing

Looking back

Berta and Emil both suffered childhood illnesses. They overcame their frailties but often stretched their physical abilities far beyond their strength. Because they had the means, they were able to replenish their physical forces in beautiful locations and their soul forces in Dornach. All this ended when Emil died. Berta continued active for a while, sending pleading letters to government officials and attending meetings. For a while she still visited her family members and published Emil's early memoirs, but she longed for him and felt at odds with the world.

She was bereft, having lost her husband, her son, her grandchild, her school, her society and, in reality, her country. She began to withdraw. Eventually Dora took her to a facility where she was cared for and where friends could visit. Dora had married Max Emil Kimmich and both taught in the school until its closure. Then he was recruited and, too soon, became a casualty of the war. Later Dora and her son moved to her sister Lisa's, in Spring Valley. It is her memoir which allows us a very small insight into Berta's last days.

Berta's final years as described by her niece, Dora Kimmich

Berta survived her husband by three years.

She suffered the closing of the school by the Nazis but her trust in the future of the school was unbroken. She remained in contact with the teachers and worked on her husband's memoirs, bringing the early years out in private editions. In October 1938 I saw my Aunt Berta, who had just returned from a difficult trip. After lying sick for weeks she had pulled herself together to take care of what she needed to do. Here she was, lovely as ever, but very weak. In the summer of 1939, just before the war began, her illness took its final course. I saw her again on July 16th. Her mood was free, almost happy, with a loving interest in everything. She told us of Walter and his family and showed me their pictures. I sensed a longing and a desire for the child. Once we brought her our own baby, Christoph. She said gently: "I see him; he is a good one." Shortly after this visit she lost her clarity of thought. In this condition, with the soul no longer completely in the suffering body, she remained for 14 days. Her carer, Miss Lüchauer, slept in the next room from where she could be called if necessary. On August 16th, I sat with her. There was a letter from Walter. I read it to her and saw her attempt at comprehension. She seemed to be reliving youthful experiences.

Berta toward the end

On August 17th, I came again with my husband, Max Emil. He waited in the next room, chatting to someone. She listened with a questioning look. I said, "It's Emil." A joyful expression spread over her face, and she tried to get out of bed. On August 20th, 1939, my mother was with her and called us early from Stuttgart that the death was imminent. Emil and I drove in and found Count Bothmer in attendance. It was a beautiful summer day. Toward noon the breathing stopped. Her face was not listening and smiling as Uncle's had been. It was serious but with a wonderful expression. Many came into the house, many roses were sent. Felix and Hans Thielemann came and helped. She died without being touched by the imminent war.

* .* *

Die Frau des Initiators der ersten Waldorfschule war von rührender zarter inniger Schönheit. In ihren tiefen dunklen Augen leuchtete die Sehnsucht nach dem Geist, glänzte ein warmer Strom von Liebe, die allen Menschen entgegenschlug.

[Berta Molt] was of a touching, delicate inner beauty. In her deep dark eyes the longing for the spirit shone forth. A bright stream of warmth and love radiated toward everyone. – Marie Steiner, 1939

Interestingly, Berta's sister Emma died on the same day that Berta's funeral was held. It was also the day on which the first soldiers were mobilized in Stuttgart.

Renewal

The anthroposophical initiatives that were attempted early in the 20th century went underground during World War II. When the war finally ended, all of Europe was on its knees again. Large areas of the continent had been annihilated and cities such as Dresden were the fiery graveyard of thousands. But in Stuttgart, parents, teachers and Waldorf friends cleaned up the rubble that had been their school, and a few months after the war they reopened the school in donated army barracks. Had the teachers sacrificed the school's ethos to the Nazis in 1933-38, it is very likely that the school would have been lost.

With that flagship school leading the way, well over 1000 Steiner/ Waldorf schools have opened in all continents, making it the largest non-denominational private school system in the world. The research and practice of biodynamic farming provides wholesome sustainable food throughout many countries. The Weleda company makes medicines and body care products in facilities around the world. Hospitals and clinics, special-needs communities, ethical banks and many other ventures based on Steiner's suggestions, have been developed over the years. The Goetheanum remains a vibrant gathering place for anthroposophy, regularly serving as a venue for studies, conferences and cultural offerings.

The Threefold Social Order, of which Emil was to be the "Curator," is perhaps the least developed of all aspects of anthroposophy. Steiner regarded it as his most significant contribution and yet it is not being practiced in any of the institutions or in the world. It should become an integral part of the Steiner/Waldorf high school curriculum, both in theory and practice. Otherwise these three domains of culture, rights and business, will continue to be entangled in an inappropriate manner to the detriment of society. This is an area still to be developed and work to be done.

Appendix

An Appeal to The German Nation and to the Civilized World
by Rudolf Steiner

Germany believed herself secure for time without end in her empire, which was founded half a century ago. In August 1914 she thought the war she was faced with would prove her invincible. Today all she can do is look upon its ruins. Such an experience calls for self-reflection. For such an experience proved that an opinion held for fifty years, and especially the ideas that had prevailed during the war, had been a tragic error. Where can the reasons for this fateful error be found?

This question must now call forth a process of self-evaluation within the soul of every German. Will there be enough strength left for such introspection? Germany's very existence depends upon it. Germany's future also hinges upon the sincerity of the questioning mind—how did we fall prey to such fatal misconceptions? If reflection upon this inquiry starts immediately, then it will come in a flash of understanding: yes, we did found an empire half a century ago, but we neglected to give it a task springing from within the very essence of its national spirit.

The empire was founded. During the first years of its existence, care was taken to shape its inner possibilities according to demands posed, year after year, by old traditions and new endeavors. Later, progress was made to safeguard and enlarge the outer positions of power that were based on material resources. Linked to it were policies regulating the social demands of the new era, policies that did take into account the requirements of the day, to some extent, but lacked a greater vision.

A goal could have been defined had there been enough sensitivity to the growing needs of the new generation. Thus the empire found itself in the larger world arena without an essential direction or goal to justify its existence. The debacle of the war revealed this truth in an unfortunate way. Until the war, other nations saw nothing to suggest that Germany had a historic world mission that ought not to be swept away. Her failure to manifest such a mission, according to those with real insight, was the underlying cause of Germany's ultimate breakdown.

Immeasurably much depends now on the ability of the German people to assess this state of affairs objectively. Disaster should call forth an insight that never appeared during the previous fifty years. Instead of petty thoughts about the immediate concerns of the day, the grand sweep of an enlightened philosophy of life should surge through the present, endeavoring to recognize the evolutionary forces within the new generation, and dedicating itself to them with a courageous will. There really must be an end to all the petty attempts to dismiss as impractical idealists everyone who has his eye on these evolutionary forces. A stop must be put to the arrogance and presumption of those who consider themselves to be practical, yet who are the very ones whose narrow-mindedness, masked as practicality, has led to disaster. Consideration must be given to the evolutionary demands of the new age as enunciated by those who, although labeled impractical idealists, are actually the real practical thinkers.

For a long time, "pragmatists" of all kinds have foreseen the emergence of new human needs. However, they wanted to meet them with traditional modes of thought and institutions. The economic life of modern times gave rise to these needs. It seemed impossible to satisfy them following avenues of private initiative. It seemed imperative to one class that, in a few areas, private labor should be changed over into social labor; and where this class's own philosophy deemed it profitable, the change became effective. Another class wanted radically to turn all individual labor into social labor. This group, influenced by recent economic developments, had no interest in the preservation of private goals.

All efforts regarding humanity's new demands heretofore have one thing in common: they all aim at the socialization of the private sector in the expectation that it will be taken over by communal bodies (the state or commune); however, these have their origins in preconceptions that have nothing to do with these new demands. Nor is any consideration given to the fact that the newer cooperatives, which are also expected to play a role in the takeover, have not been formed fully in accordance with the new requirements, but are still imbued with old thought patterns and habits.

The truth is that none of the communal institutions influenced in any way by these old patterns can be a proper vehicle for the new ideas. The forces at work in modern times urge recognition of a social structure for all humanity that comprehends something entirely different from prevailing views. Heretofore, social communities have been largely shaped by human social instincts. The task of the times must be to permeate these forces with full consciousness.

The social organism is articulated like a natural organism. Just as the natural organism must take care of the process of thinking through its head and not through its lungs, so the social organism must be organized into systems. No one system can assume the work of the other; each must work harmoniously with the others while preserving its own integrity.

Economic life can prosper only if it develops according to its own laws and energies as an independent system within the social organism, and if it does not let confusion upset its structure by permitting another part of the social order—that which is at work in politics—to invade it. On the contrary, the political system must function independently alongside the economic system, just as in the natural organism breathing and thinking function side by side. Their wholesome collaboration can be attained only if each member has its own vitally interacting regulations and administration. However, beneficial interaction falters if both members have one and the same administrative and regulatory organ. If it is allowed to take over, the political system is bound to destroy the economy, and the economic system loses its vitality if it becomes political.

These two spheres of the social organism must now be joined by a third that is shaped quite independently, from within its own life-possibilities—the cultural sphere, with its own legitimate order and administration. The cultural portions of the other two spheres belong in this sphere and must be submitted to it; yet the cultural sphere has no administrative power over the other two spheres and can influence them only as the organ systems coexisting within a complete natural organism influence each other.

Today it is already possible to elaborate at length upon the necessity of the social organism and to establish a scientific basis for it in every detail. Here, however, only guidelines can be offered for those who want to pursue the important task.

The foundation of the German Empire came at a time when the younger generation was already confronted with these necessities. However, its administration did not understand how to give the Empire a mission with a view to these needs. Understanding it would not only have helped provide the right inner structure; it would have guided Germany in a justified direction in world politics. Given such an impetus, the German people could have lived together with other nations.

Disaster ought to give rise now to introspection. The will to make the social organism possible must be strengthened. A new spirit—not the Germany of the past—should now confront the external world. A new Germany with cultural, economic and political systems, each with its own administrations, should now begin the work of rebuilding relationships with the victor. Germany failed to recognize in time that, unlike other nations, she needed to become strong through the threefold articulation of the social order; therefore, she must do so now.

One can imagine the so-called pragmatists saying how these new concepts are too complicated, and how uncomfortable they are merely thinking about a collaboration of three spheres. Shying away from the real demands of life, they want to pursue complacently their own habits of thought. They must awaken to the fact: either one must deign to submit one's thinking to the demands of reality, or nothing will have been learned from the debacle, and this self-inflicted misery will be endlessly perpetuated and compounded.

Bibliography

Rudolf Steiner

At the Gates of Spiritual Science, Forest Row, UK: Rudolf Steiner Press, 1970, 1986.

The Calendar of the Soul, available in many translations and editions; also available online at the Rudolf Steiner Archive https://rsarchive.org.

Christianity as Mystical Fact and the Mysteries of Antiquity, Guildford, UK: White Crow Books, 2011.

Education and Practical Life from the Perspective of Spiritual Science. The Hague, 1921.

The Foundations of Human Experience (trans. Robert F. Lathe and Nancy Parsons Whittaker), Great Barrington, MA: Anthroposophic Press, 1996.

The Gospel of Saint John: Ten Lectures, GA 103, Hamburg, Germany, 1908, Great Barrington, MA: Anthroposophic Press, 1962.

How to Know Higher Worlds: A Modern Path of Initiation, Great Barrington, MA: Anthroposophic Press, 1994.

Intuitive Thinking as a Spiritual Path: A Philosophy of Freedom, Great Barrington, MA: SteinerBooks, 1995.

The Karma of Untruthfulness, V.1. Forest Row, UK: Rudolf Steiner Press, 1988.

Life Between Death and Rebirth. Vienna: GA 153, 1914.

The Mission of the Folk Souls in Relations to Teutonic Mythology, Forest Row, UK: Rudolf Steiner Press, 2005.

The Philosophy of Freedom: The Basis for Modern World Conception, Forest Row, UK: Rudolf Steiner Press, 2011.

The Renewal of the Social Organism. Spring Valley, NY: Anthroposophic Press, 1985.

Rudolf Steiner in the Waldorf School: Lectures and Addresses to Children, Parents, and Teachers 1919-1924. Great Barrington, MA: SteinerBooks, 1996.

The Spiritual Communion of Mankind, Rudolf Steiner Archive https://rsarchive.org.

The Study of Man. Forest Row, UK: Rudolf Steiner Press, 1966.

The Tension Between East and West. London: Hodder & Stoughton, 1963.

Towards Social Renewal: Rethinking the Basis of Society. Forest Row, UK: Rudolf Steiner Press, 2000.

The Younger Generation, Educational and Spiritual Impulses for Life in the Twentieth Century, Great Barrington, MA: SteinerBooks, 1967.

Steiner, Rudolf and Marie von Sievers-Steiner, *Correspondence and Documents 1901–1925.* Great Barrington, MA: SteinerBooks, 1988.

Steiner, Rudolf and Ita Wegman, *Fundamentals of Therapy.* Whitefish, MT: Kessinger Publishing, LLC, 2010.

Other authors

Bielenberg, Christabel. *The Past Is Myself: The Personal Story of an English Woman Living in Nazi Germany.* London: Corgi Books, 1968.

Emmichoven, J.E. Zeylmans van. *Wer war Ita Wegman I-III.* Verlag am Goetheanum, 1992.

Foch, Ferdinand. (translated by T. Bentley Mott). *Memoirs of Marshal Foch.* London: Heinemann Ltd, 1931.

Goebel, Nana. *Die Waldorfschule und ihre Menschen: Geschichte und Geschichten weltweit 1919–2019.* Berlin: Weinmeisterstr, no date.

Keynes, John Maynard. *The Economic Consequences of the Peace.* Heritage Illustrated Publishing, Open Library, 2014.

Kiersch, Johannes. *A History of the School of Spiritual Science,* London: Temple Lodge Books, 2006.

Landau, Rom. *God Is My Adventure: A Book on Modern Mystics, Masters and Teachers.* Landau Press, 2007.

Lutters, Frans. *An Exploration into the Destiny of the Waldorf School Movement*. Hudson, NY: Waldorf Publications, 2015

Meyer, T.H., editor, *Light for the New Millennium, Rudolf Steiner's Association with Helmuth and Eliza von Moltke*. Forest Row, UK: Rudolf Steiner Press, 1998.

Moltke, Generaloberst Helmuth von, *Moltke Erinnerungen–Briefe– Dokumente 1877–1916, Ein Bild vom Kriegsausbruch, erster Kriegsfuehrung und Persoenlichkeit des ersten militaerischen Fuehrers des Krieges, Herausgegeben und mit einem Vorwort versehen von Eliza von Moltke geb Graefin Moltke-Huitfeld*. Stuttgart: Der Kommende Tag A.-G. Verlag, 1922.

Muehlon, Wilhelm. *The Vandal of Europe*. http://www.archive.org/stream/ cu31924027829740#page/n357/mode/2up

Nicolson, Harold. *Portrait of a Diplomatist: The Life of Sir Arthur Nicolson*. New York: Houghton Mifflin Company, 1930.

Pfeiffer, Ehrenfried. *On Rudolf Steiner's Mystery Dramas, Lectures*. Spring Valley, NY: Mercury Press, 1948.

Polzer-Hoditz, Ludwig Graf. *Memories of Rudolf Steiner, Reminiscences of an Austrian*. Spring Valley, NY: St. George Publications, 1987.

Schoeffler, Heinz Herbert, *Guenther Wachsmuth, Ein Lebensbild*. Dornach: Verlag am Goetheanum, no date.

Stein, Walter Johannes. *The Ninth Century and the Holy Grail*. London: Temple Lodge Books, 2009.

————. *Reminiscences of Life as an Aid to the Understanding of Our Time*. Spring Valley, NY: St. George Publications, 1987.

Sulzbach, Herbert. *With the German Guns: Four Years on the Western Front*. Barnsley, South Yorkshire, UK, Pen and Sword Books, reprint 2012.

Tautz, Johannes, editor. *Molt, Emil: Entwurf Meiner Lebensbeschreibung*. Stuttgart: Verlag Freies Geistesleben GmbH, 1972.

Von Eschenbach, Wolfram. (translated by H. Mustard and C. Passage) *Parzival*. New York: Vintage Books, 1961.

Vreede, Elisabeth. *Anthroposophy and Astrology; the Astronomical Letters of Elisabeth Vreede*. Great Barrington, MA: SteinerBooks, 2001.

Wachsmuth, Guenther. *The Life and Work of Rudolf Steiner*. New York: Whittier Books, 1955

Werner, Uwe, in collaboration with Christoph Lindenberg. *Anthroposophen in der Zeit des Nationalsozialismus, unter Mitwirkung von Christoph Lindenberg, (1933–1945)*. Place: R. Oldenbourg Verlag, 1999.

Suggestions for further reading on Waldorf education

Awakening Intelligence: The Task of the Teacher and the Key Picture of the Learning Process by Magda Lissau

Child Development at a Glance by Christian Breme

Educating the Will by Michael Howard

Education, Teaching and Practical Life by Rudolf Steiner

Kicking Away the Ladder: The Philosophical Roots of Waldorf Education by Frederick Amrine

Learning to See the World through Drawing by Elizabeth Auer

Learning about the World through Modeling by Arthur Auer

Pedagogical Theater by Arthur Pittis

The Seven Core Principles of Waldorf Education by the Pedagogical Section Council of North America, edited by Elan Leibner

Teaching Language Arts in a Waldorf School edited by Roberto Trostli

Trailing Clouds of Glory: Essays on Human Sexuality and the Education of Youth in Waldorf Schools edited by Douglas Gerwin

Waldorf Education: An Introduction by Henry Barnes

Waldorf Education: An Introduction for Parents edited by David Mitchell

Windows into Waldorf edited by David Mitchell

Also visit

www.waldorfpublications.org
www.waldorflibrary.org
www.waldorfresearchinstitute.org
www.waldorfresources.ch
www.awsna.org

Addendum

One hundred years after its inception, Waldorf education has grown to over 1100 schools and many more individual kindergarten programs around the world. The curriculum meets the children at every phase of their development for maximal health in body, mind, and spirit.